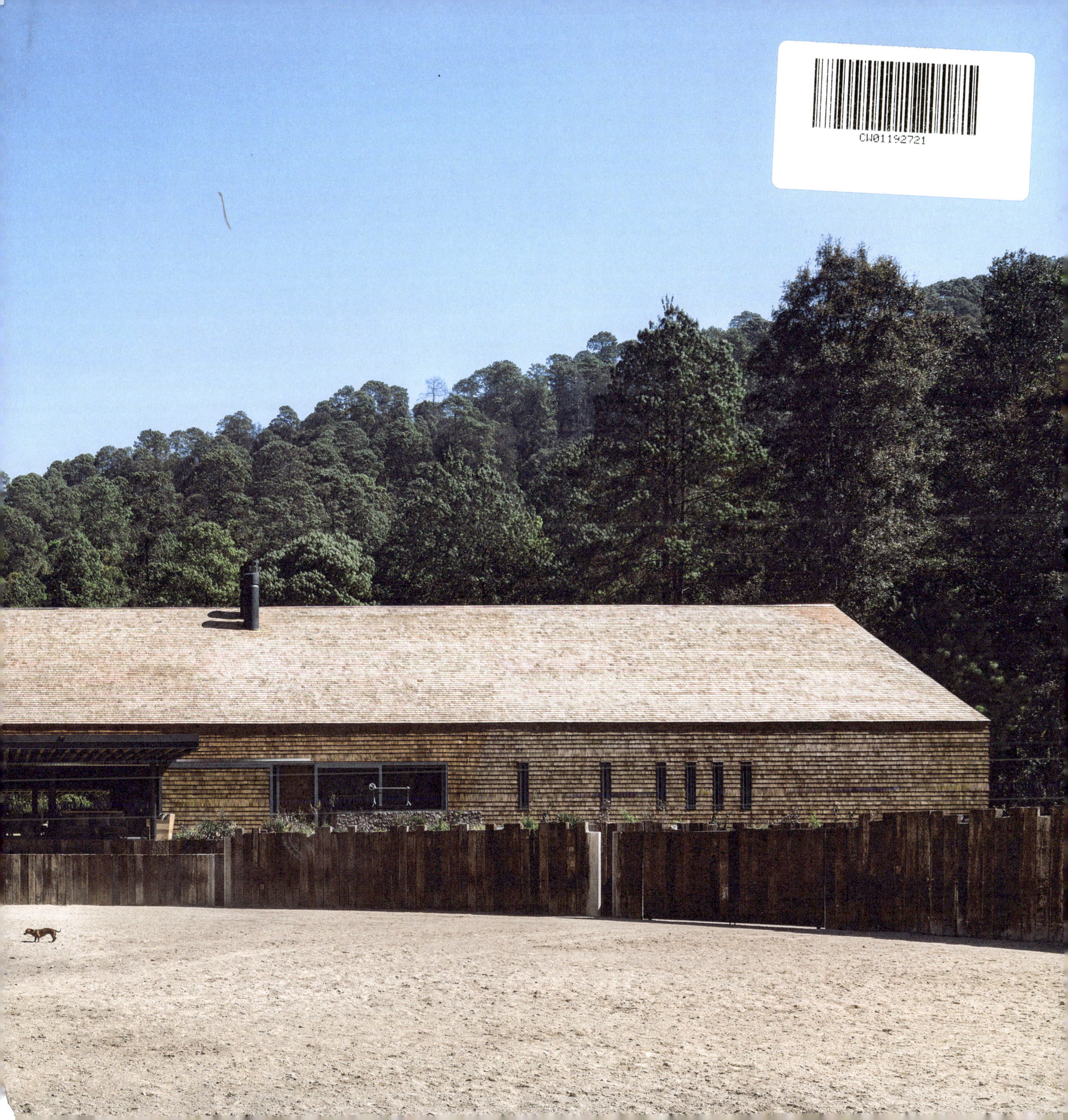

STABLES

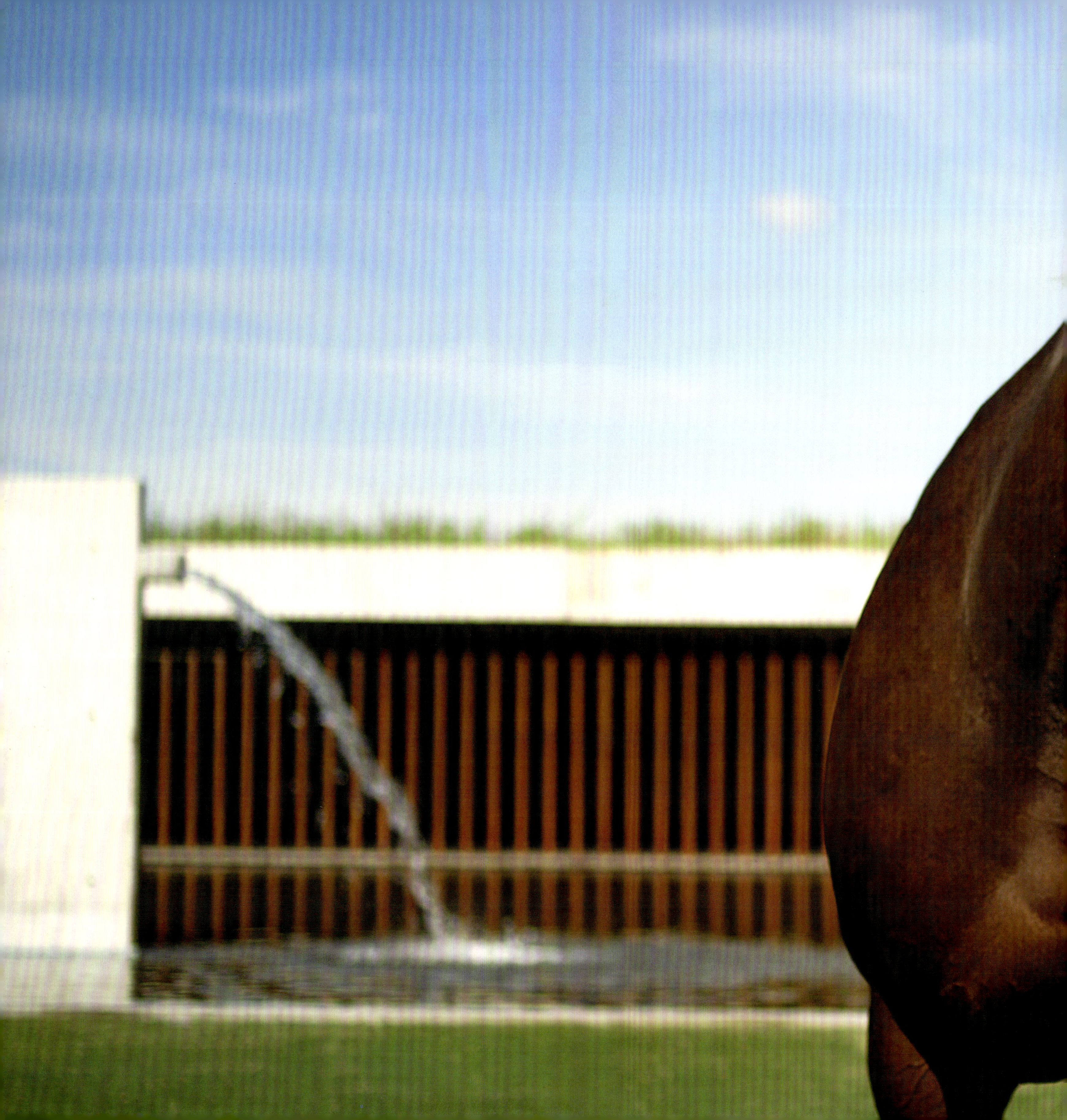

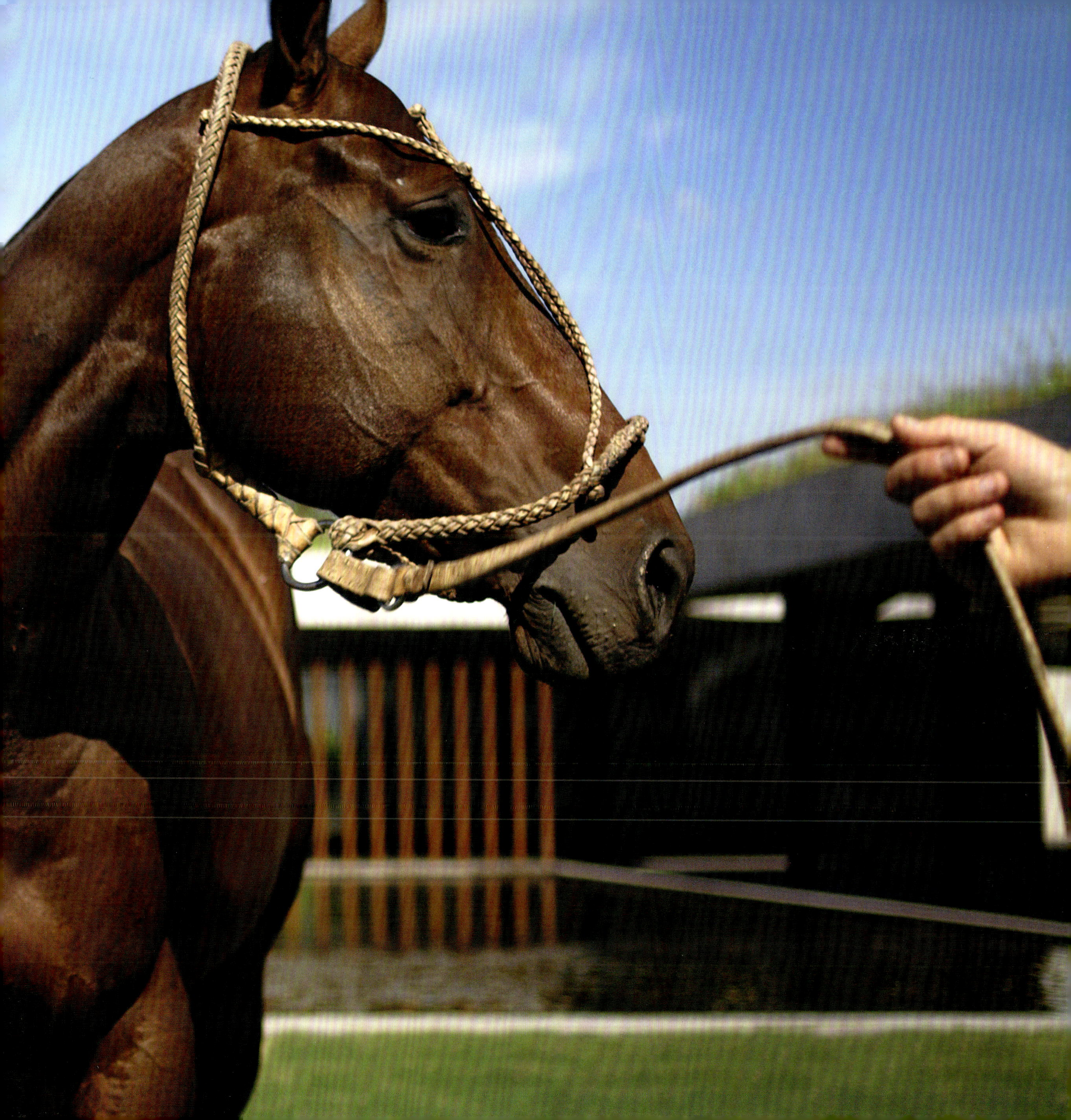

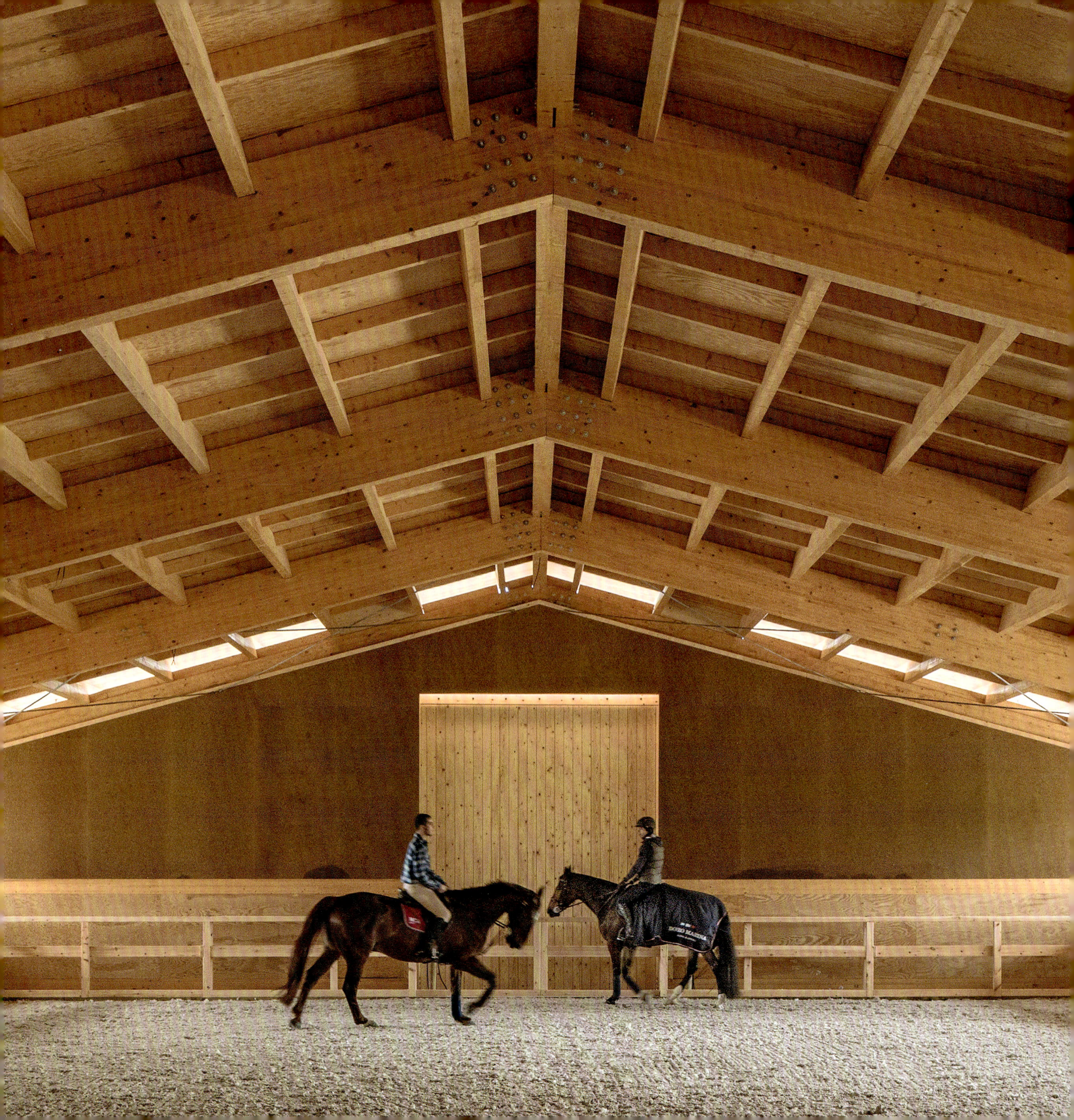

STABLES
High Design for Horse and Home

Oscar Riera Ojeda & Victor Deupi

Rizzoli
NEW YORK

New York · Paris · London · Milan

TABLE OF CONTENTS

INTRODUCTION / VICTOR DEUPI	8
STABLES	14
ARCHITECTS' PROFILES	264
AUTHORS' PROFILES	269
BOOK CREDITS	272

Introduction
Victor Deupi

When a man has found a horse to his mind, bought him and taken him home, it is well to have the stable so situated with respect to the house that his master can see him very often; and it is a good plan to have the stall so contrived that it will be as difficult to steal the horse's fodder out of the manger. (Xenophon, *De equis alendis*, 4.1)

Human dependence on horses has been a relatively stable constant since the dawn of urban civilization in the fourth and third millennia BCE. Hunting, fishing, gardening, and herding all contributed to the communal food supply for early societies whose population exceeded the amount of readily available land for self-sustenance. Surplus was a necessity and storage space for food supply and pack animals became a requirement for any trading civilization. Most sedentary societies had ordinary stables for the simple purpose of housing horses and other working animals. These early structures accommodated such basic functions as individual stalls and loose boxes for the animals, as well as storage space for food and equipment, and even lodgings for people. Moreover, a good stable would honor the horse by allowing for food, water, drainage, and a constant temperature with controlled ventilation. Stalls were divided by wooden partitions, and the horses typically faced the wall where a rack of hay and troughs for feed and water were located. Horses have always been praised for their strength and beauty, and stables were designed for both practicality and display, as horses—like art—were recognized as valuable possessions and installations.

Ancient writers extolled the virtues of horsemanship in both the private realm, for instance in managing one's estate, traveling or exercise, and in the public sphere, as in mounted cavalry, military processions, equestrian sport, and entertainment. Pliny the Younger described in a letter his sumptuous seaside villa in Laurentum, outside of Rome, and the ease with which he could arrive on horseback. Though he never described the stable buildings in his estate, we do know that Roman country houses such as the villa and farmstead near Chedworth in Gloucestershire, England, had stables for horses and other working farm animals. The Roman writer Vitruvius, noted specifically in his treatise on architecture that:

Stables are to be so placed as to have the warmest part of the farm buildings, provided they do not look towards the hearth. For when draught horses are stabled next to the fire, they lose their sleekness.[1]

For villas and country estates then, stables were simply located within rustic farm buildings or otherwise free-standing outbuildings, whereas in city residences they were situated within the property boundary, often within the house, as we see in several cases in Pompeii. These types of residences often had a dual purpose of living and some other commercial or workshop activity, and they are distinguished by purpose-built ramps that allowed for vehicular access in the form of horse or mule-drawn carts. Often architecturally sumptuous with atriums, peristyle courts, suites of dining rooms, private baths, gardens, service quarters, and stables, these houses were typically built for people of a social and economic status higher than the norm. In the case of Roman fortified military camps, horses were stored in the same barracks as their riders, with the horses in the front rooms and their riders behind, making the animals available for instant deployment if necessary. Roman camps were spread about the empire, and with the establishment of an intricate and comprehensive road system, Rome could maintain peace and stability throughout their territories.

There were of course not only private and military stables but imperial ones as well. The Bible, for instance, mentions that King Solomon in his great wisdom built his stables on the southeast corner of the Temple Mount in Jerusalem to house "four thousand horses and chariots, and twelve thousand cavalry horses."[2] The Roman emperor Augustus had an extensive stable facility built nearby the Circus Maximus in Rome to house the horses that raced in the ancient stadium. Arenas for the performance of trained horses were pervasive throughout the ancient world and we find some of the best examples in Delphi, Mérida, Spain, and Constantinople. Yet perhaps the most intriguing account of stables from the ancient world comes in the myth of Hercules' labors in which the legendary strong man redirected a river to clean out the stables of King Augeas shedding light on the less glamorous aspects of horse stables and the herculean task of maintaining them clean and in order.

Throughout history, the housing of horses was an important element in the exhibition of wealth and power by kings, clergy, and the nobility. Medieval castles and cloisters contained stables for war, hunting, and transport, though the representation of the noble animal was equally important as we see in tapestries and other forms of illustration. In the early modern period, at least since the mid-fifteenth century, horse stables began to take on a more architectural character, especially in Italy where popes, rulers, and aristocratic families all sought to emphasize their humanist inclinations through elaborate building projects. The Medici family in Florence, the Montefeltro Dukes of Urbino, and the Gonzagas of Mantua, all had sumptuous stables in their city palaces and country estates. The Vatican in Rome contained papal coach houses and stables underneath the new wings of the *Cortile del Belvedere* that the architect Bramante designed to connect the Vatican Palace with the Villa Belvedere further up the hill. Further north, the Venetian architect, Andrea Palladio, made *barchese* (service buildings with colonnades, usually containing stables and other domestic uses) a requisite element of country villas, and his influence spread throughout England and the Americas, finding great favor in figures such as the English architect James Gibbs and the American Thomas Jefferson.

In the seventeenth and eighteenth century, palaces and country houses throughout Europe contained impressive stables that played an important role in maintaining a sense of royal grandeur. The French architect, Louis Le Vau, designed the barrel-vaulted stable block at Vaux-le-Vicomte (1656–61) outside of Paris, while Jules Hardouin-Mansart designed the Royal Stables at Versailles for Louis XIV (1679–82), a project that is considered the greatest housing for horses ever undertaken. Built opposite the palace with semi-circular courts, here one could find very long and high stable buildings in which hundreds of horses could be viewed. Other impressive examples include the stable court at Blenheim Palace (1705–22) designed by Sir John Vanbrugh for the Dukes of Marlborough just outside of Oxford, the Royal stables by Filippo Juvarra at La Venaria Reale, near Turin (1720–29), and the free-standing complex of stables at Chantilly (1721–35), placed at the edge of a vast lawn. In Spain, the Royal Palace of San Ildefonso "La Granja" (the farm) was built by the Spanish Bourbons (1720–45) and modelled on Versailles with military barracks, royal stables, several pleasure gardens, and an extensive hunting park. The Bourbons in Italy also built the Royal Palace at Caserta (1752–72), with gardens extending 3 km to a waterfall at the back, and in the front an oval forecourt housing barracks, stables and roads radiating outwards like the Place d'Armes at Versailles.

The nineteenth and twentieth centuries saw a return to more private, utilitarian, and functional stable buildings, with urban structures like the English mews (a stable behind a terrace house that contained horses and coaches and accessed by an alley) providing an alternative to the more conventional carriage house that in cities and towns throughout North America would be found adjacent to the main house or nearby on a side street. As travel still relied on horses as a principal means of transport, private urban stables proliferated. New functions were added such as wash stands, harness rooms, cleaning rooms, and lavatories for the grooms. Yet the growth of cities and rail expansion also allowed for an increasing number of horses to work as "machines" in mills and factories, to deliver freight, pull streetcars, and enable police departments and the military to maintain order. The livery stable, or a stable where horses, teams, and carriages were for hire, but also where privately owned horses could be boarded for a short time, emerged as a variant to the private stable.

Often, the families who owned such industries as railroad and commercial manufacturing also kept horses in their private country estates, transforming the physical landscape of equestrian recreation and sport. New hunt clubs emerged in exclusive suburban and semi-rural areas, providing a rustic complement to the elegant social clubs of the city. Breeding and training farms supported the racing industry which increased significantly in the late-nineteenth and early-twentieth centuries. The combination of agricultural and recreational activities became the standard of twentieth century stables, and the variety of stable buildings in terms of the arrangement and number of stalls and ancillary uses reflected the variety of architectural styles in which they were designed and built.

Today, stables continue to flourish around the world in private estates, stud farms, equestrian centers, riding clubs, military camps, and even royal estates. The modern stables featured in this book provide a glimpse into the current state of stable building across the globe, built by people of a variety of social classes for the purpose of housing horses and to fulfill their passion for the art of horsemanship. Yet it is the architecture as much as the horses that stand out in this book, as the commitment to building can be seen in every case to complement the dedication to animal husbandry. The care and craftsmanship that is so clearly discernible in the making of these modern stables is equivalent to the attention that is given to breeding, training, and maintaining these majestic creatures.

In the pages that follow, one will find a variety of architectural projects in North and South America, Europe, and Oceania, that range from modest rustic timber stables to grand equestrian riding centers, but you will not find any princely or aristocratic stables. Nor will you find military or police barracks. Rather, all the projects contained in this book are privately owned and situated in rural bucolic settings, where the landscape seems to extend directly from the stables out towards the horizon. And even though one example in Sweden belongs to a municipality, its siting on a peninsula surrounded by water makes it seems as if it was a rural property. Some stables pertain to existing farm complexes, while others are simply additions to private residences, some with pre-existing buildings in place. Some of the stables are for sport horses that are used in polo, shooting, or show jumping, and others are for exhibition and competition.

The architecture of the stables featured in this book ranges from traditional to highly modern with most of the projects hovering somewhere in between. Though this is not so much a book about architectural style as it is about architectural approach. In most cases there is a great sensitivity to the existing landscape and historical context of the region in which the stables are situated, and therefore bridging the gap between the past and the future is a concern of both the architects and their clients. The use of materials also dictates quite often the form and structure of many of the stable buildings, with wood, metal, and stone being the most common elements employed on both the exterior and interior. Climatic conditions also inform the choice of materials, and the necessity for neutral light, controlled ventilation, and other mechanical necessities, appear as natural as the dirt on which the horses train. Occasionally concrete and other manufactured materials are blended in to give the buildings a distinctly industrial appearance—after all, barns are highly functional structures. Yet regardless of the architectural approach, all the projects featured in this book show as much care and sensitivity to the individual horse stalls as they do to the entirety of the site and related programs, with indoor and outdoor arenas, paddocks, service buildings, and gardens providing a humane face to the otherwise functional buildings. Social spaces for the horses, riders, and visitors also play an important role in filling out the projects, making stables not just places for sport but also of entertainment and leisure.

There is a beauty and serenity in all these projects that reflects the majesty of these animals, the distinctive landscapes in which they are set, and the creative visions of the owners, architects, and designers who have all brought them into being. It is clear from the projects that follow that the modern stable is a building type whose popularity is on the rise and who's creative potential seems limitless, this despite the relative simplicity of the building's basic needs. But isn't that always the case with architecture that emerges from the soil around it, when necessity dictates the need for invention,

and beauty is the result of the most unpredictable and satisfying circumstances. To be sure, the allure of housing horses is a story of architecture, design, landscape, and a unique way of living in magnificent places—and spaces—that are made exclusively for horses and for those who love them.

[1] *De architectura*, 6.6.4
[2] 2 Chronicles 9.25.

Previous spread: Equestrian Complex, Main Stables Perspective, Alireza Sagharchi-Stanhope Gate
This spread: Maha Equestrian Resort, Estudio Ramos

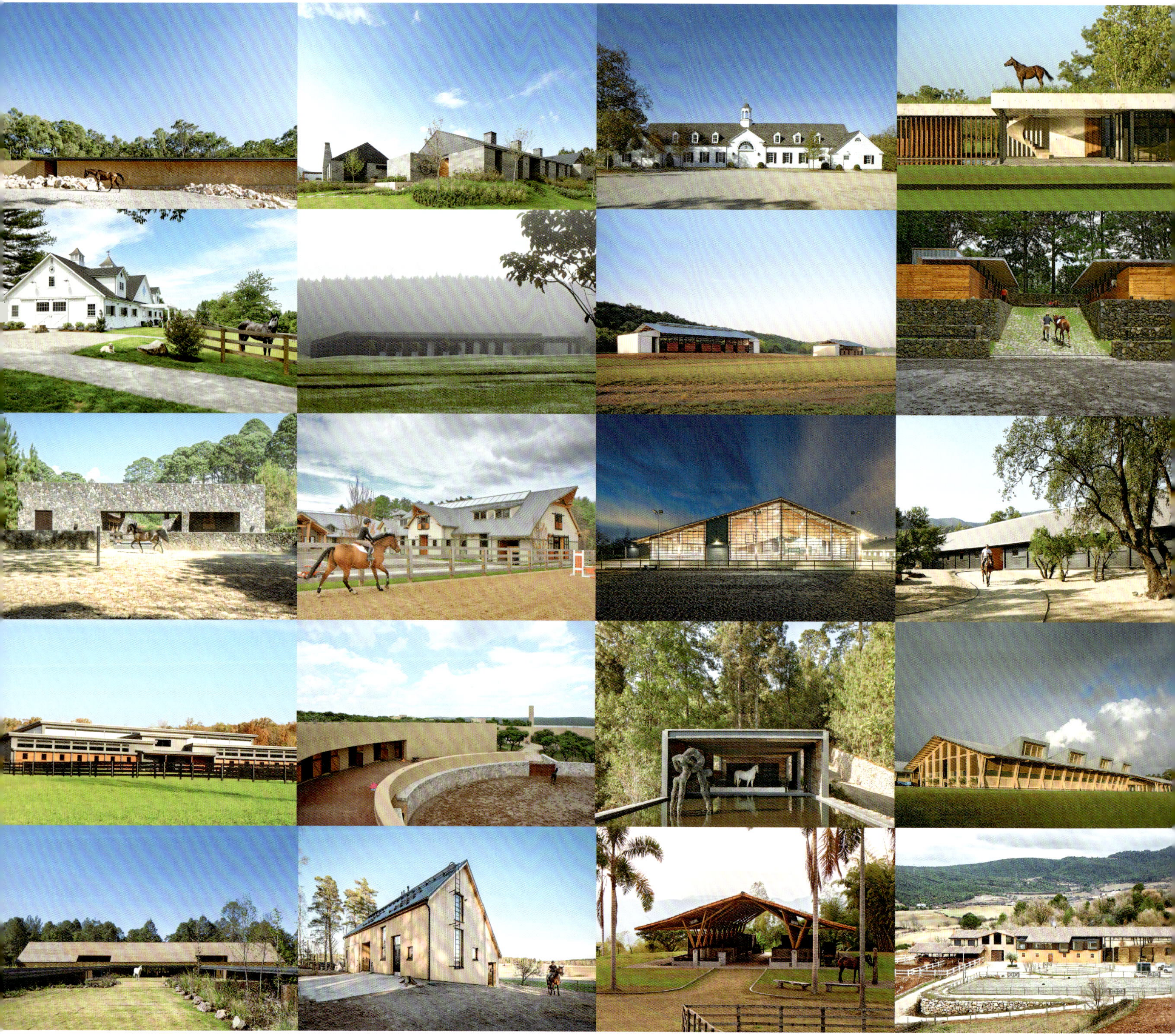

STABLES

Ecuestre Puebla	**16**
San Francisco Ranch	**26**
Shooting Stable in Alabama	**40**
Figueras Polo Stables	**50**
Merricks Equestrian Center	**64**
DarkHorse	**76**
Fazenda Boa Vista	**88**
Air Barns	**102**
Hípico del Bosque	**108**
Horse Riding Field in Cattle Farm	**120**
House In Cerro Gordo	**126**
Beechwood Stables	**136**
Klagshamn Equestrian Center	**148**
MSporthorses	**154**
Cannery Barn	**164**
Pegaso Farm	**168**
La Rosilla	**176**
Pabellon El Mirador	**186**
Equestrian Centre	**198**
La Stella Ranch	**206**
Proyecto Ecuestre	**216**
Kekkapää Stables	**230**
Caballerizas Sanint	**236**
Hípica La Llena	**246**
Cutting Horse Ranch	**252**

Ecuestre Puebla
Manuel Cervantes Estudio

Puebla, México

Building Area:
3,586 m²

Site Area:
10,949 m²

Architect in Charge:
Manuel Cervantes Céspedes

Project Team:
Helena Rojas, Jose Luis Heredia, Oswaldo Flores

Photographer:
Rafael Gamo

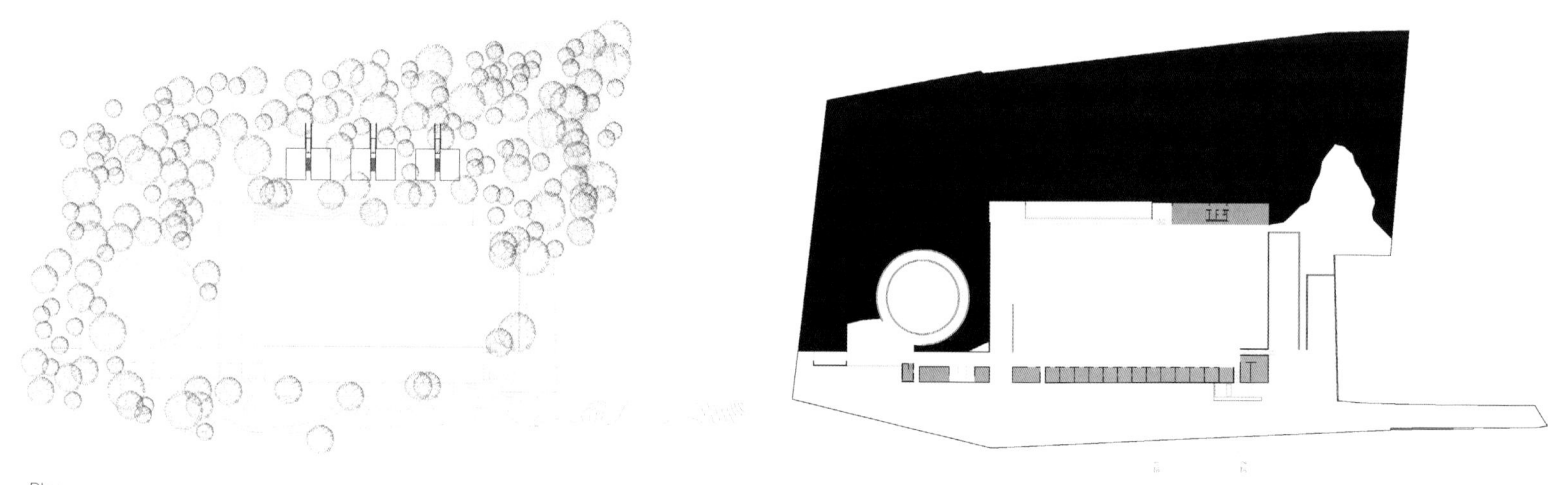

Plan

This extraordinarily elegant project is located on a rocky site in the western highlands of the city of Puebla, Mexico, adjacent to a large natural reserve. The client's intended purpose was to create a modern yet rustic equestrian center that integrated residential life with equestrian life. The program included a 35 x 70-meter riding arena, a circular track, stables, a stage, and a small private housing development. The site's topographic slope presented a challenge in locating the large open arena and track, requiring significant site cuts and immense retaining walls. The project can be clearly understood in section where each function is placed in a level according to the existing topography and tree canopy, seeking the right conditions for each program's use. In plan the project is centered on the riding arena with the stables lining the long side facing downhill and the housing development on the opposite side climbing up the hill. The stables were placed alongside the arena in a repetition of 4 x 4-meter modules under a wood and steel sloping roof. This allowed additional modules to be added throughout the process, according to the client's wishes. Six houses were placed at the highest part of the site, formed in pairs overlooking the open space. Privacy is maintained through the abundant landscape surrounding the houses. At one short end of the arena, there is a circular track and at the opposite end a large enclosed water basin and stone stairs climbing up the hill. More than anything, though, this incredibly compelling project is linked directly to the rustic site through its use of natural materials, with all the rock that was cleared when the track was built used on the stable's foundation and retaining walls. The contrast of the flat linear planes of the architecture with the organic stone surfaces and scattered rock piles throughout, give the impression that the equestrian center is situated among ancient Mesoamerican ruins.

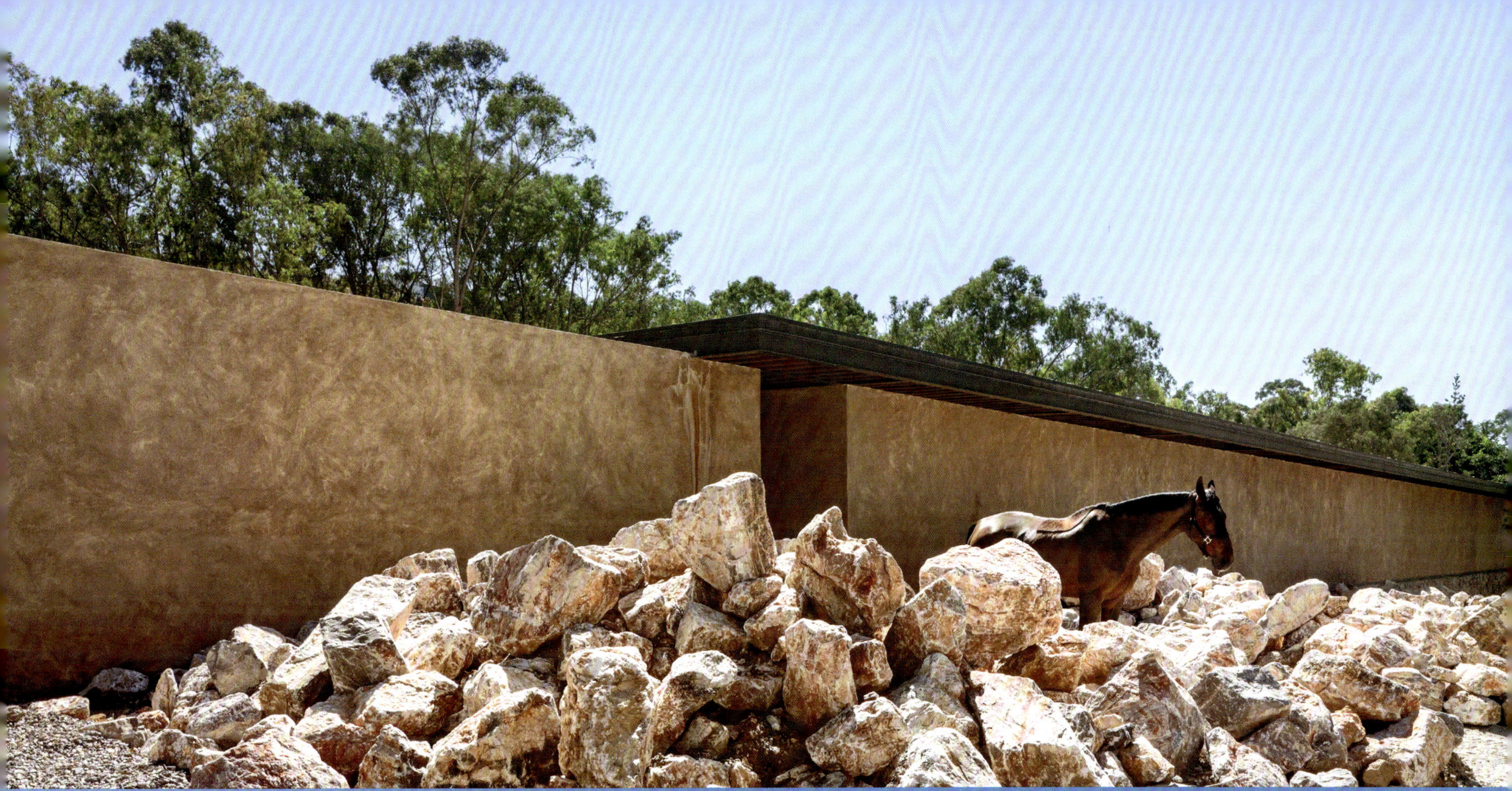
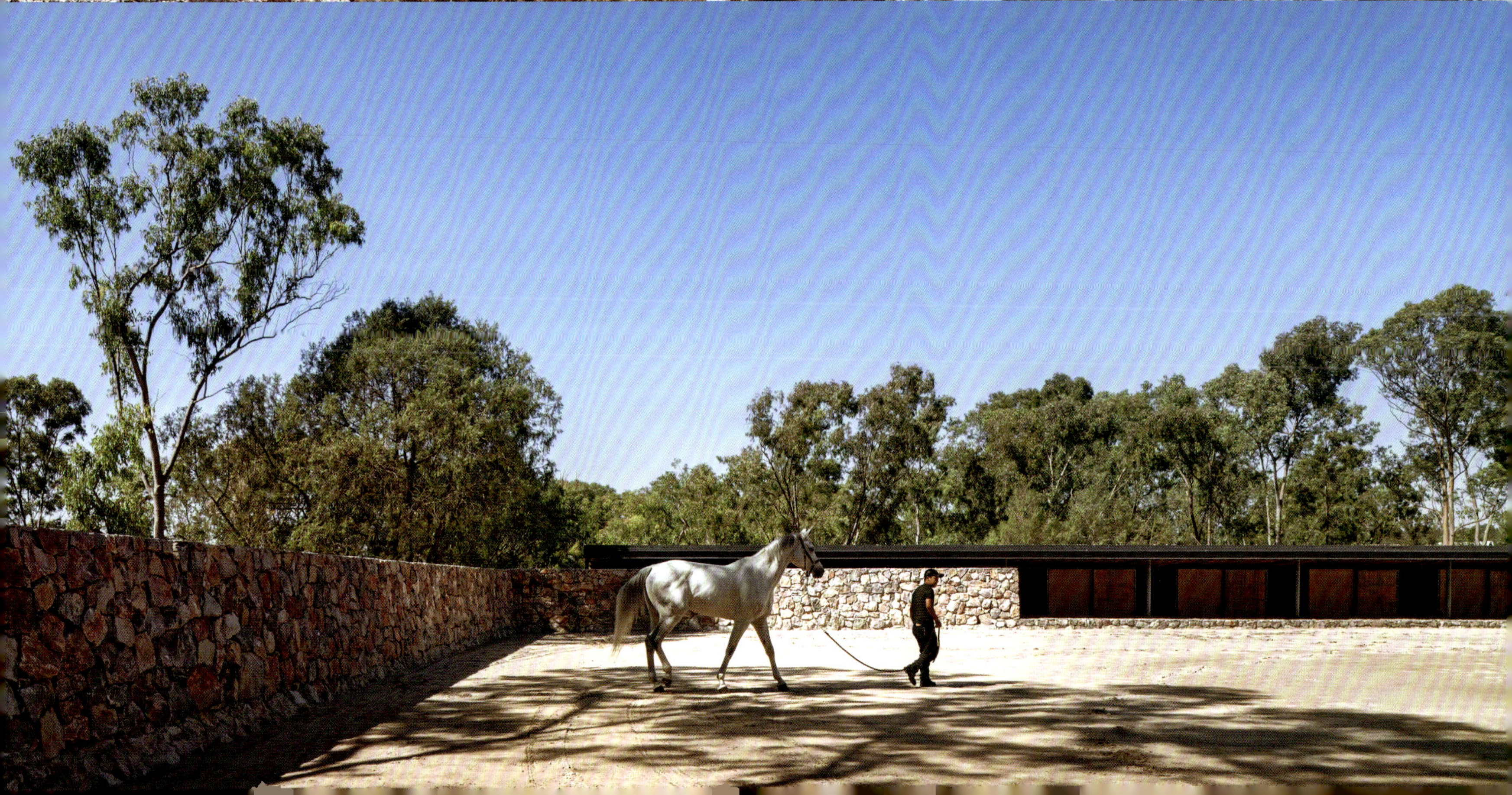

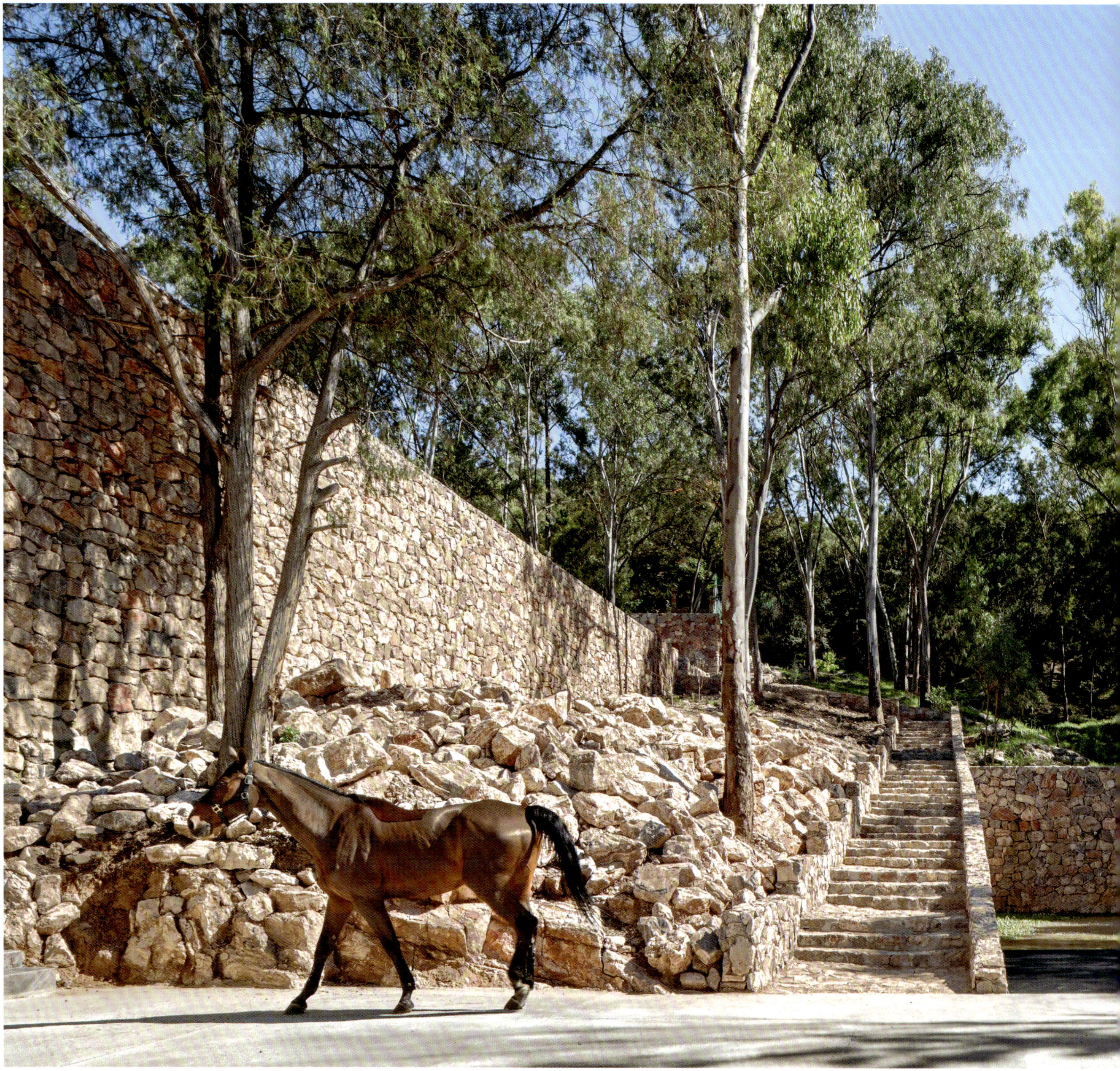

ECUESTRE PUEBLA 21

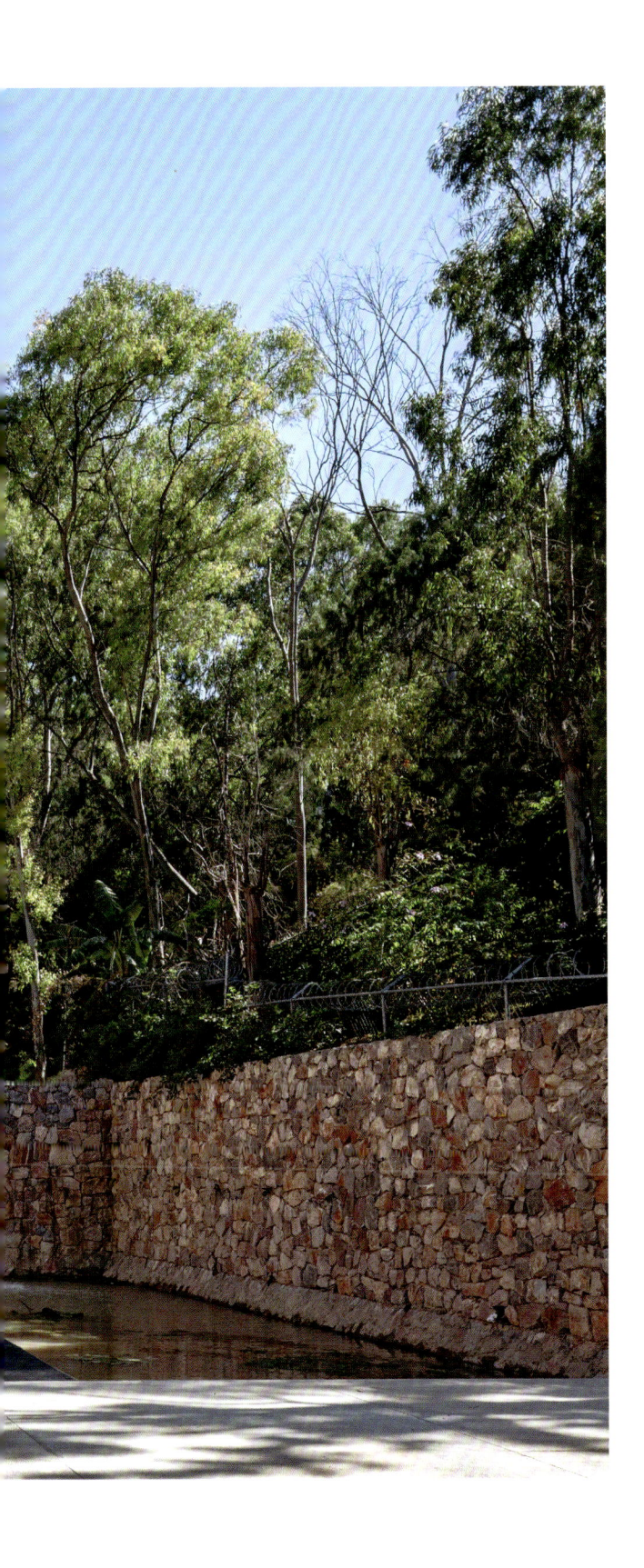

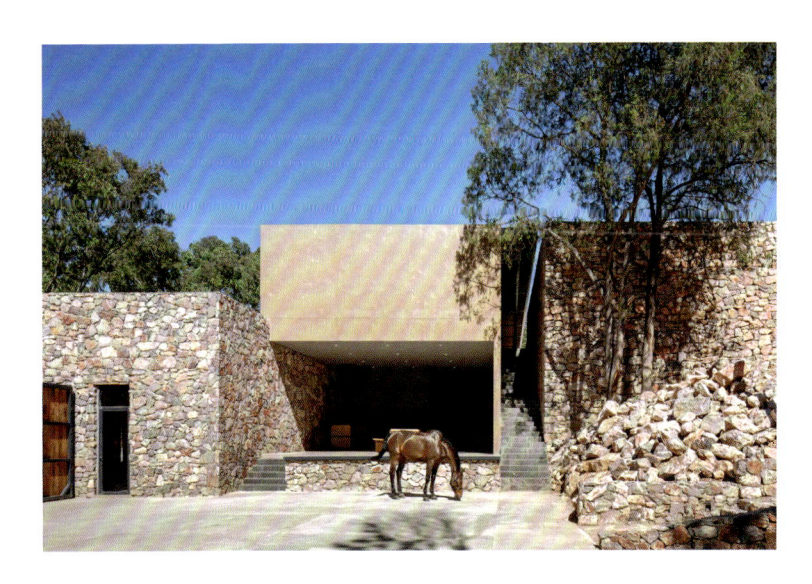

22 MANUEL CERVANTES ESTUDIO

ECUESTRE PUEBLA

24 MANUEL CERVANTES ESTUDIO

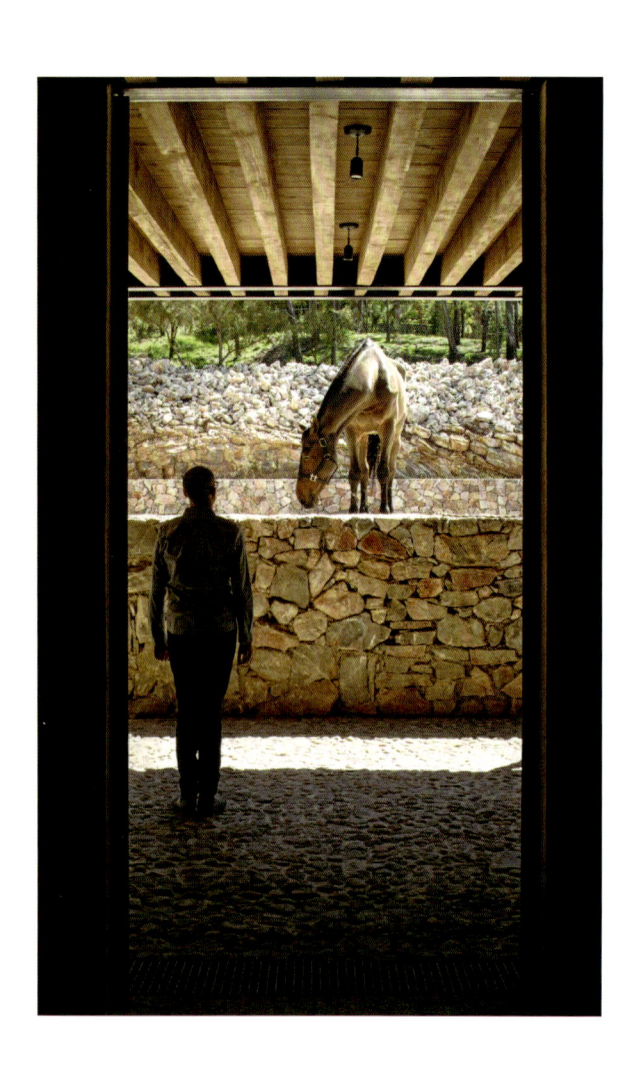

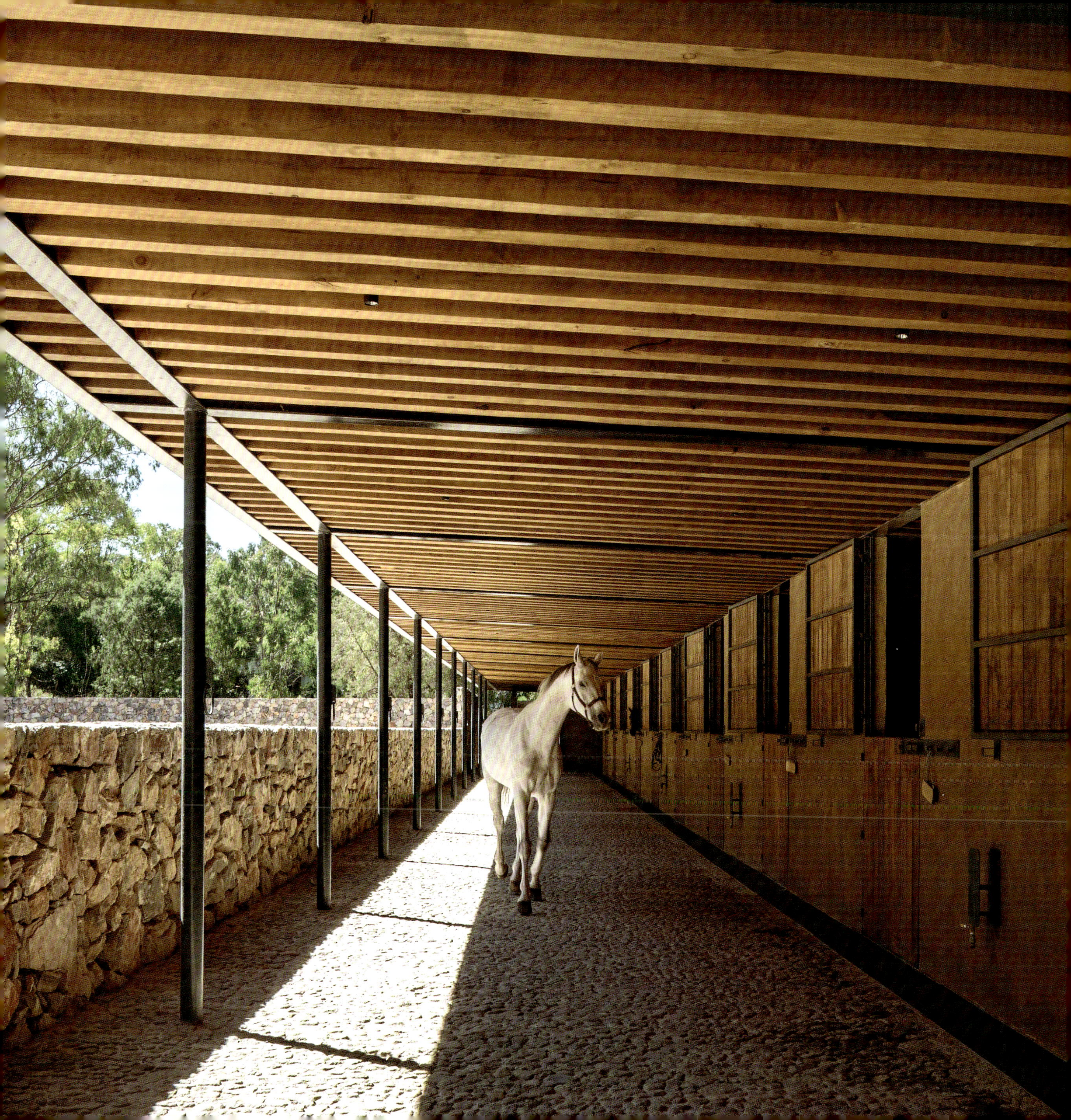

San Francisco Ranch

AE Arquitectos

Tapalpa, Jalisco, Mexico

Building Area:
1,030 m²

Site Area:
23,507 m²

Architect in Charge:
Andrés Escobar

Project Team:
Alejandra Rojas, Josué Carrillo
Silvia Sitten

Interior Designer:
Mumo Interiorismo

Landscape Designer:
Bonsai Paisajismo

Photographer:
Lorena Darquea

Plan

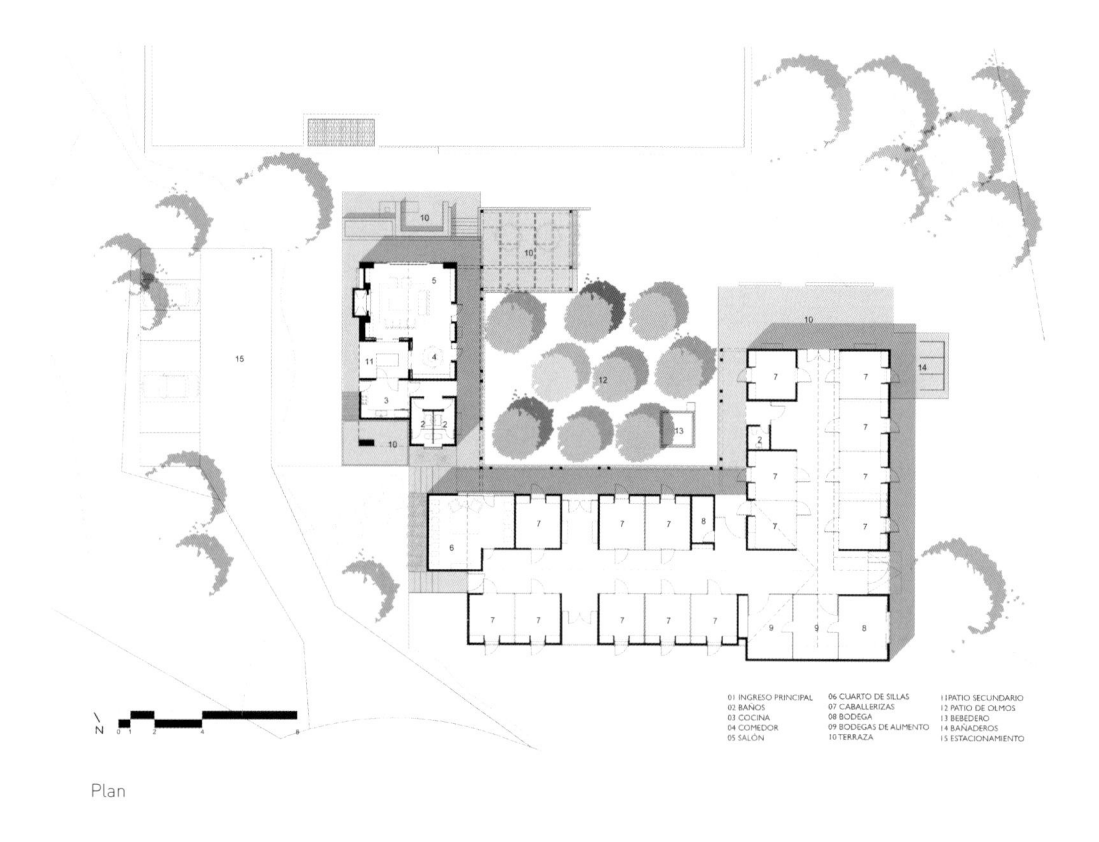

01 INGRESO PRINCIPAL	06 CUARTO DE SILLAS	11 PATIO SECUNDARIO
02 BAÑOS	07 CABALLERIZAS	12 PATIO DE OLMOS
03 COCINA	08 BODEGA	13 BEBEDERO
04 COMEDOR	09 BODEGAS DE ALIMENTO	14 BAÑADEROS
05 SALÓN	10 TERRAZA	15 ESTACIONAMIENTO

San Francisco Ranch is located just north of the city of Tapalpa, in the Mexican state of Jalisco, in a residential development of large private lots with shared common areas that encourages each property to focus inwardly. Surrounded by mountains and pine tree forests, the area is recognized for the equestrian lifestyle of the local inhabitants. For this reason, the project takes advantage of the gently sloping conditions of the site, integrating the stables to the natural landscape and creating a harmony among the buildings. The project is located over a slightly raised area surrounded by forest, with rough and heavy volcanic stones serving as the walls of the structure. In plan the project is organized like a large courtyard house with an open patio at the center and buildings surrounding it on three sides, all connected by covered wooden porticoes. The central patio is filled with elm trees, reinterpreting the forest at the core of the project. A fountain underneath the elms brings the environment to life by embracing the animals and their horsemen after a long day of riding. The stable building is L-shaped with a central passageway and stalls on either side, all of which wraps around the patio. The main house occupies the third wing around the courtyard and contains a main gathering room that is open to it with a large walk-in fireplace at the opposite wall. A covered wooden dining terrace partially encloses the fourth side of the court. On the exterior, the massive chimney stands out from the gable roof, reminding the viewer of the primitive origins of architecture in fire and coexistence. The use of simple masonry, wood, and tile reinforces the vernacular character of the project. Yet beyond its use as a stable building and residence, the main purpose of this project is to conjure up memories through the recognizable domestic-scaled architecture. The porticos, interior spaces, and patios all recall the idea of the traditional Mexican house, where the landscape plays a fundamental role in the arrangement of the whole.

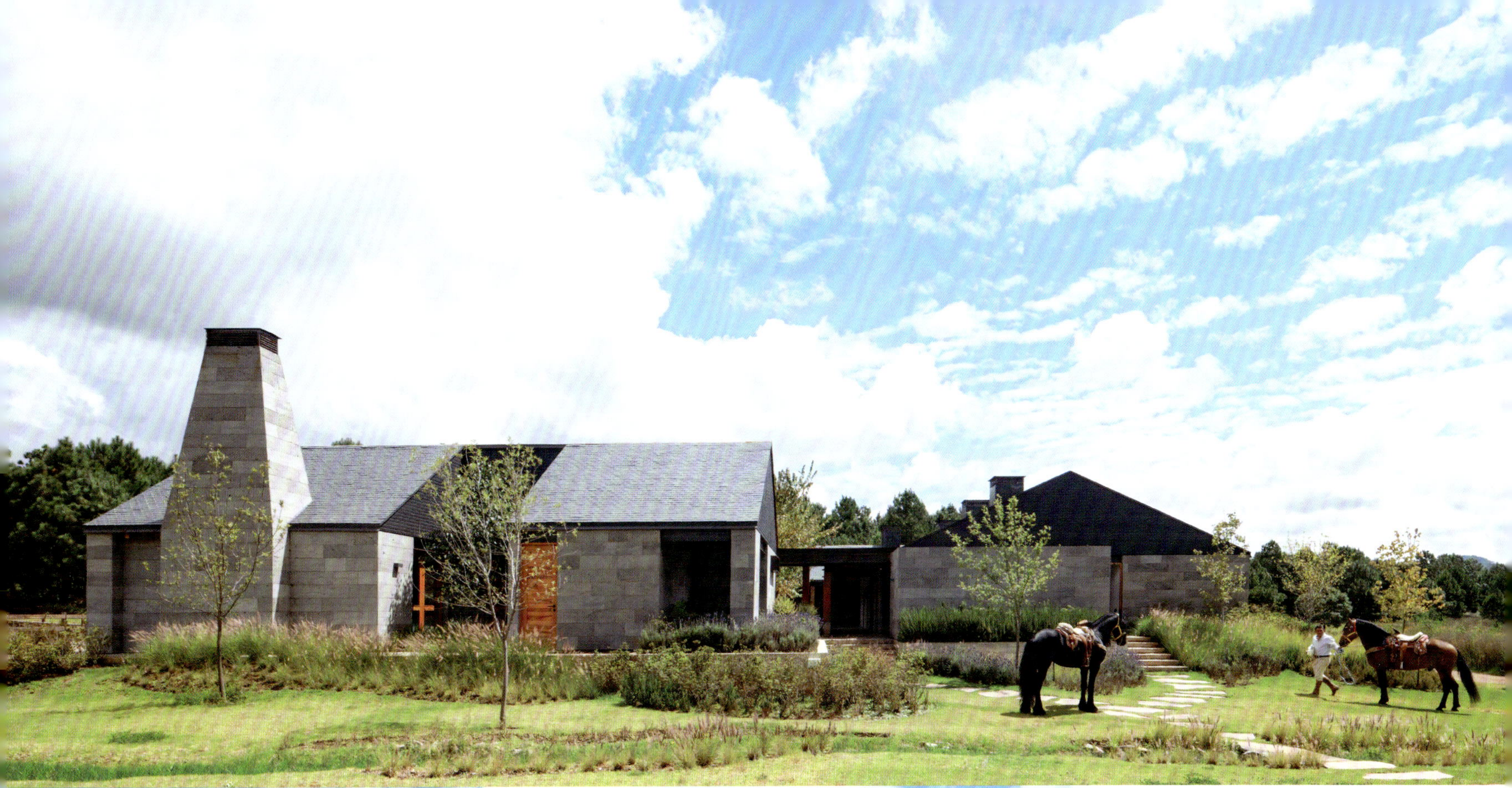

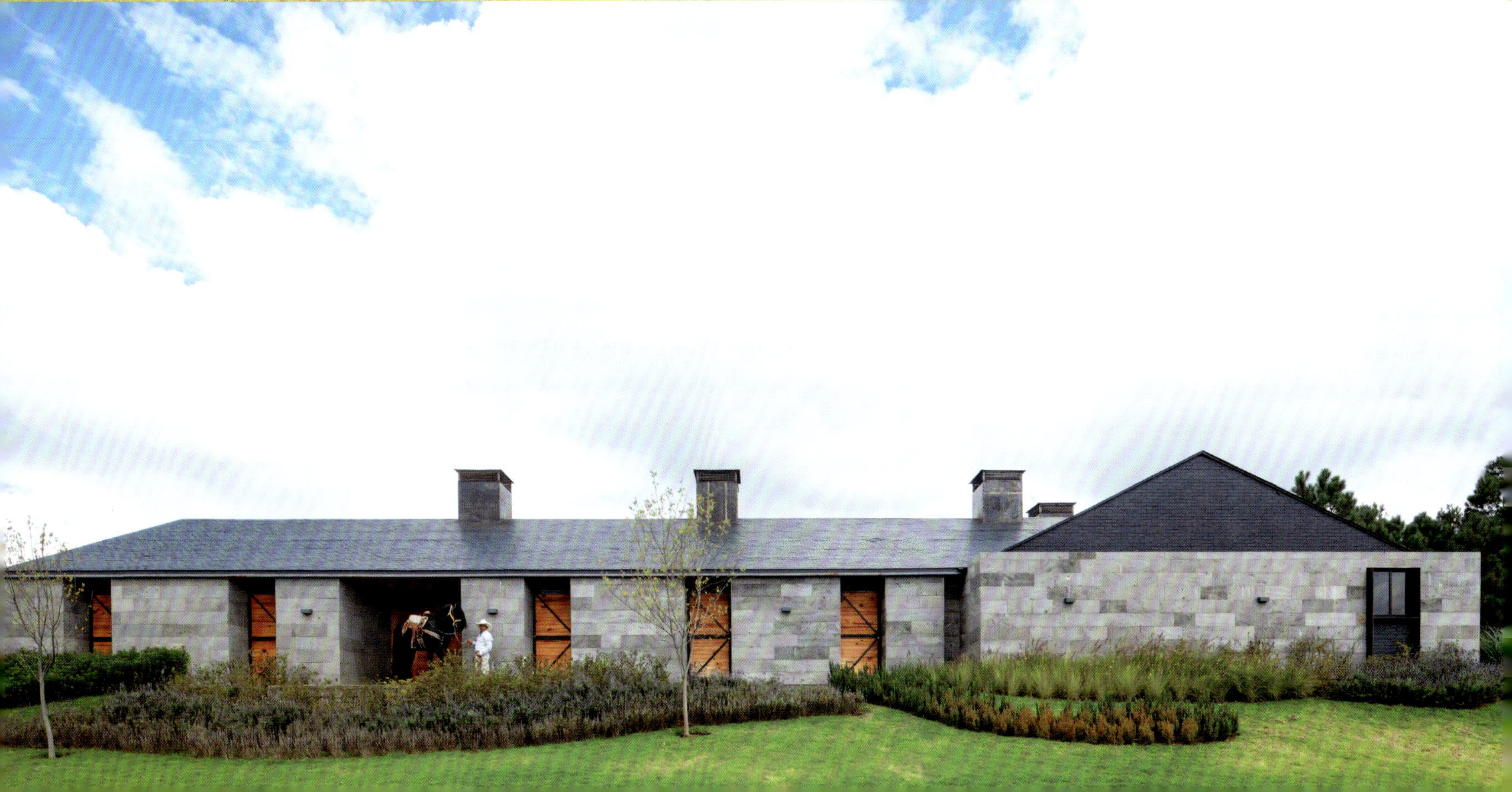

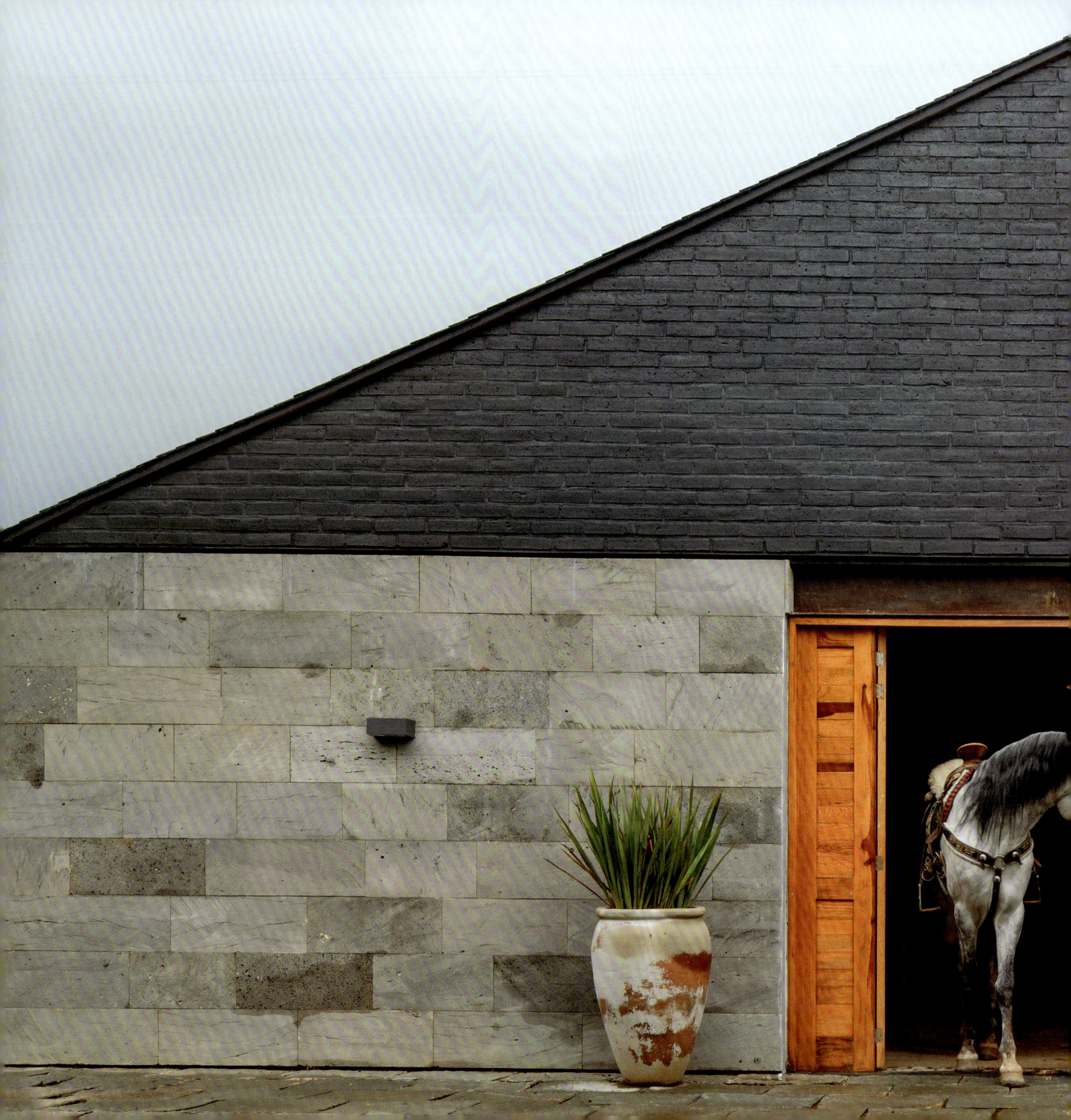

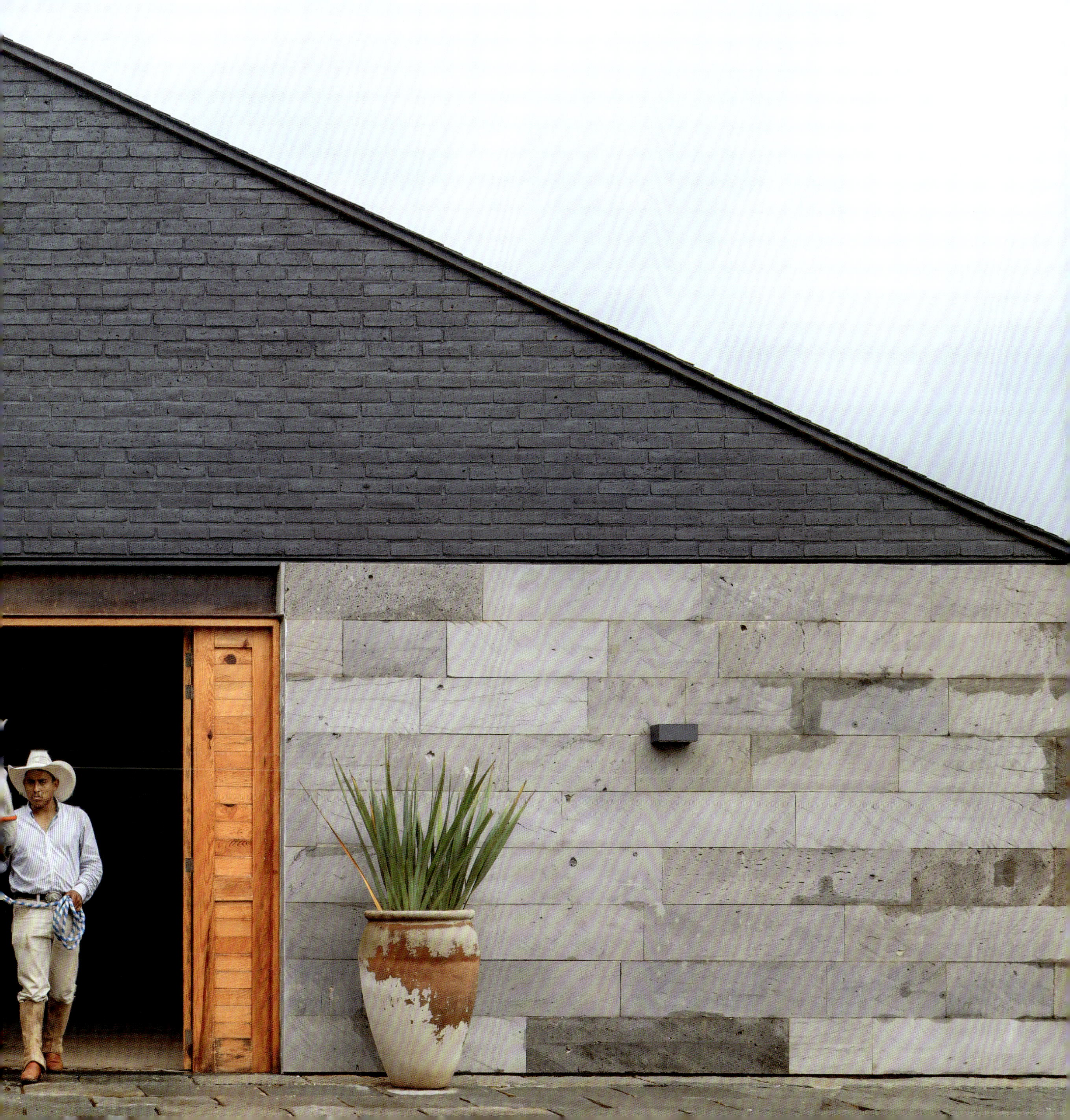

32 AE ARQUITECTOS

SAN FRANCISCO RANCH

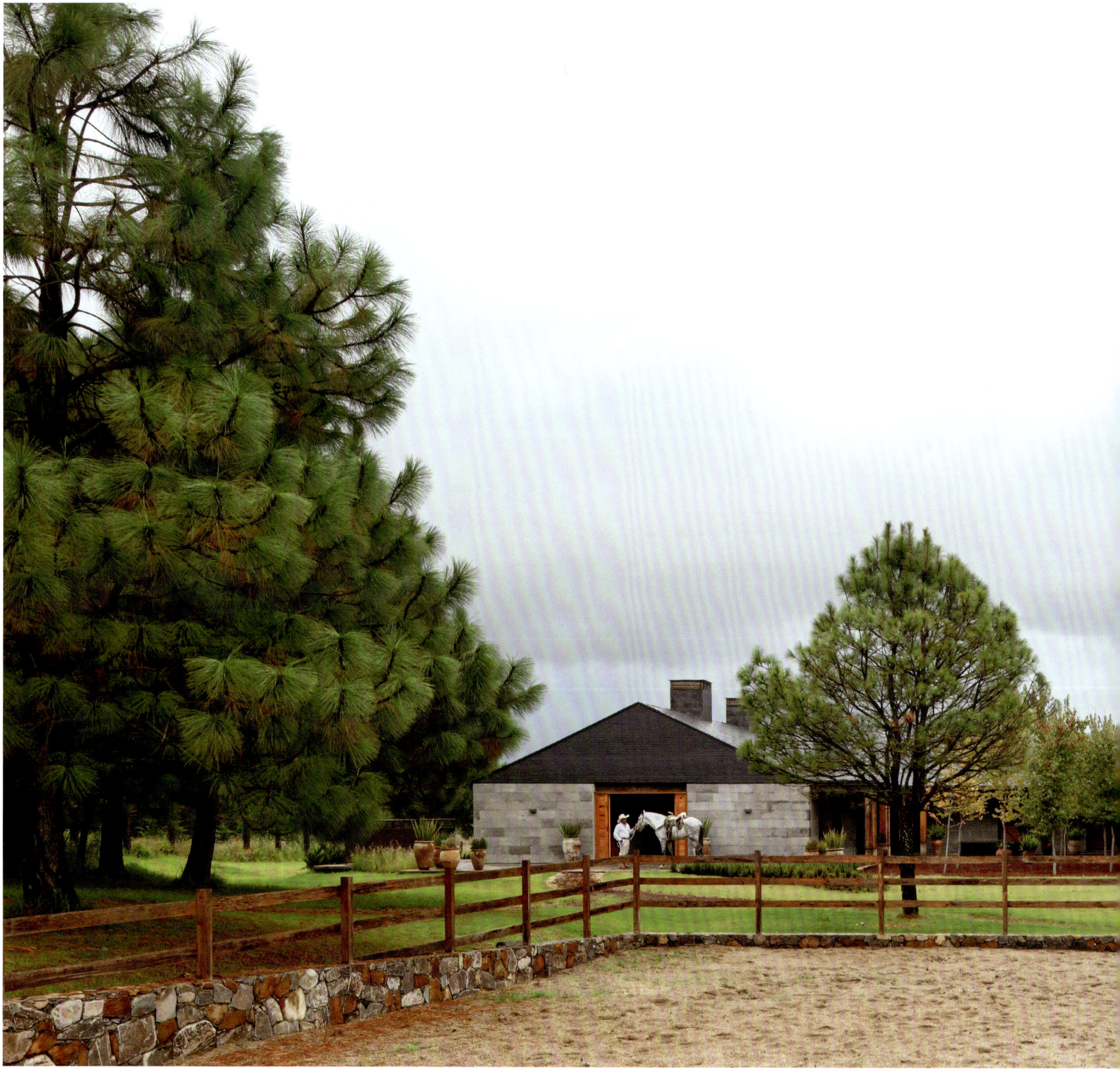

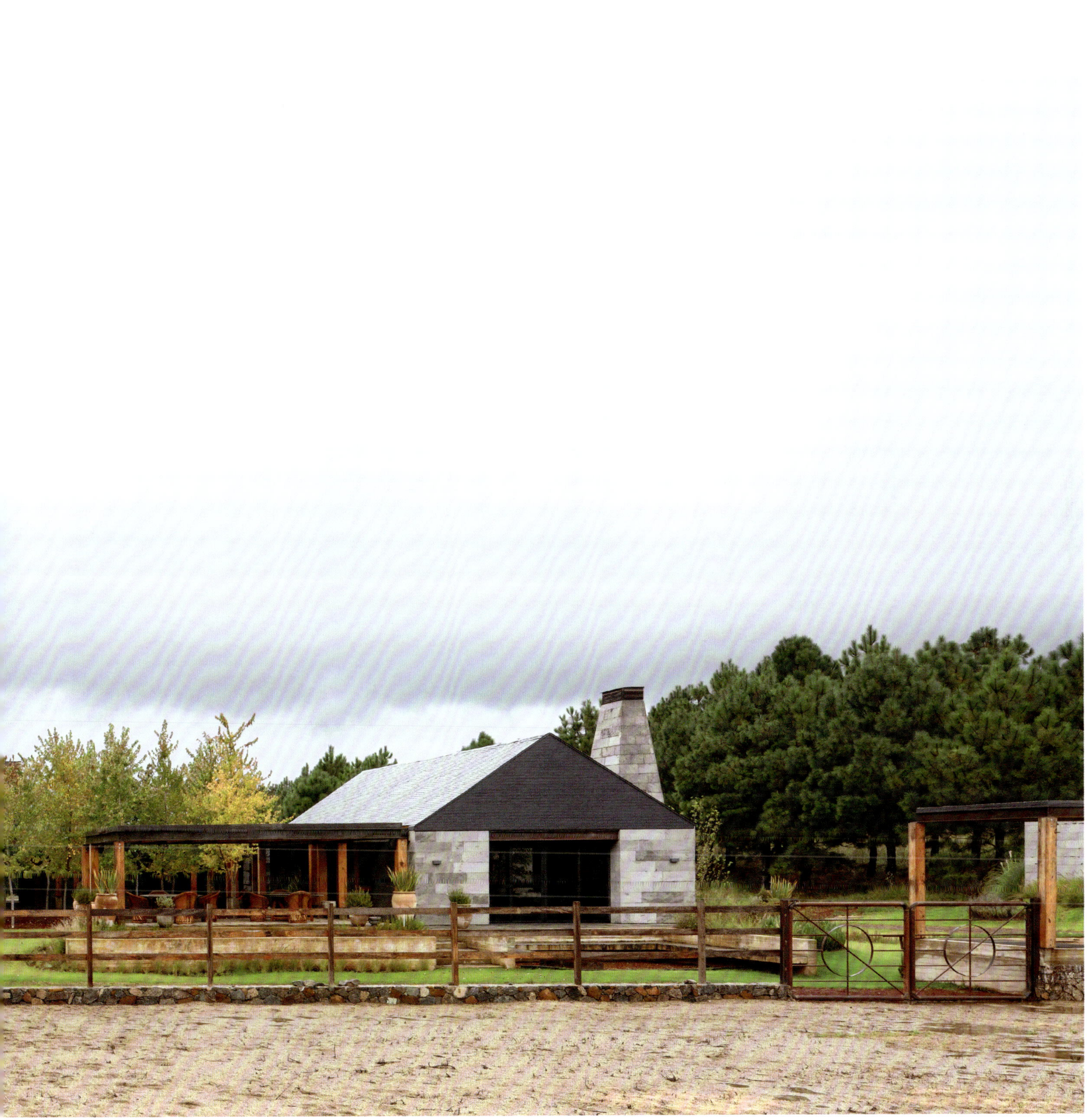

36 AE ARQUITECTOS

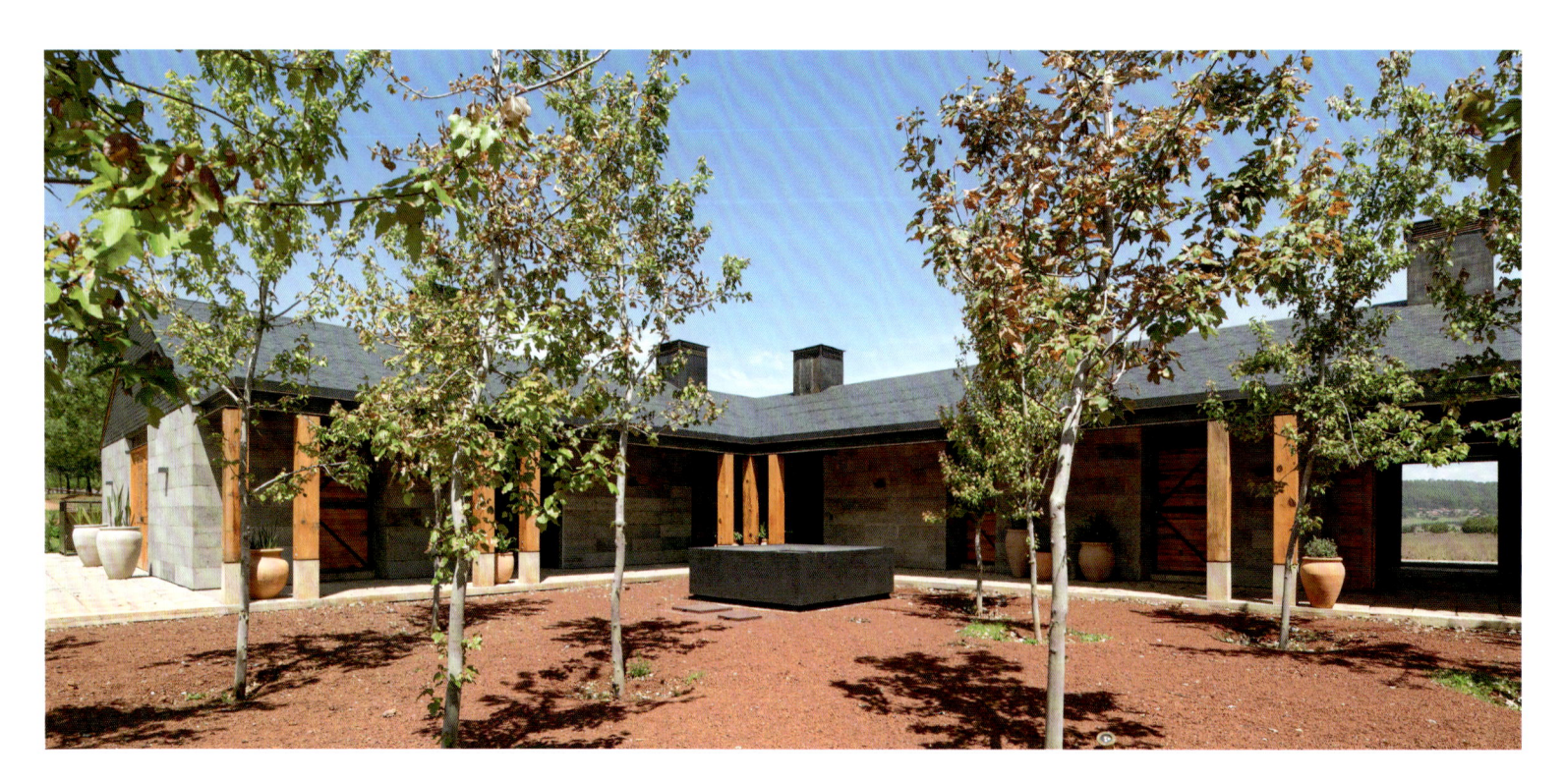

SAN FRANCISCO RANCH

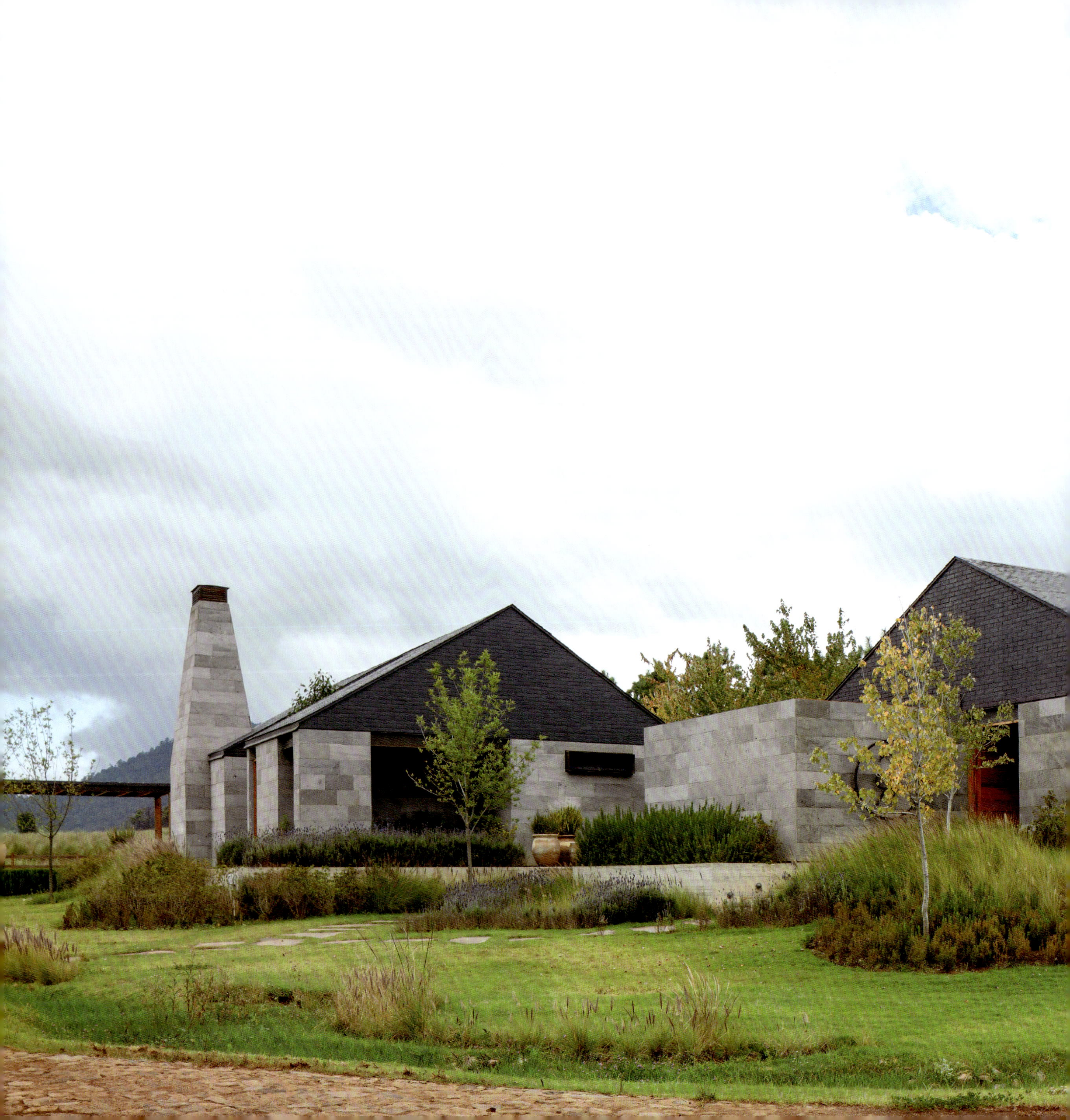

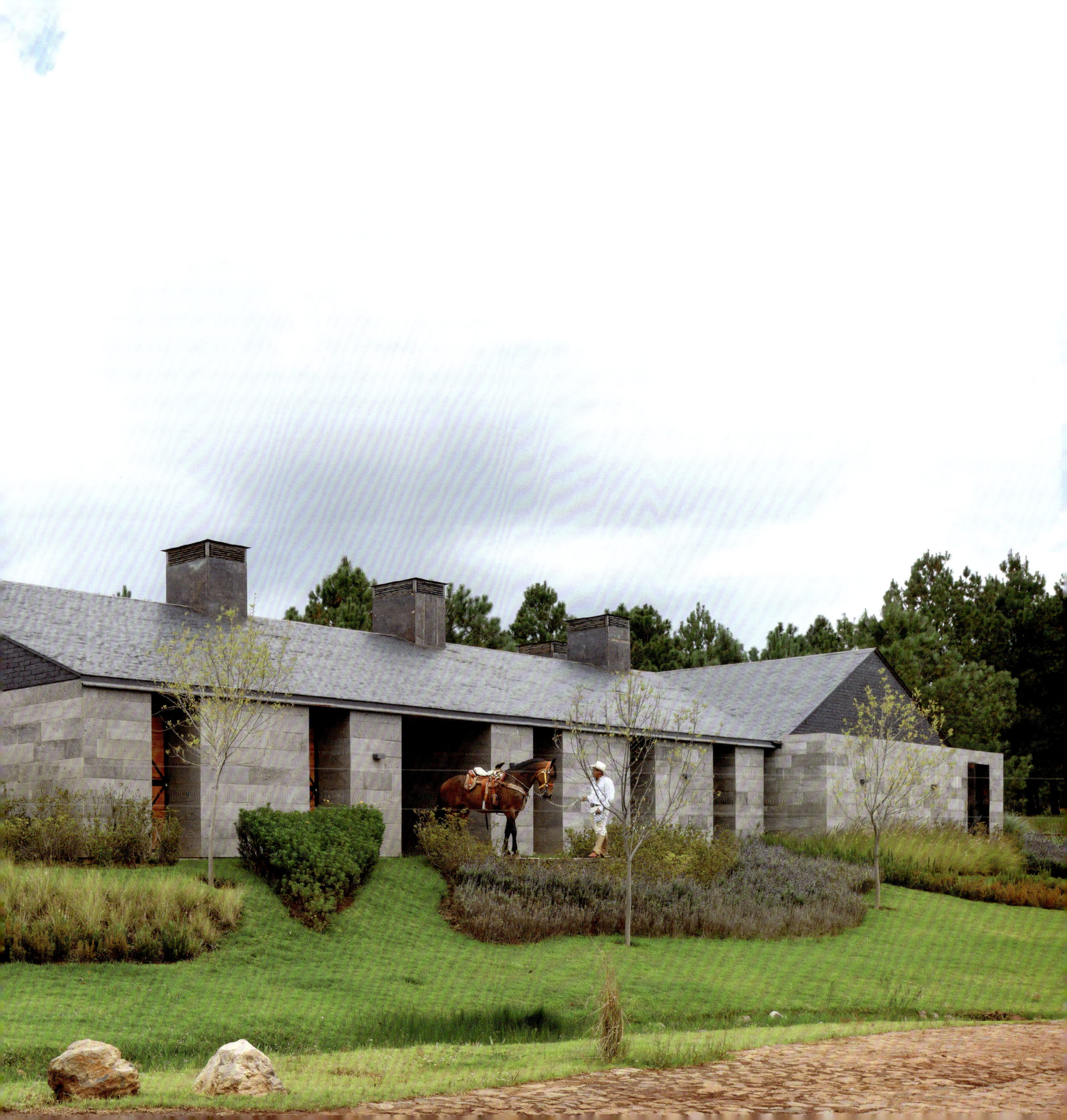

Shooting Stable in Alabama
James F. Carter

Union Springs, Alabama, United States

Building Area:
1,068 m²

Architect in Charge:
James F. Carter

Project Team:
James F. Carter,
Scott Boyd

Photographer:
Jean Allsopp

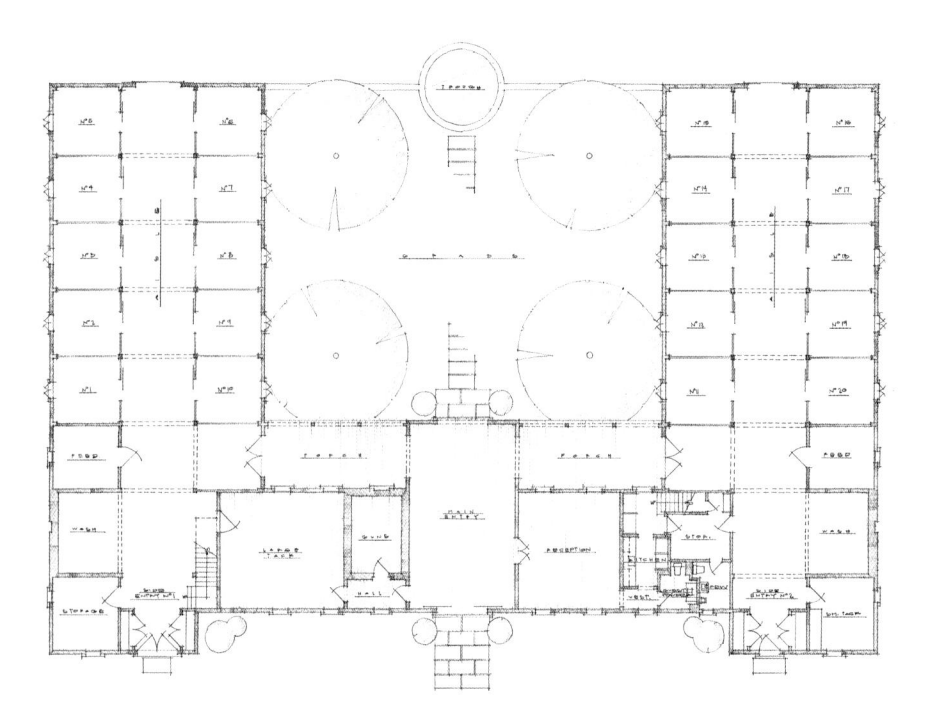

Plan

This entirely traditional project consists of a new stable as part of a planned farm group to serve as the signature building on a historic Southern shooting plantation. The programming requirements included space for 20 horses with necessary equipment, feed, wash and storage areas along with a place to entertain guests. The design intent and material selections hearken to the original 1920s colonial revival structure on the property and reflect the casual personality of the owners. In plan, the project is conceived as a large U-shaped complex of volumes with an open entry hall at the center and stable wings on either side. Service functions are in between the hall and the two stable wings, with wooden porticoes opening out to the open court overlooking the horse fields. Strong axial relationships are developed within the symmetry of the overall composition. From the gravel motor court out front, visitors are treated to a distant view through the arched openings of the main entry. Landscaping components, including fencing, gates, trees and a large watering trough, further enhance the main building's axial centerline. Two smaller projecting gables on the long front elevation, and the use of large shuttered windows, custom wood doors, wood detailing, and roof cupola are some of the architectural aspects incorporated to maintain a more residential scale and downplay the inherently large size of the facility. The two rear (stall) wings of the building are timber framed and integrate seamlessly with the front portion of the building, framed predominately with conventional lumber. Stud walls are covered with wood boards, both interior and exterior. The use of weathering shake roof shingles and copper elements on the exterior with reclaimed wood boards (in unpainted areas) and salvaged brick flooring at interior spaces provide a sense of age, warmth, and character. This project shows how new buildings designed in a traditional manner can still provide inventive and clever solutions to age-old problems.

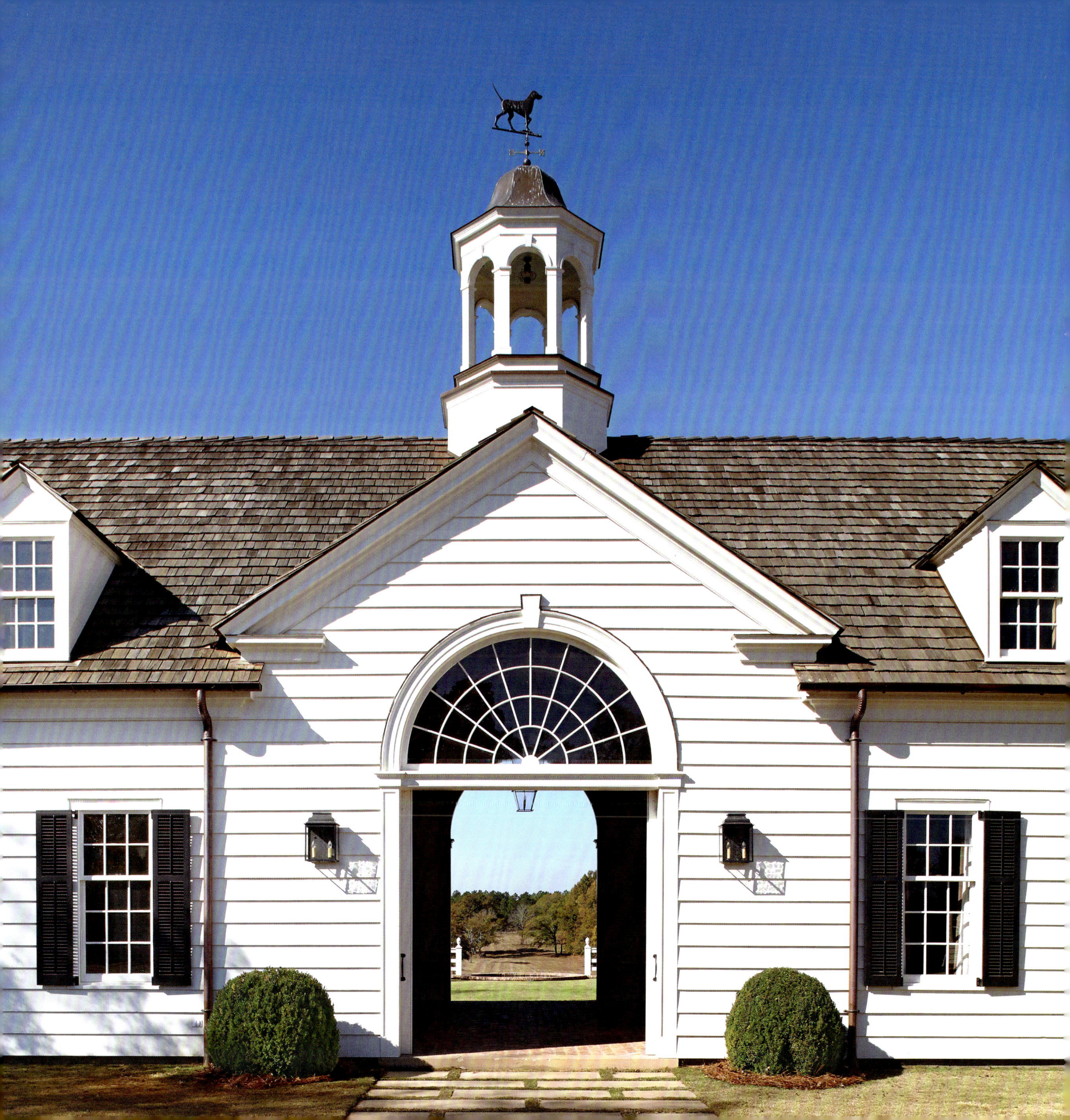

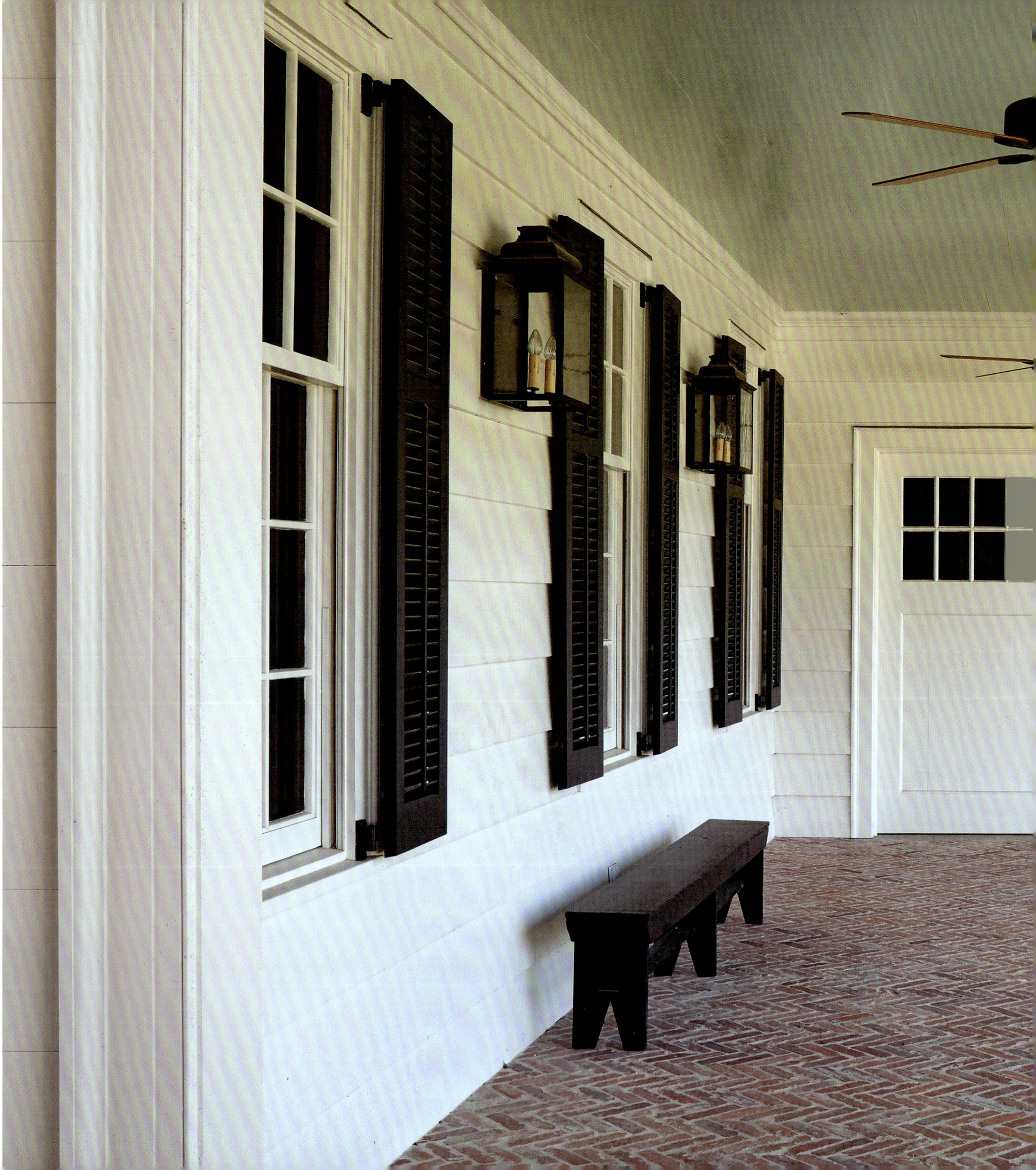

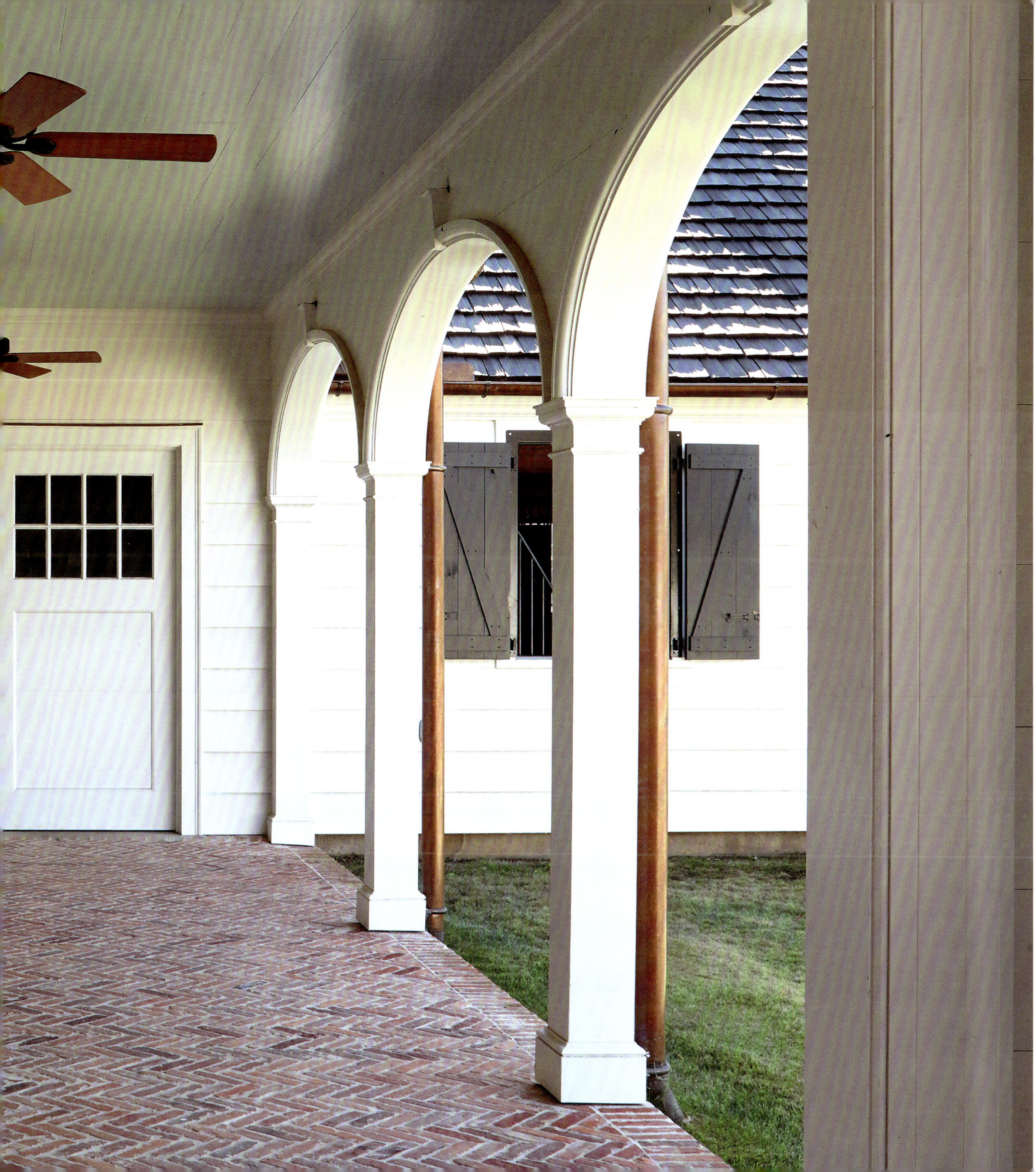

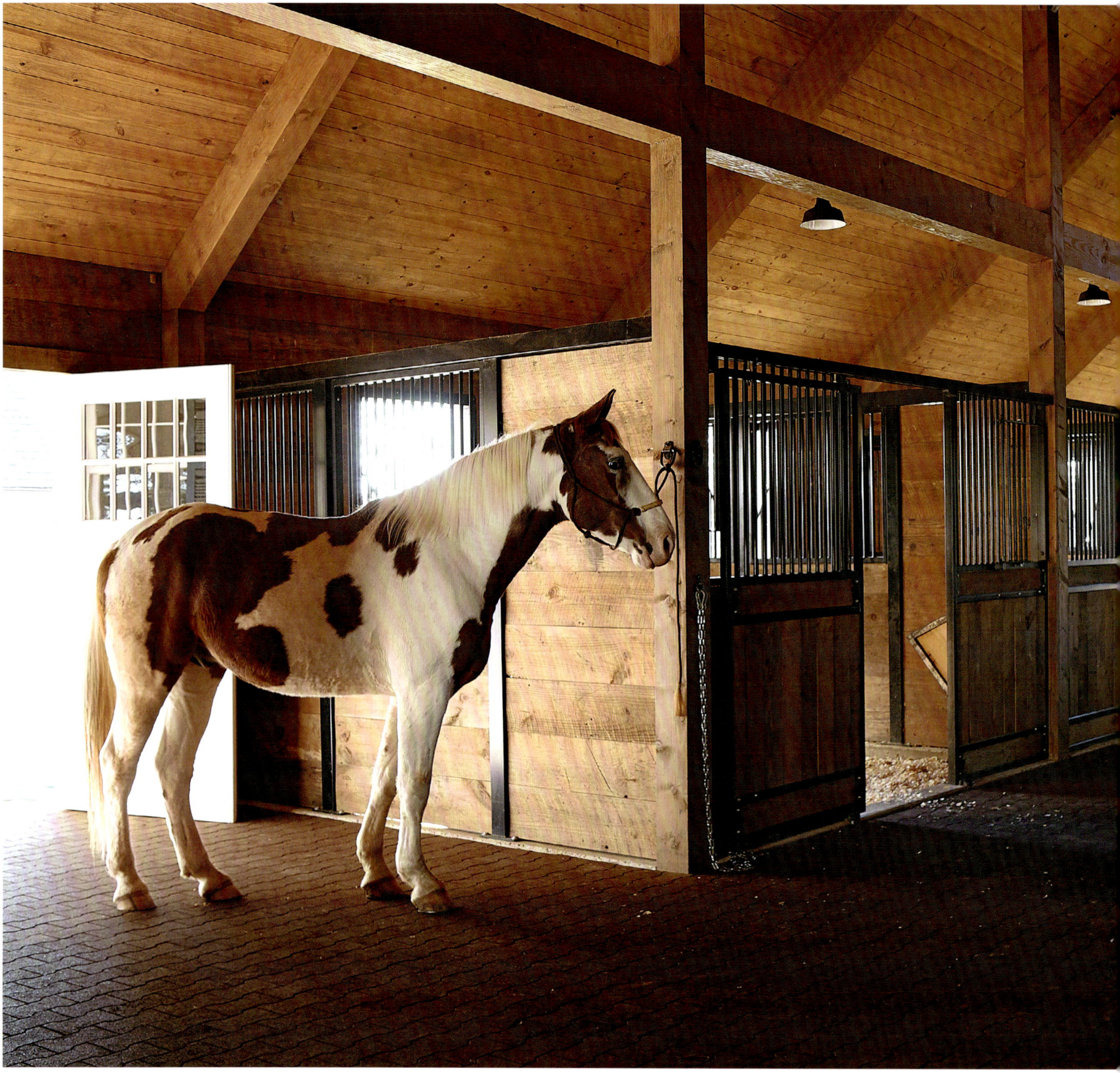

SHOOTING STABLE IN ALABAMA 47

48 JAMES F. CARTER

SHOOTING STABLE IN ALABAMA   **49**

Figueras Polo Stables
Estudio Ramos

General Rodríguez, Buenos Aires, Argentina

Building Area:
3,850 m²

Site Area:
12 hectares

Architect in Charge:
Juan Ignacio Ramos, Ignacio Ramos

Project Team:
Mercedes Martty, Sofia Ordoñez, Luis D'Adamo, Sol Mendizabal, Lucia Stafforini

Interior Designer:
Estudio Ramos

Landscape Designer:
Ernestina Anchorena

Photographer:
Daniela Mc Adden, Oberto Gili, Matias Lixklett

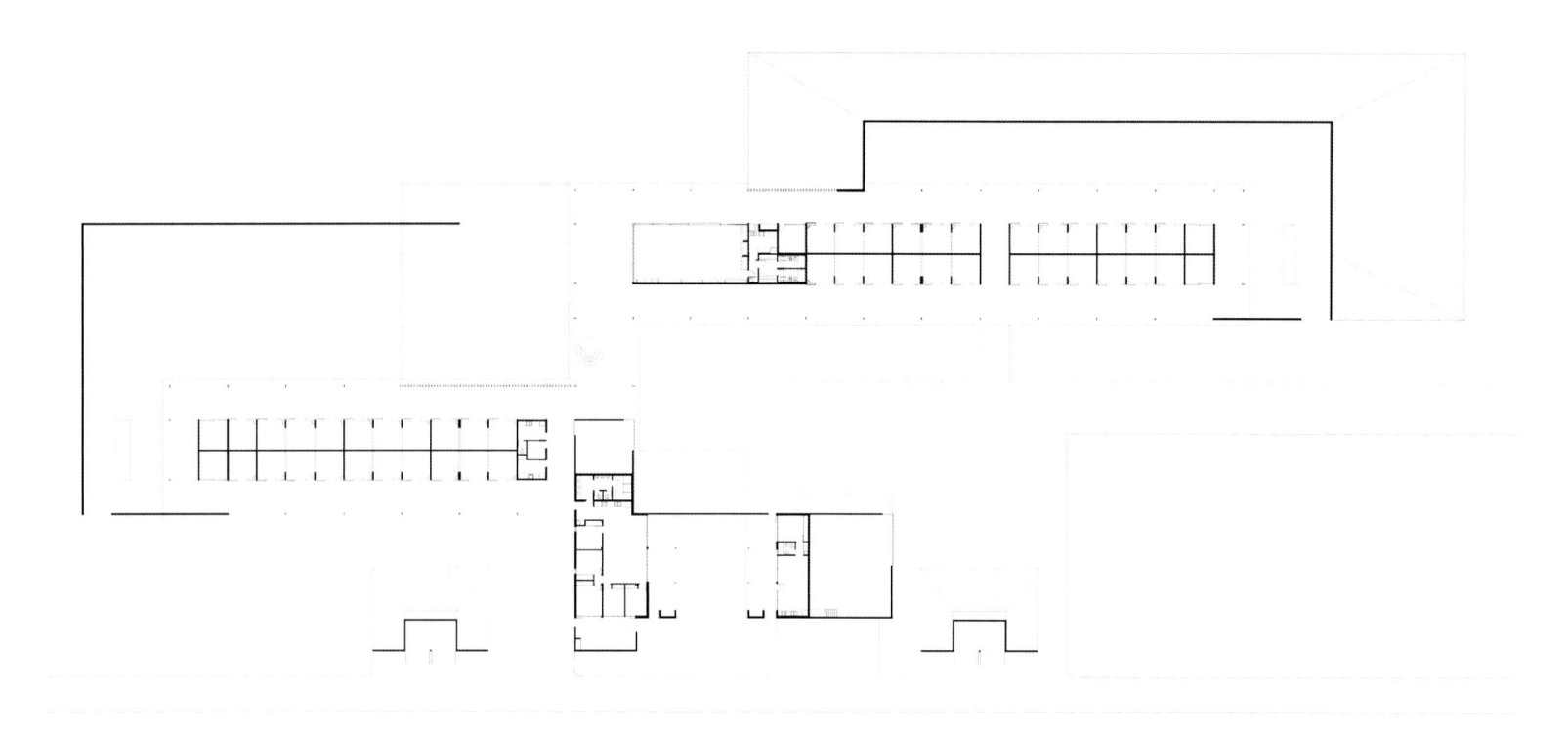

Plan

The Figueras Polo Stables is located in the region of General Rodríguez (Buenos Aires), Argentina, known as "The Pampas." Pampa is an indigenous word meaning plains or flatland. Along with its mild climate and fertile soil, the area is ideal for agriculture. When traveling through this area, there is an overwhelming feeling of a never-ending horizontality. The Argentine singer, song-writer, and writer Atahualpa Yupanqui referred to this landscape as "serene and pensive." This thoroughly modern project then, with its pronounced horizontality and simplicity of elements, attempts to reference these poetic and cerebral themes. The complex houses mainly polo horses with 44 stalls, comprising an area of 3850 square meters. The stables are composed of two long volumes with freestanding walls, which when manipulated, create diverse spaces and situations. The project has two main functions as well. One has a more social use and overlooks the polo field, and the other, facing the back of the property, houses work facilities and groom's quarters. The volumes that face the field are partially hidden behind extended walls and a massive planted earth slope, which not only provide privacy to the stables, but also subtly reduces the building's impact on the landscape. Only the center of the building is revealed, where a large water and gravel pond is located next to the covered exterior terraces and tack room. The roofs are planted with wild native grasses in an intentional contrast to the perfection of the sleek walls and polo field's smooth turf. The slopes serve as both access to the roof and as natural stands from which to observe the polo matches. Water, the universal symbol of life, purity, and harmony, is used to connect and articulate these spaces, as well as to create a serene atmosphere. Two basic materials were similarly used for the construction of the project: exposed concrete and local hardwoods. These materials were chosen because of their aesthetic properties, low maintenance and beautiful aging quality. The principle aim of the project was to create a very special and intimate connection between the horses and the people who train and take care of them, through powerful spaces that contain and nurture that relationship.

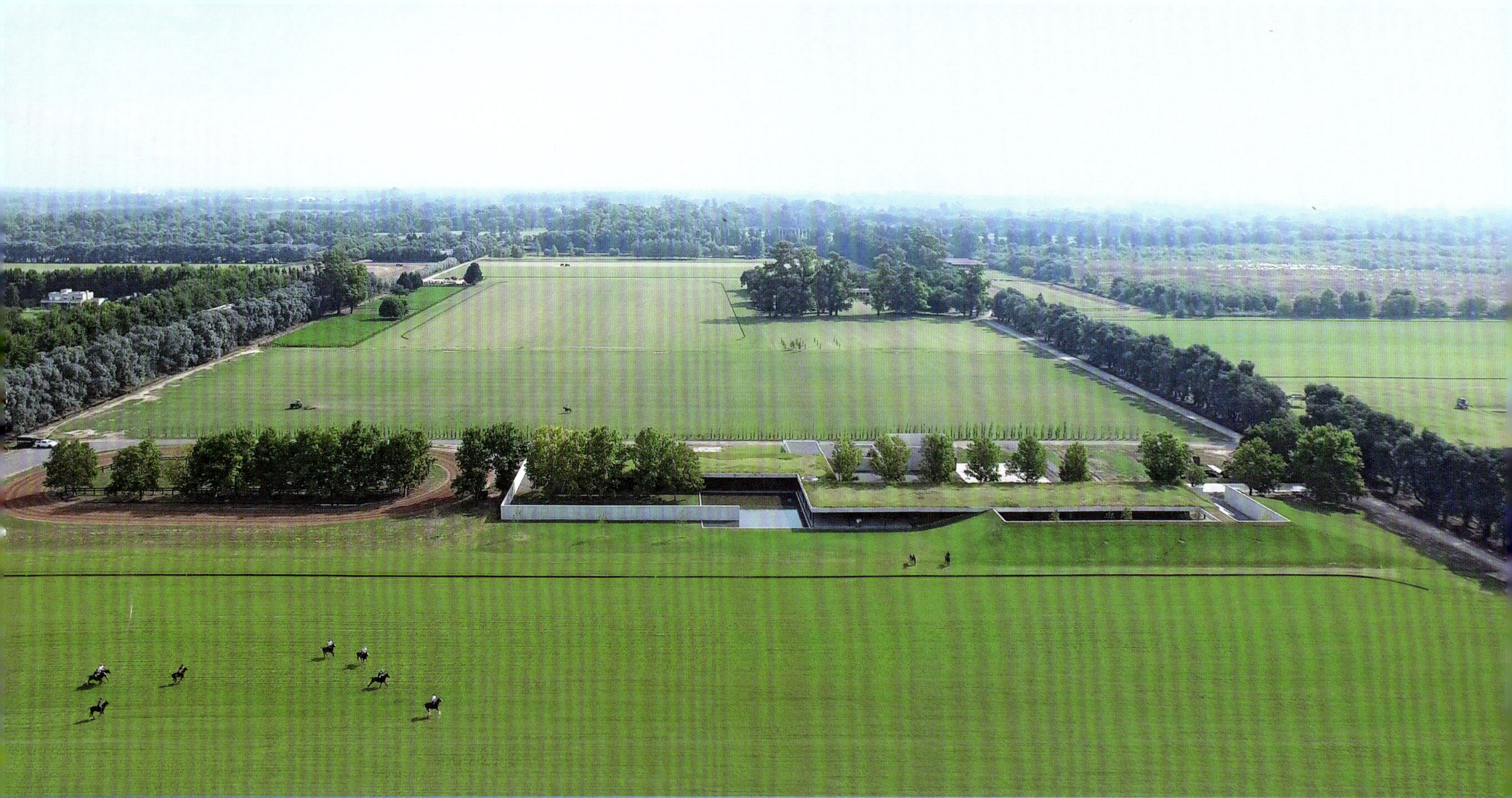
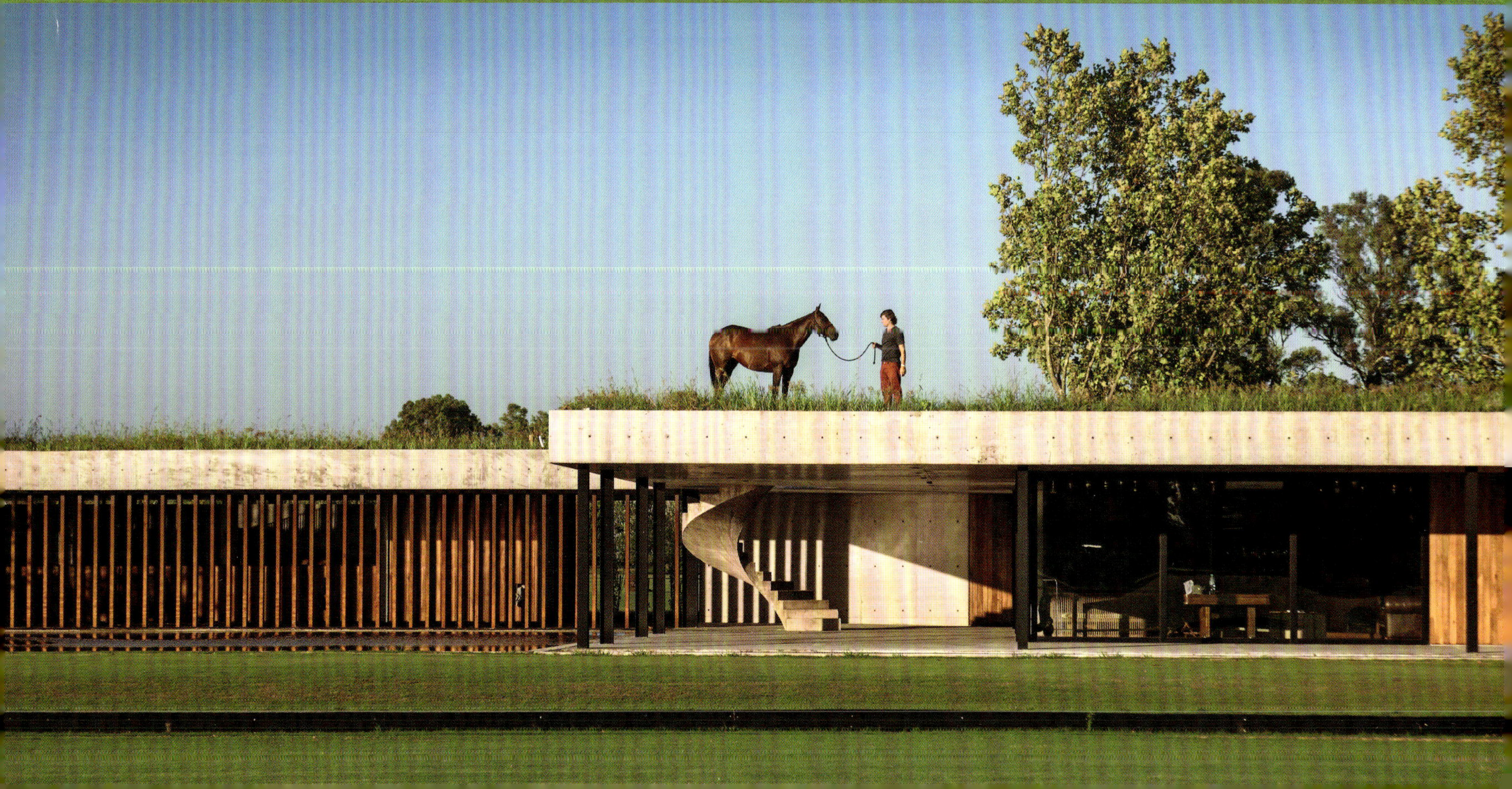

54 ESTUDIO RAMOS

FIGUERAS POLO STABLES 55

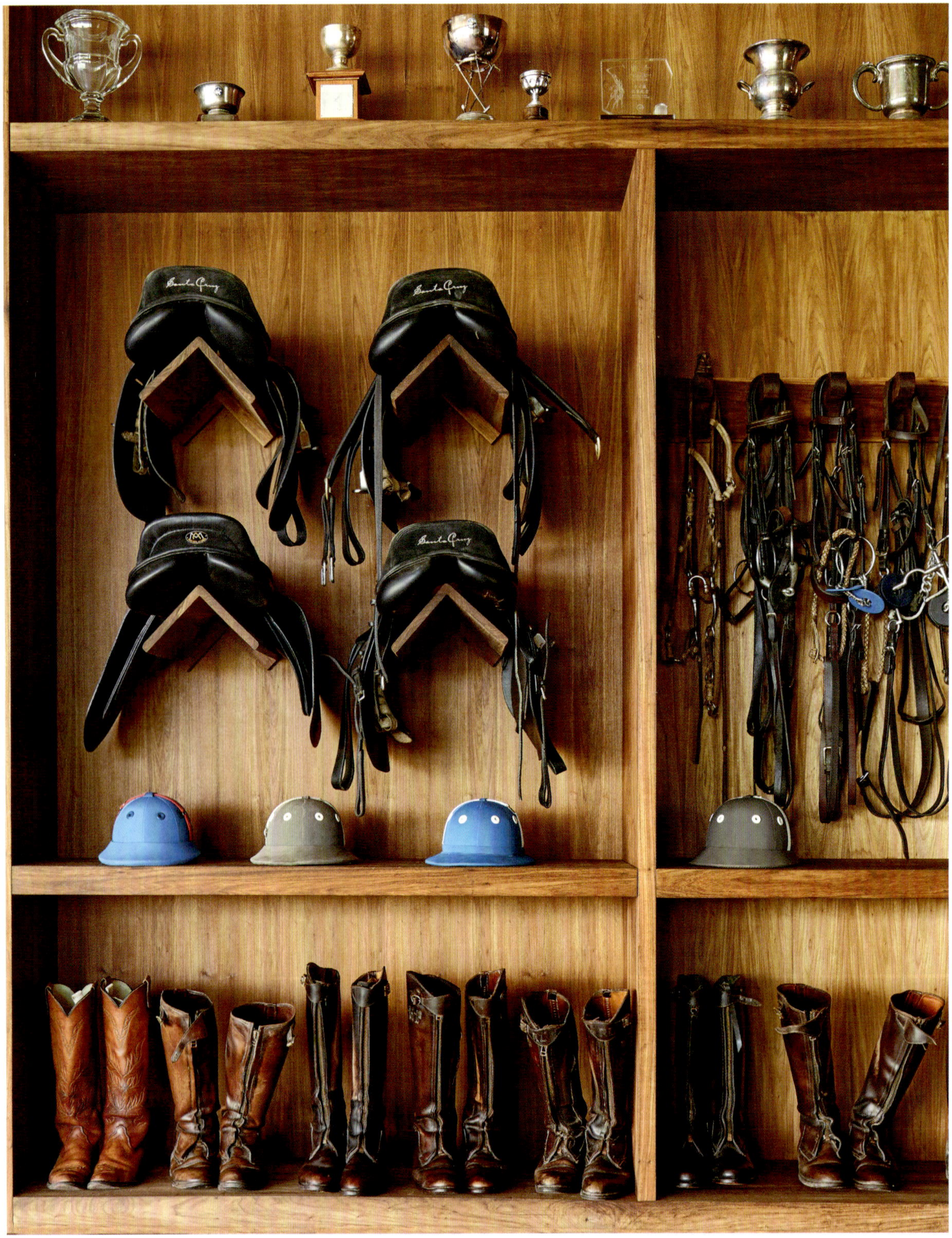

FIGUERAS POLO STABLES

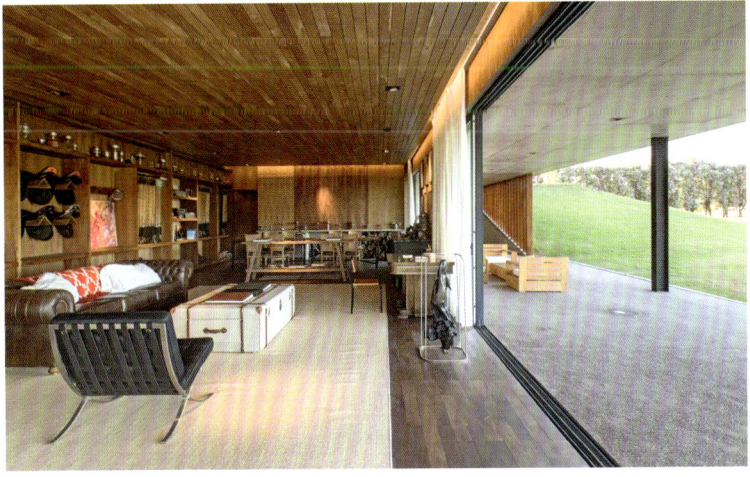

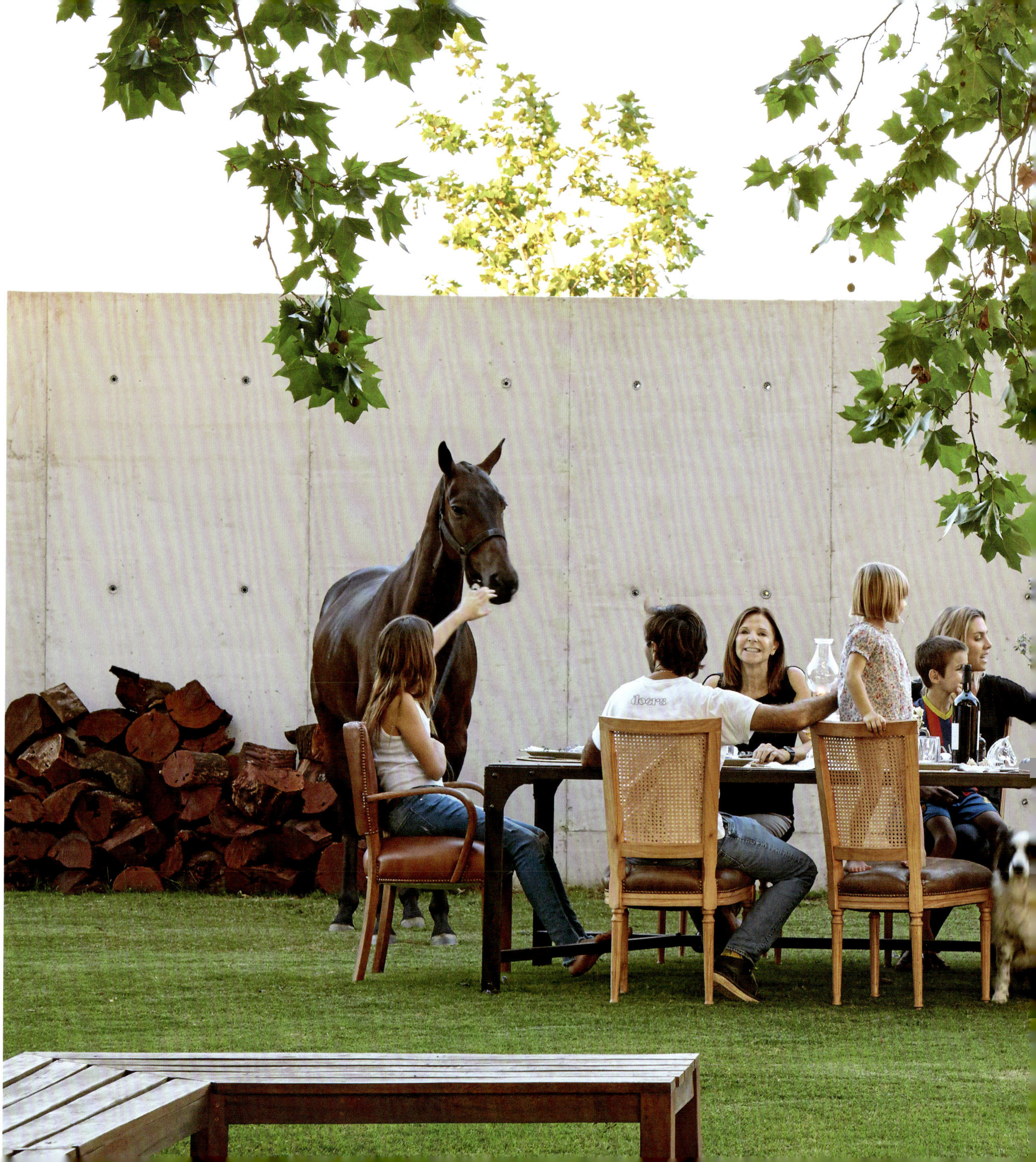

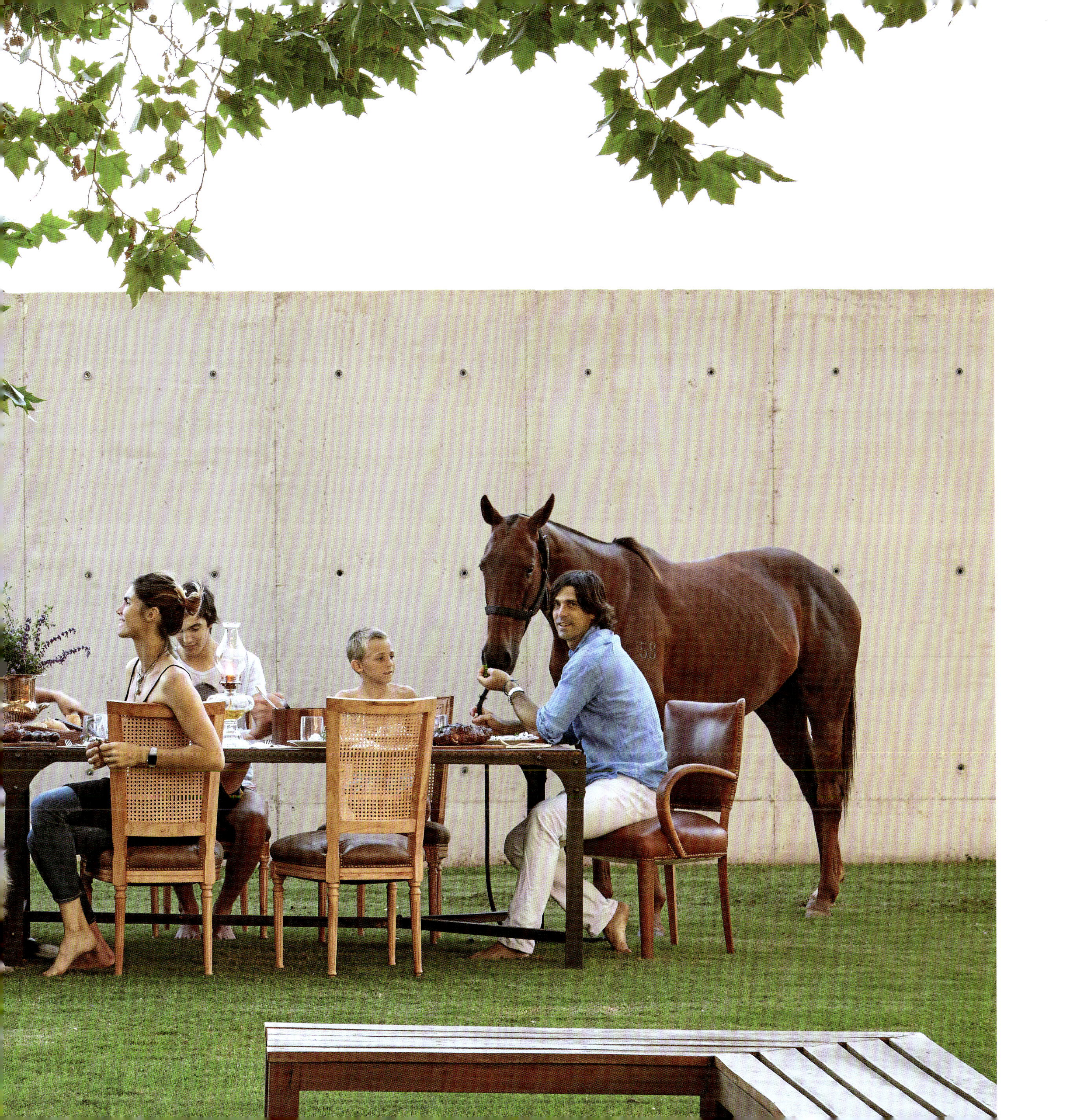

60 ESTUDIO RAMOS

FIGUERAS POLO STABLES 61

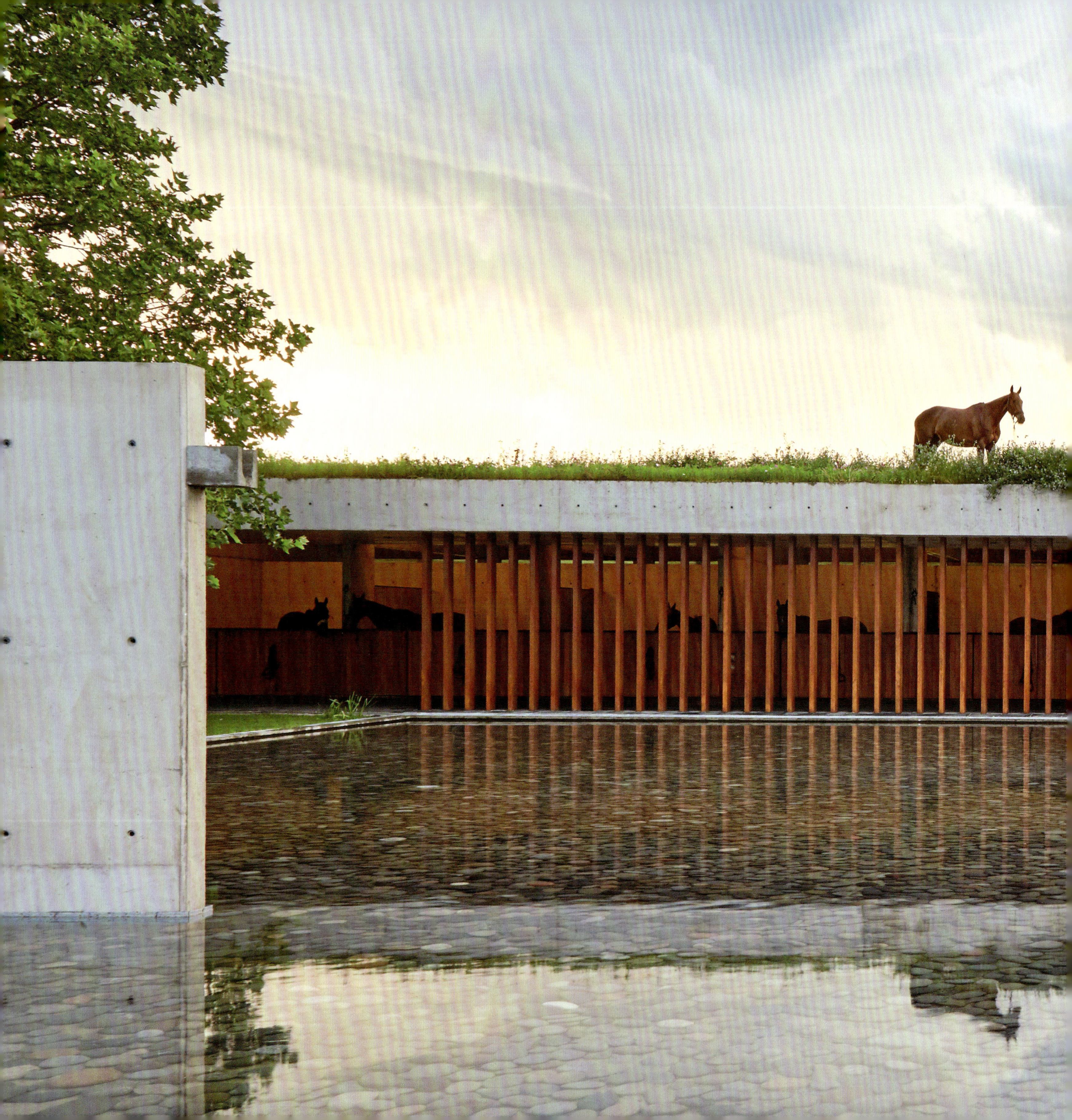

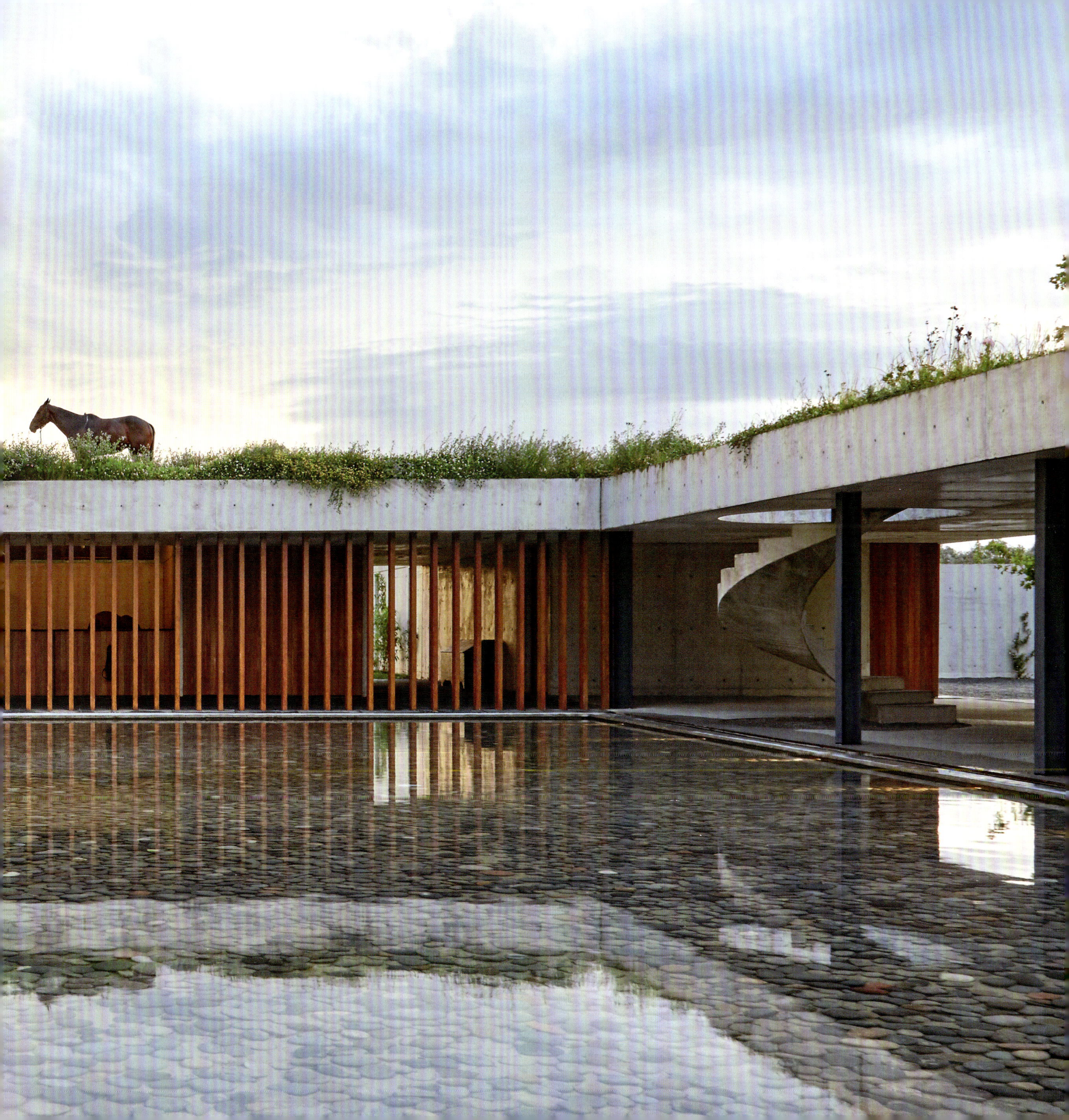

Merricks Equestrian Center

Seth Stein Architects in association with Watson Architecture+Design

Mornington Pensinsula, Victoria, Australia

Building Area:
616 m²

Site Area:
51 acres

Architect in Charge:
Robert Watson

Project Team:
Seth Stein, Nico Warr, Richard Vint, Tim Sidebottom

Photographer:
Lisbeth Grosmann, Justin Smallman

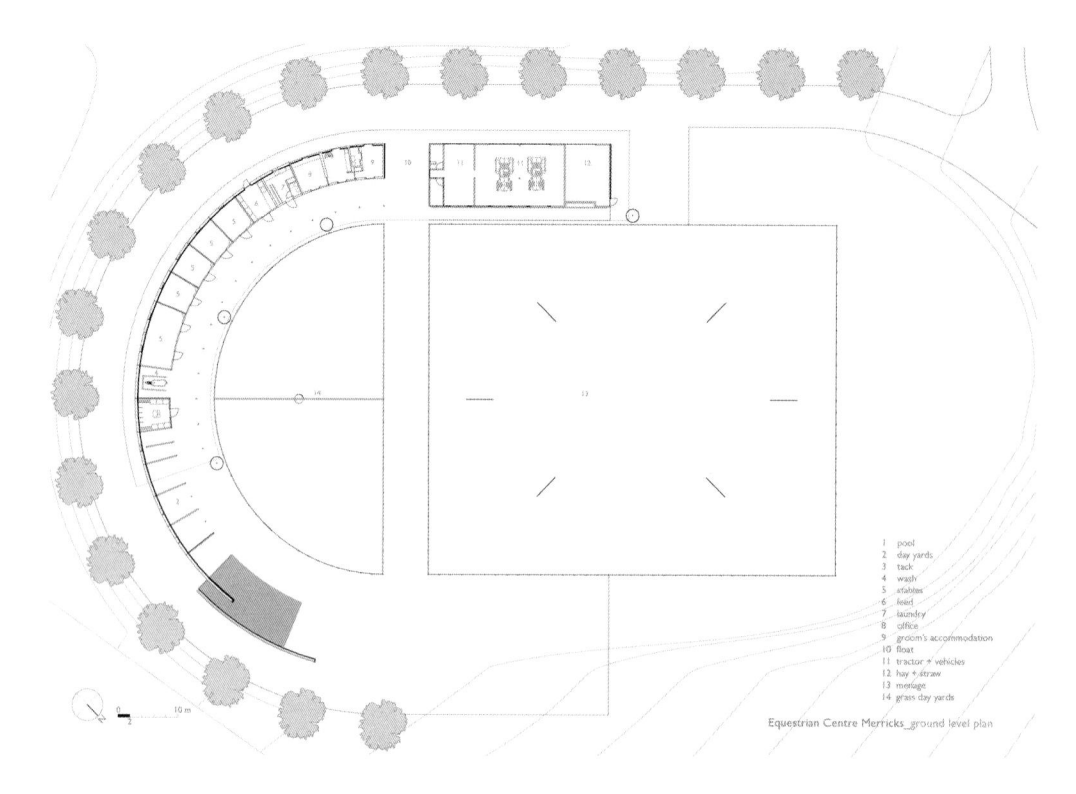

Plan

Located on the Mornington Peninsula in Melbourne, Australia, Seth Stein Architects (UK) in association with Watson Architecture + Design (Melbourne) was commissioned to design a new equestrian center for the breeding of warm blood eventing horses. The client, based locally as well as in the United Kingdom, sought a scheme that would be functional and practical, and sympathetic to the landscape through durable and sustainable architectural form and use of materials. Due the necessity to locate the building on a large level platform within an undulating landscape, and in particular to accommodate the 3000 square meter riding arena, extensive landscaping works were required to stabilize and drain the land, which also provided an opportunity to create a large spring fed dam that is a strategic part of the whole property's water management plan. The building is arranged in a crescent shape that provides large stalls for six horses with foals, wash bay, tack room, laundry, feed room as well as a small office and groom's accommodation. A further wing separated by a covered drive-through provides straw and hay storage, work shop, and parking for farm equipment and vehicles. Externally there is a small pool for the horses, day yards (hard and grassed), as well as a large arena for combined dressage and jumping practice. The curved lineal plan is relatively compact and linked via a wide internal covered thoroughfare with all activities focused inwards towards the grass day yards and the arena beyond. Also considered in the planning has been the movement of vehicles through and around the complex to allow for the protected loading and offloading of horses. The palette of building materials has been restricted to a minimum: seen from a distance the building is strongly delineated by the arching single-pitch of the zinc roof. Apart from the curved rammed earth wall that partly forms the back façade and extends beyond the roof to the pool, the entire building is made of timber. Another of the complex's key environmentally sustainable attributes is water management. Due to the high demand for water, the 1260 square meter roof can harvest over a million liters of water on an average year's rainfall, 350,000 liters of which can be stored in large underground tanks with any excess delivered to the dam. A constant feature of the building's design is the mono-pitched roof cross section used throughout, which allows for easily controlled cross flow ventilation as well as the ability to naturally dispel hot air at high level via convection.

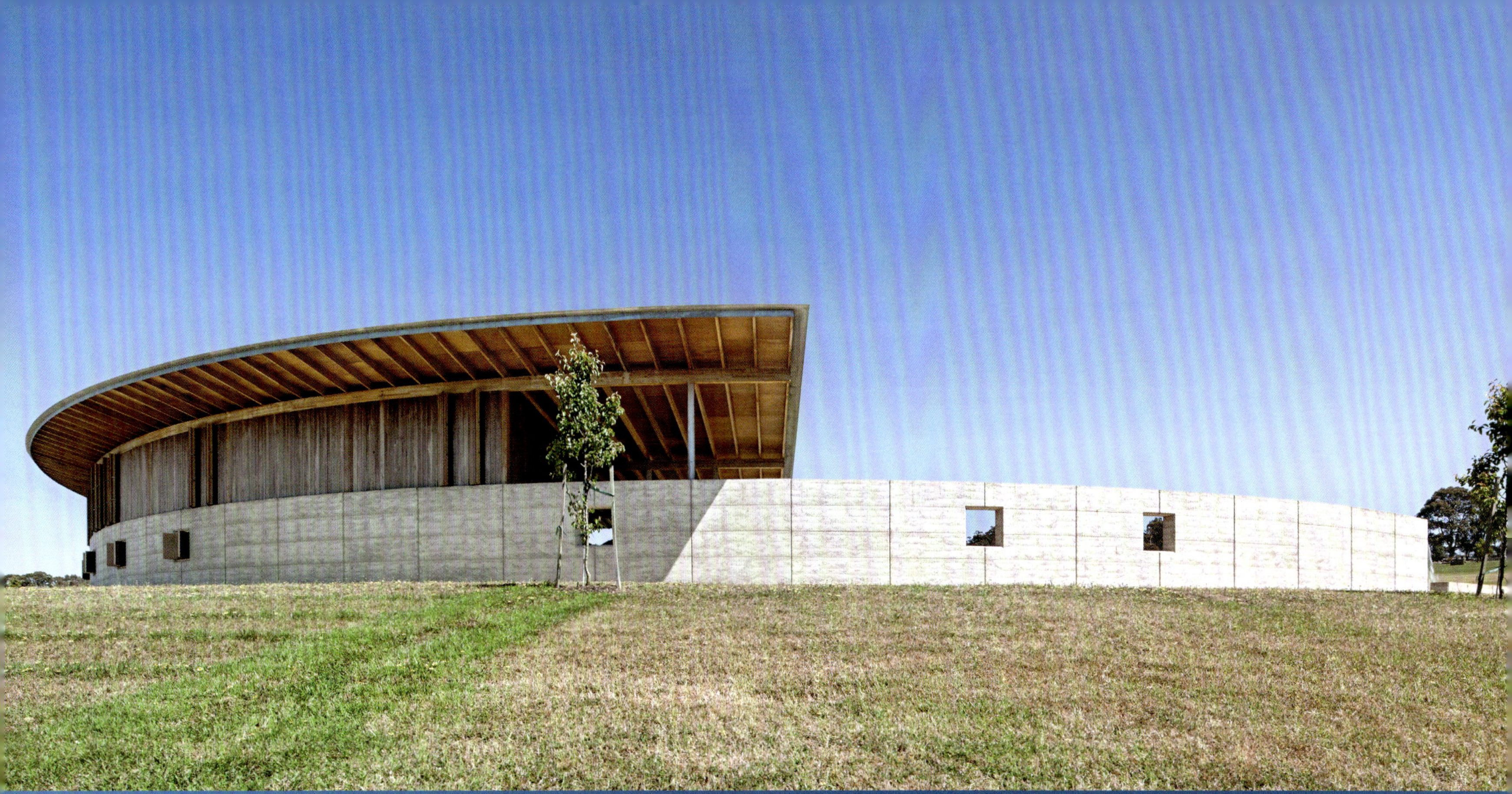

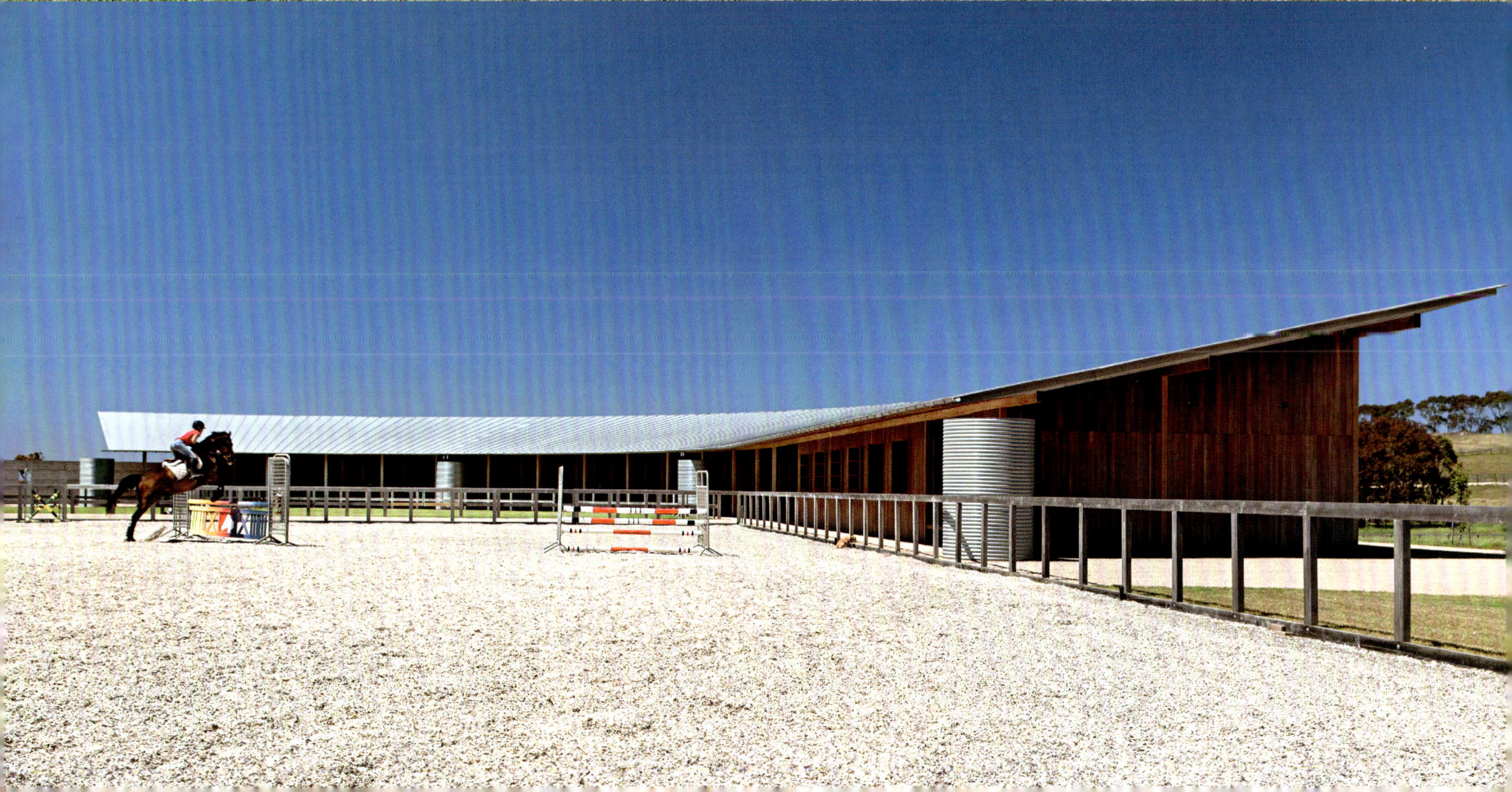

68 SETH STEIN ARCHITECTS IN ASSOCIATION WITH WATSON ARCHITECTURE+DESIGN

MERRICKS EQUESTRIAN CENTER **69**

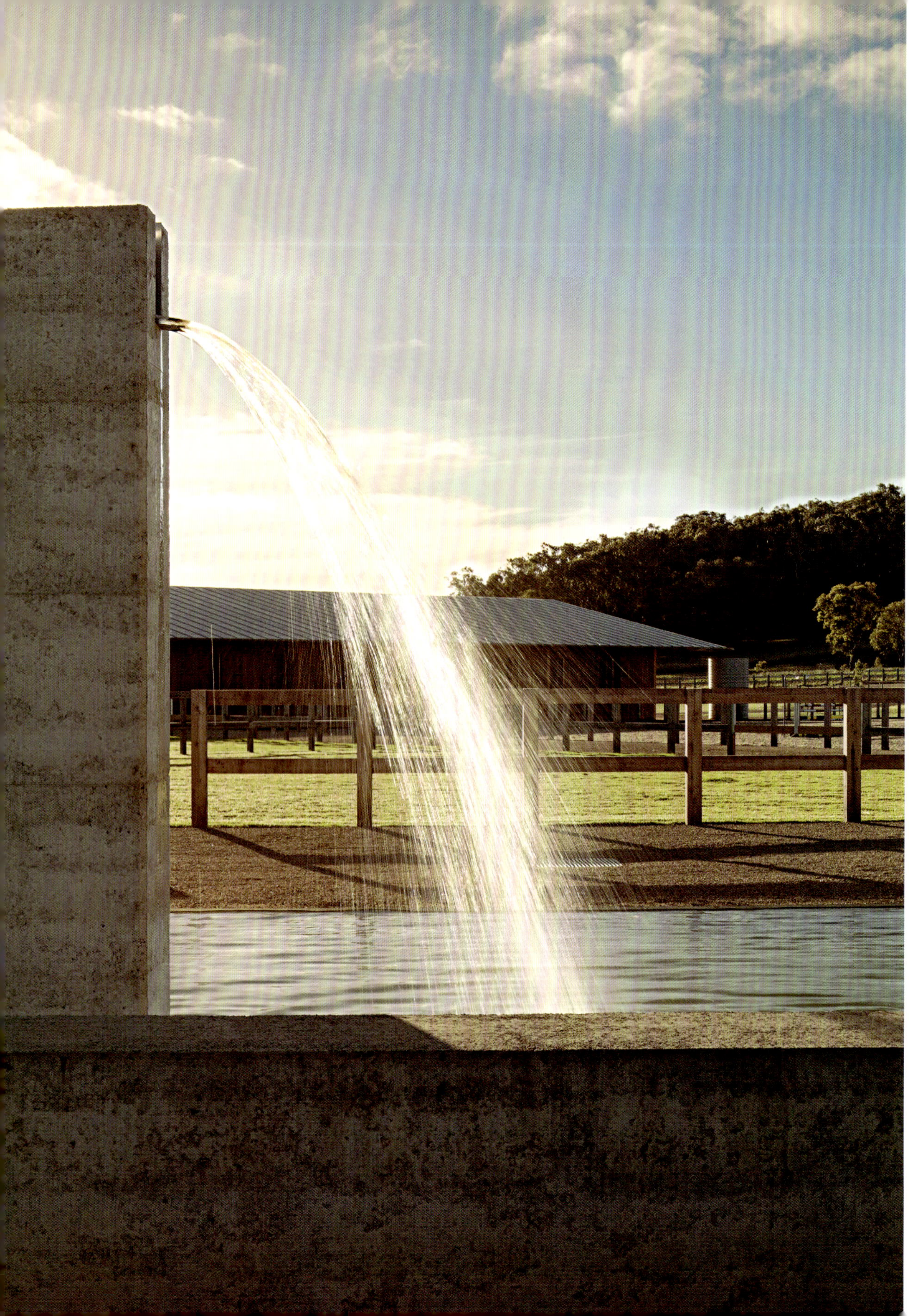

MERRICKS EQUESTRIAN CENTER 71

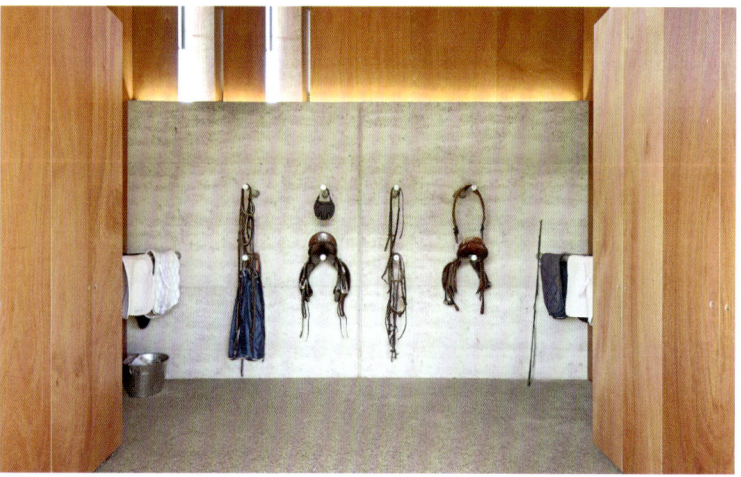

72 SETH STEIN ARCHITECTS IN ASSOCIATION WITH WATSON ARCHITECTURE+DESIGN

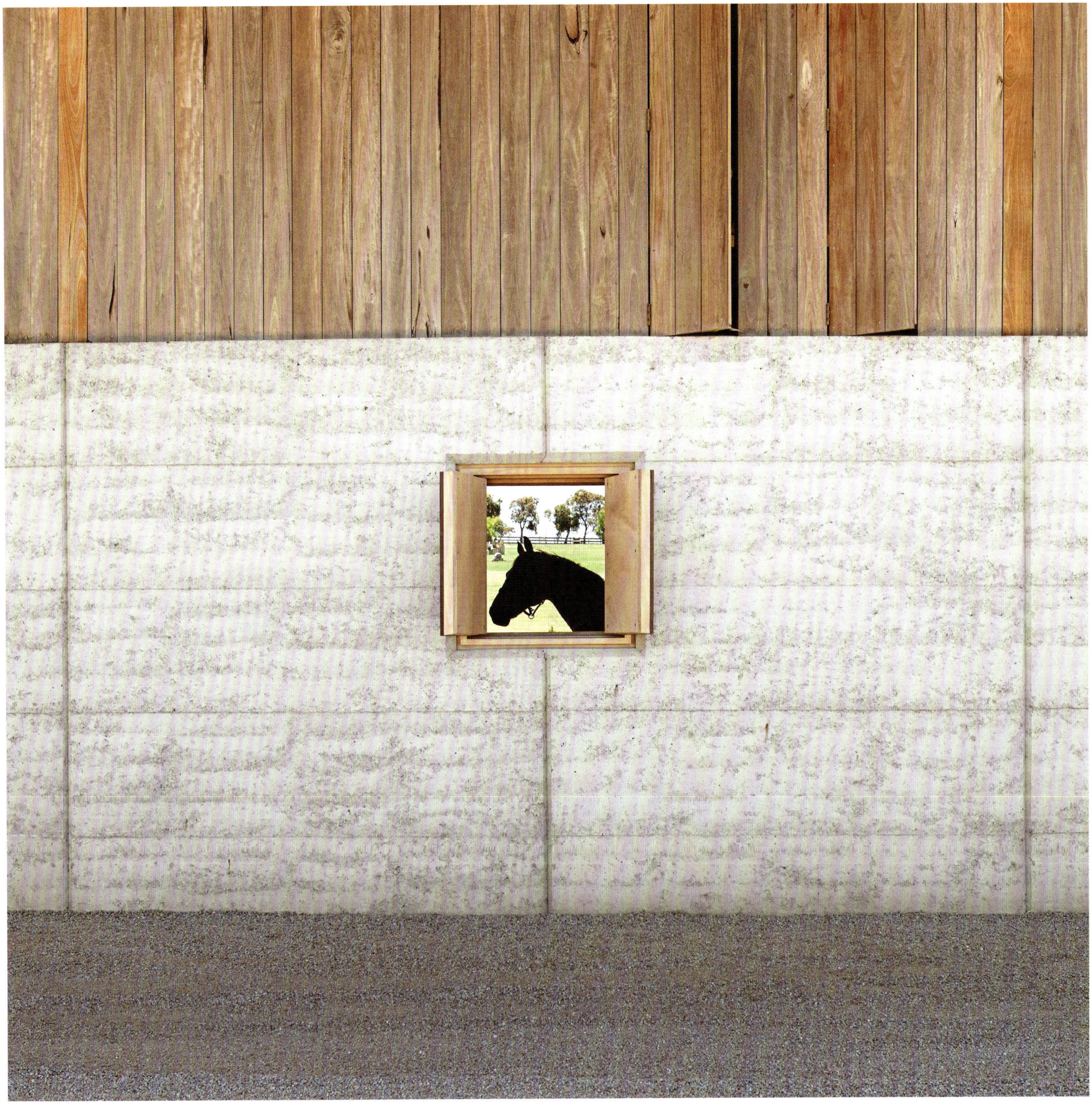

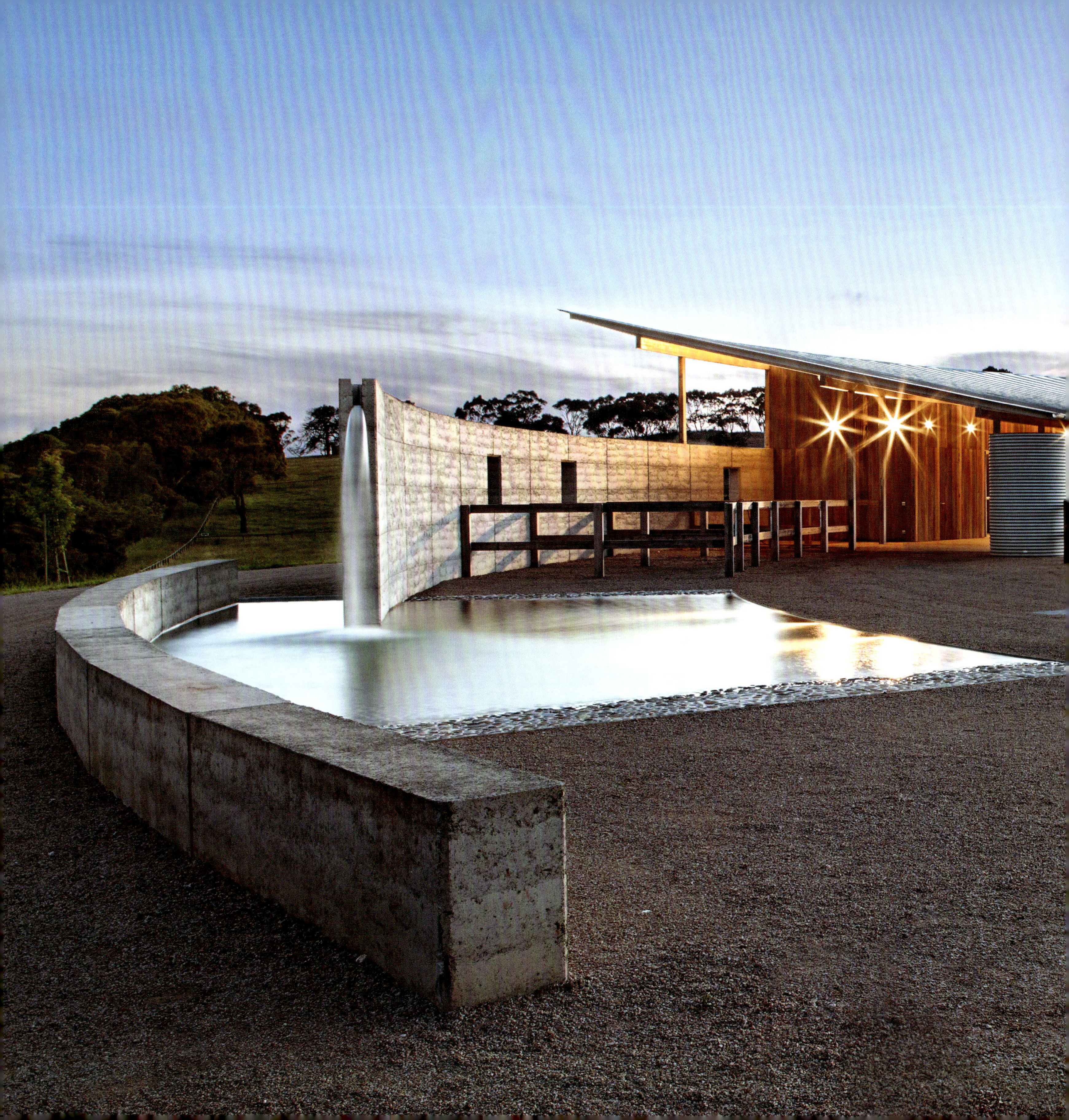

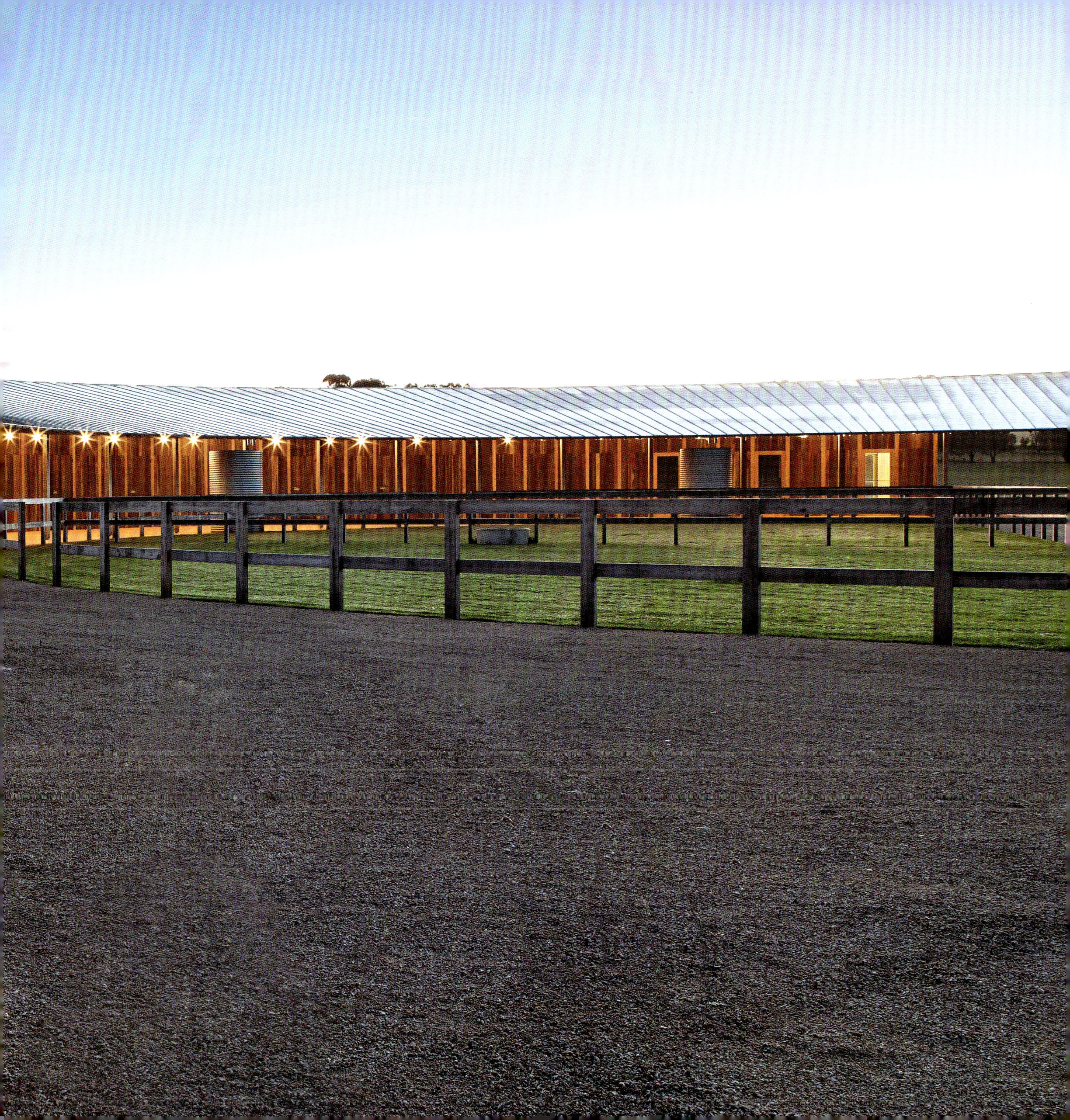

DarkHorse
Sequoia Contracting Co Ltd Design/Build

Ridgefield, Connecticut, United States

Building Area:
5 acres

Site Area:
11 acres

Architect in Charge:
Sequoia Contracting Co Ltd

Project Team:
Frank Fowler Surveyors and Engineers

Interior Designer:
Alan Megerdichian

Landscape Designer:
Alan Megerdichian

Photographer:
Tim Lenz Photography

Plan

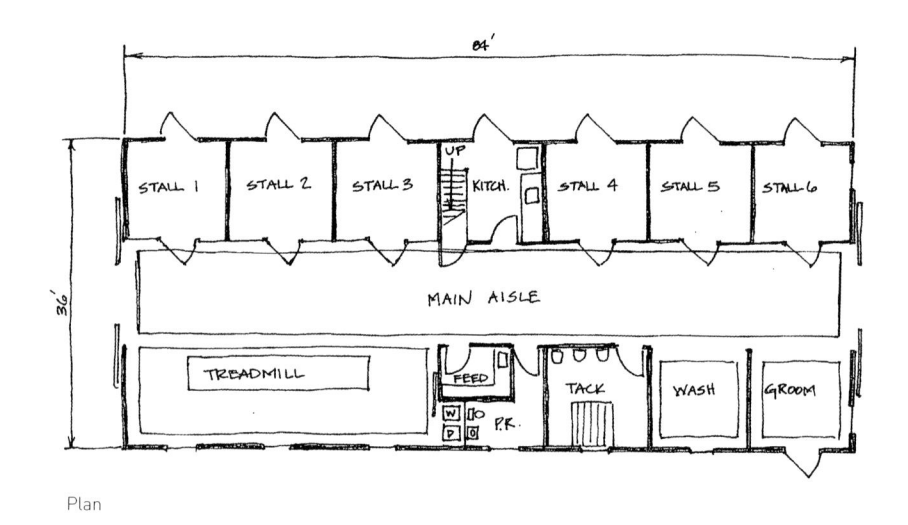

DarkHorse is an equestrian farm complex in the rolling hills of Ridgefield, Connecticut, designed by Alan Megerdichian of the Sequoia Contracting Company. Situated in a bucolic landscape surrounded by woods, the project consists of a large barn, pastures, riding arenas, and several free-standing service structures. The farm features four large paddocks that surround the main barn for easy access. The 120 x 180-foot riding arena is terminated at one end by a 12 x 24-foot jump storage shed that can double as an additional two stalls if necessary. The main barn is a 36 x 84-foot space with fourteen stalls, three of which are used to make room for an indoor treadmill. A local metal crafter fabricated a custom light fixture to go over the treadmill area as well as cabinetry pulls, shelf brackets, and coat hooks for the tack room. Alan also commissioned a glass blower to create custom shades for the light fixture over the treadmill. The barn has a tack room, powder room, feed room, kitchen, grooming stall, and wash stall. There is also an office/lounge located on the second floor. On the exterior, a central pergola hovers above a bluestone patio that overlooks the arena and paddocks. The door beneath the pergola leads directly to the barn's kitchen. Behind the barn towards the back of the property is a 76-foot lunge ring with custom galvanized panels to minimize the spacing between the bars for additional safety for the horses. A free-standing garage is used to store farm equipment, and next to it is the parking area for the horse trailers and a dumpster pad. Across from the equipment garage is a 14 x 36-foot shed used for storing hay and shavings. The bright white gabled buildings with large dormer windows, sliding barn doors, ridge lanterns, stone details, picket fences, and lush landscaping create a picturesque setting that embodies the vernacular wood building traditions of the southern New England region.

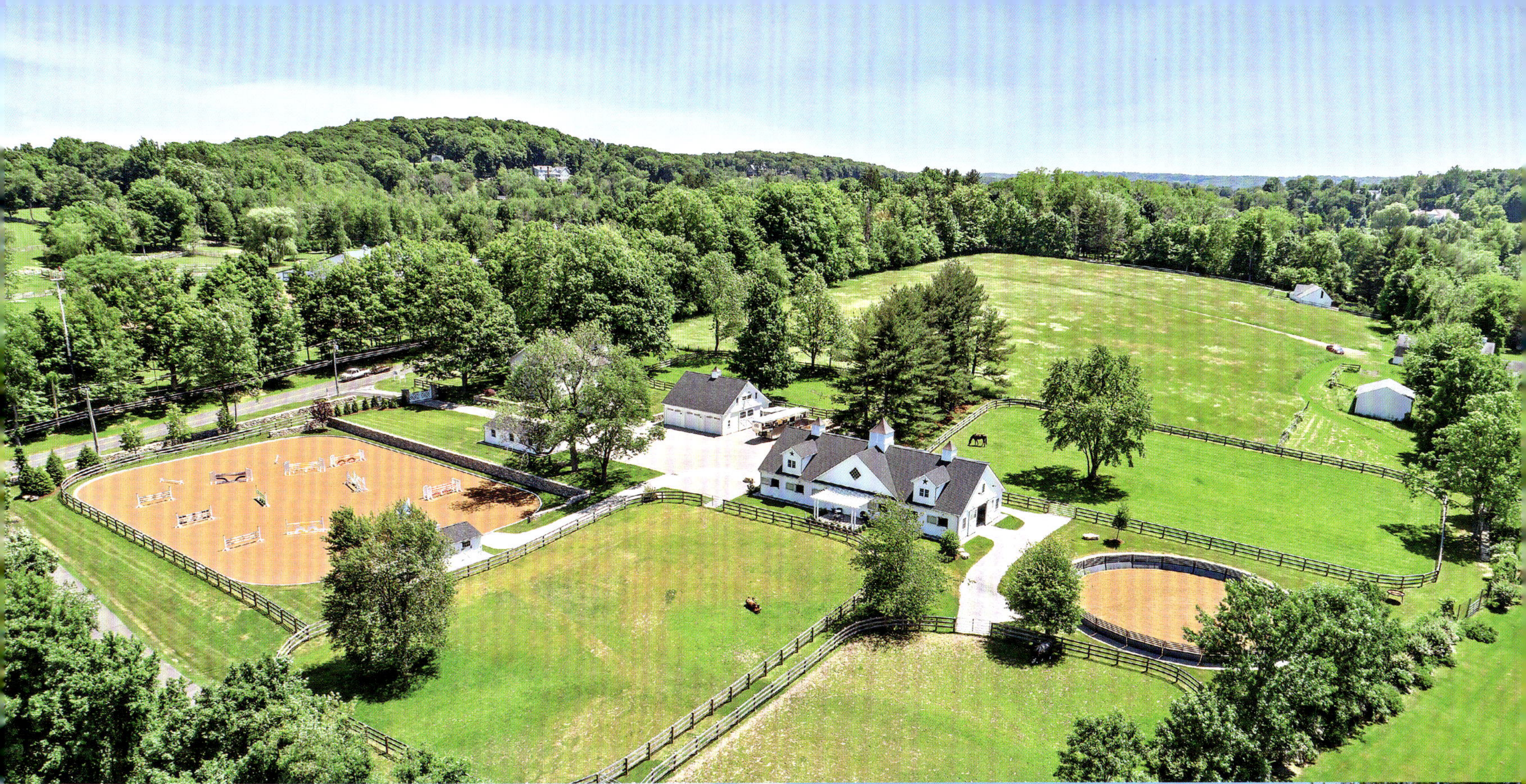

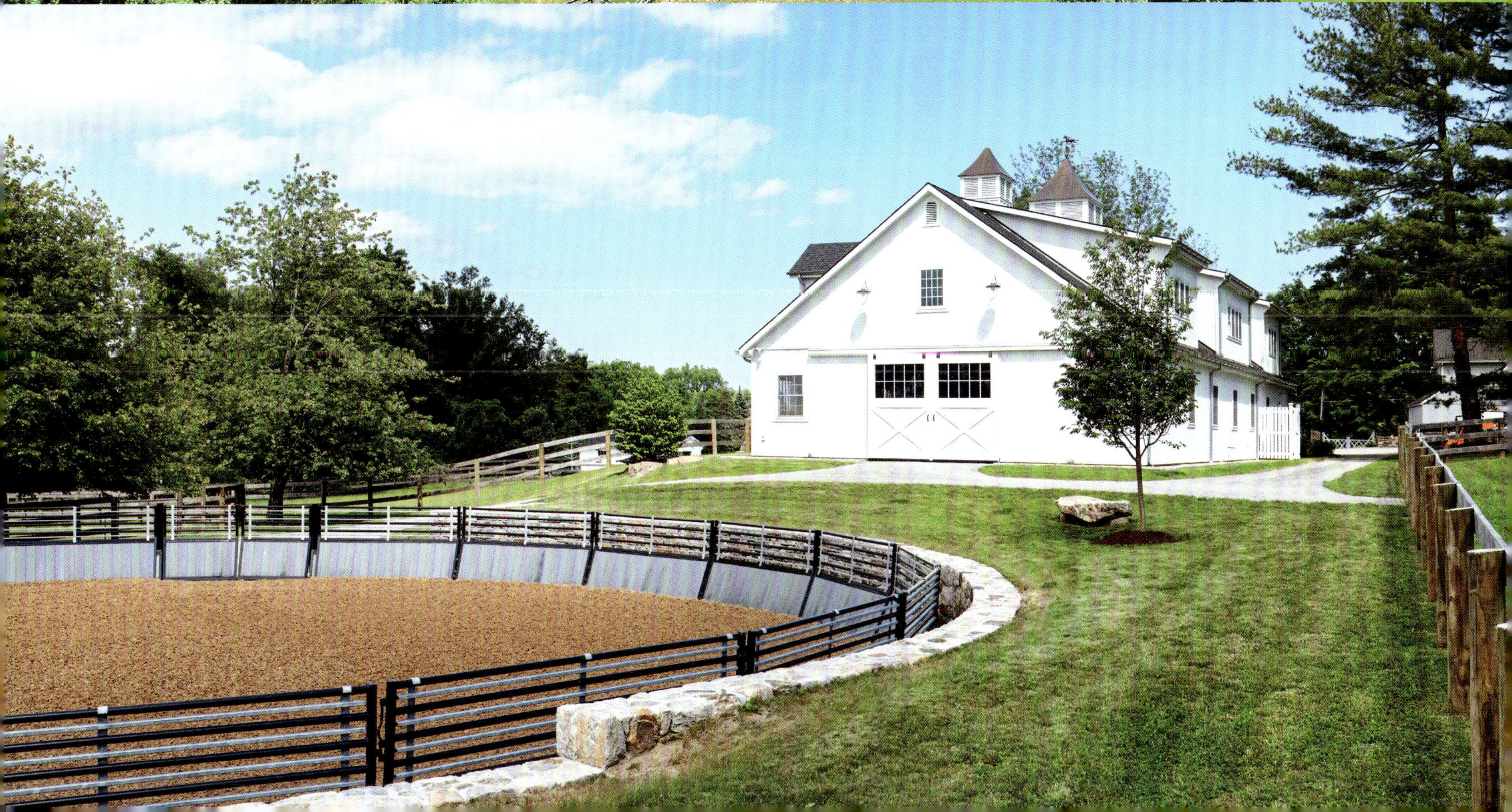

80 SEQUOIA CONTRACTING CO LTD DESIGN/BUILD

DARKHORSE 81

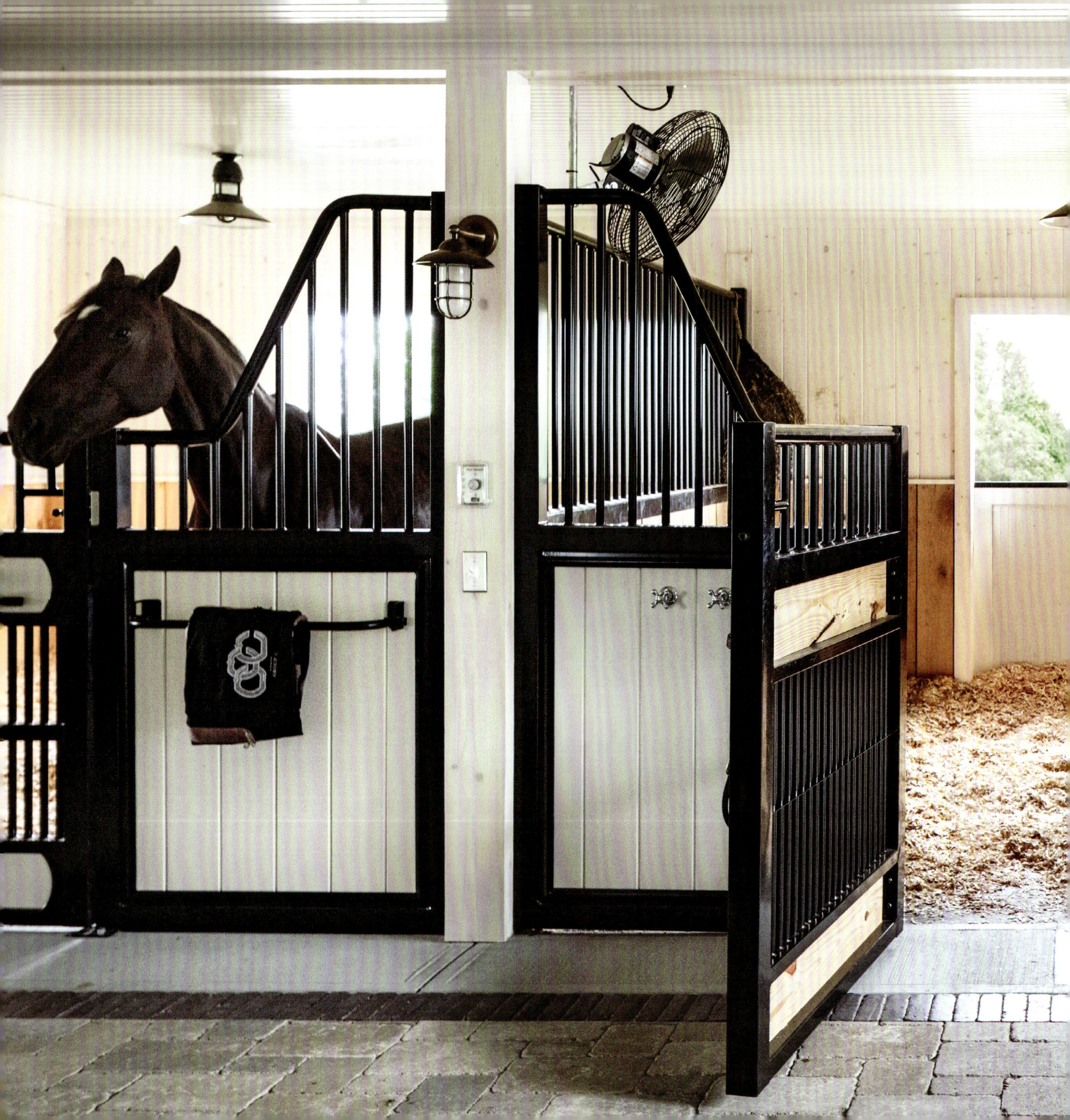

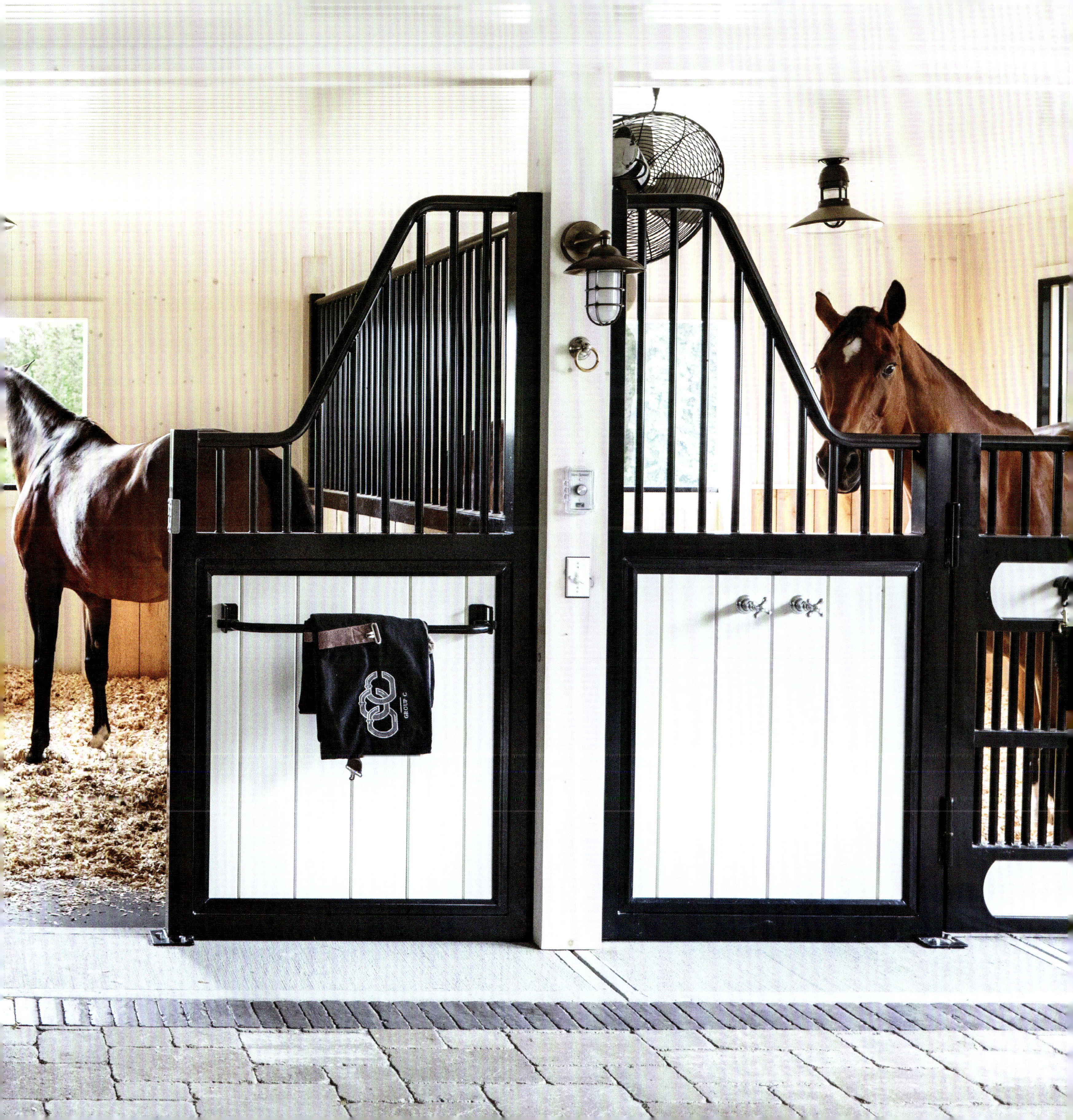

84   SEQUOIA CONTRACTING CO LTD DESIGN/BUILD

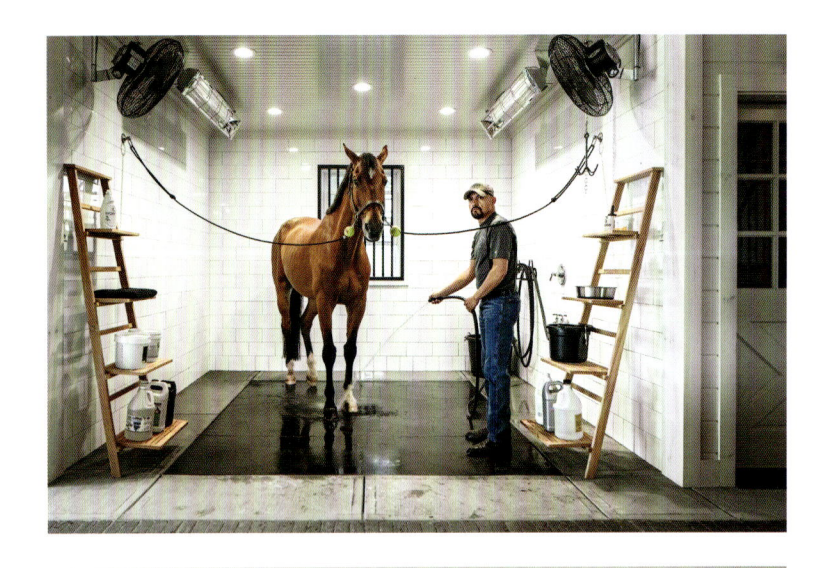

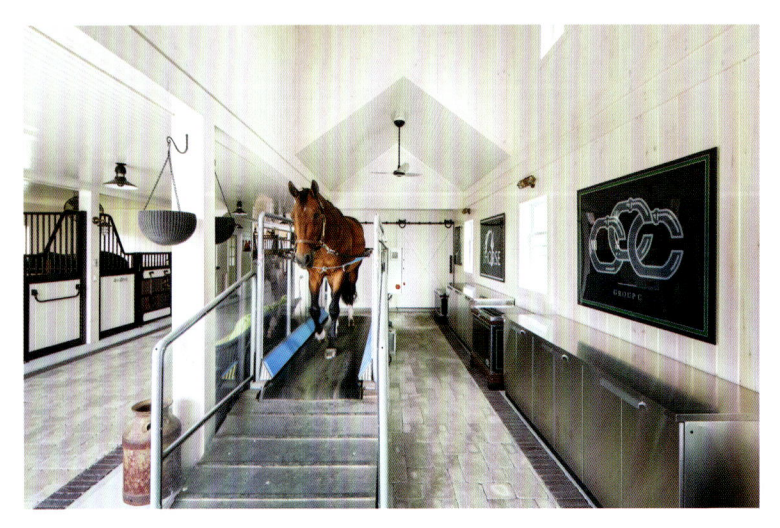

DARKHORSE 85

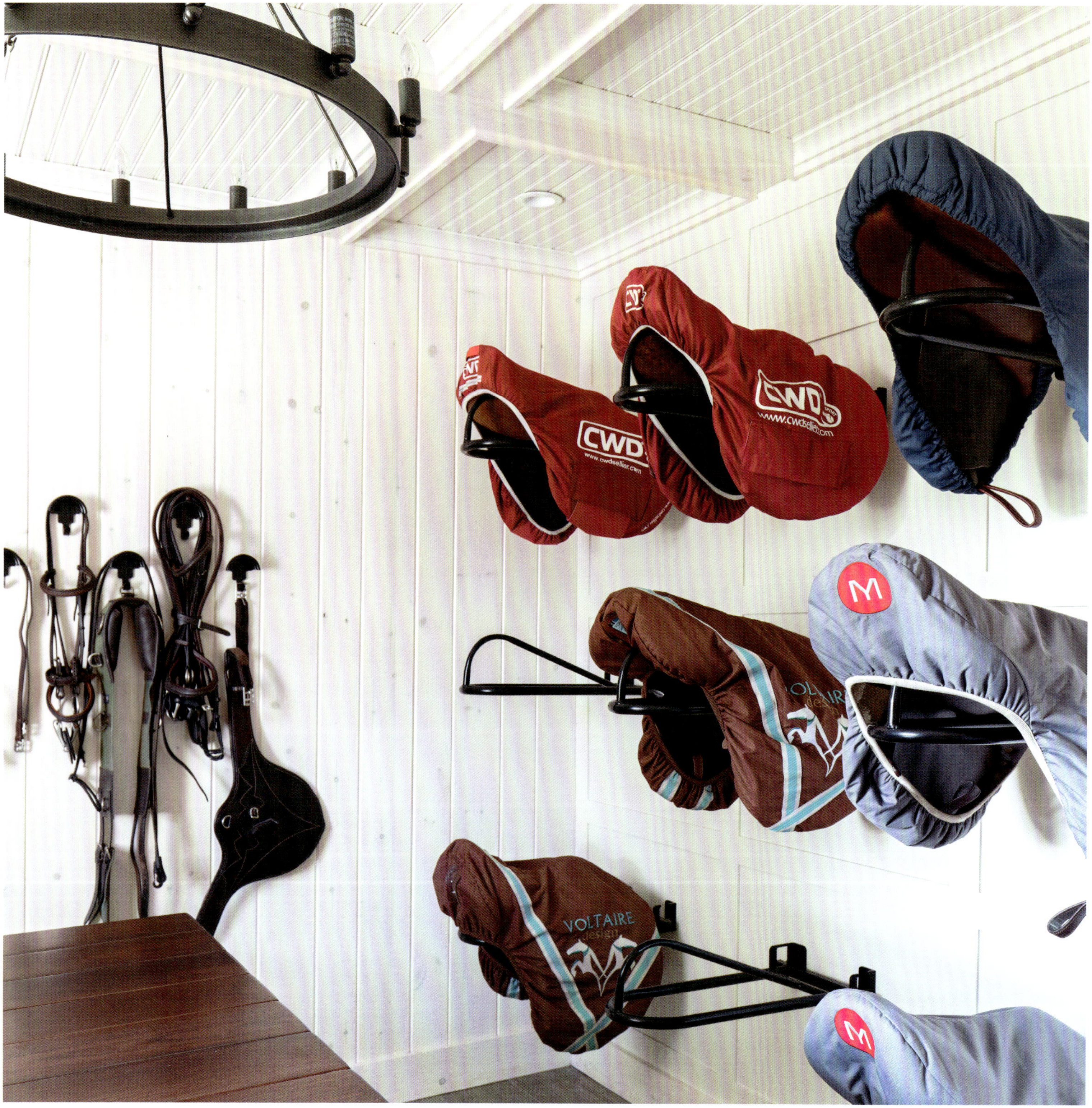
CWD
www.cwdsellier.com
VOLTAIRE
design

DARKHORSE **87**

Fazenda Boa Vista

Isay Weinfeld

Porto Feliz, Sao Paulo, Brazil

Building Area:
259.75 m²

Site Area:
644.50 m²

Architect in Charge:
Isay Weinfeld

Project Team:
Sebastian Murr, Katherina Ortner, Monica Cappa Santoni, Adriana Aun, Juliana Scalizi, Carolina Miranda

Landscape Designer:
Maria João D'orey

Photographer:
Fernando Guerra | FG+SG

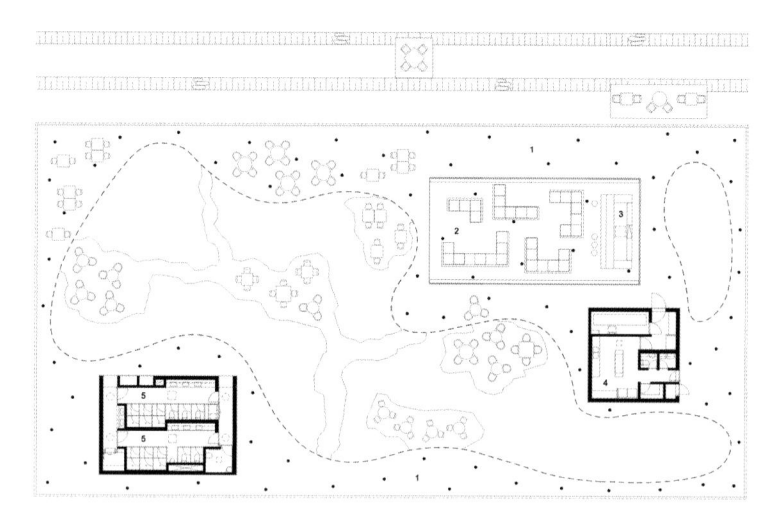

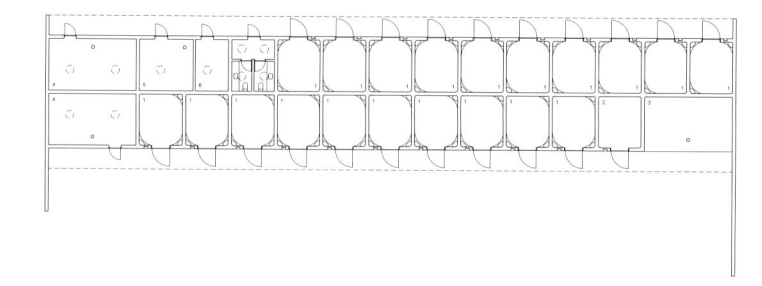

Plan

PLANTA

1. COCHEIRA
2. BANHO DE LUZ
3. DUCHAS
4. QUARTO DE SELA
5. CAIXAS E EQUIBOX
6. ALIMENTAÇÃO

Fazenda Boa Vista (the word *fazenda* means farm in Portuguese) is a residential and resort complex located in a 750-hectare site in the municipality of Porto Feliz, Brazil, 100 km west of São Paulo. Besides a hotel, the property contains private villas, a spa, a children's club, equestrian center and clubhouse, a sports center and swimming pool, petting zoo, two 18-hole golf courses and clubhouse, and a 242-hectare forest punctuated with numerous lakes. Fazenda Boa Vista's entirely modern equestrian center stands discreetly on a slight slope, overlooking the grass competition field and a dirt riding arena on one side, and two polo fields on the other. The straightforward program of the building, meant as a supporting and reception area for riders and spectators, features a lounge, bar, kitchen, restrooms and locker rooms, all under a single rectangular concrete slab roof supported by slim concrete columns. The signature feature of the roof is a large amoeba-shaped cutout that provides light to an inner garden filled with dense vegetation and leafy indigenous trees. Three cubic spaces are distributed around the garden: the locker rooms and kitchen are each housed in a wood cladded volume, whereas the bar and lounge areas are all glazed. Additional open lounging areas are distributed throughout, as are a succession of terraced platforms that descend from the clubhouse to the competition track, welcoming spectators to sit, relax, and enjoy the performances. The stables, situated on the opposite end of the competition track and riding arena consist of six rectangular bar buildings gently sloping up a hill, creating narrow outdoor service spaces between them. Like the equestrian center, the stables are covered by a simple mono-sloping concrete slab roof held aloft by thin concrete columns. Wooden doors and slats on the ceiling give the stables a rustic sensibility that contrasts with the modern character of the center.

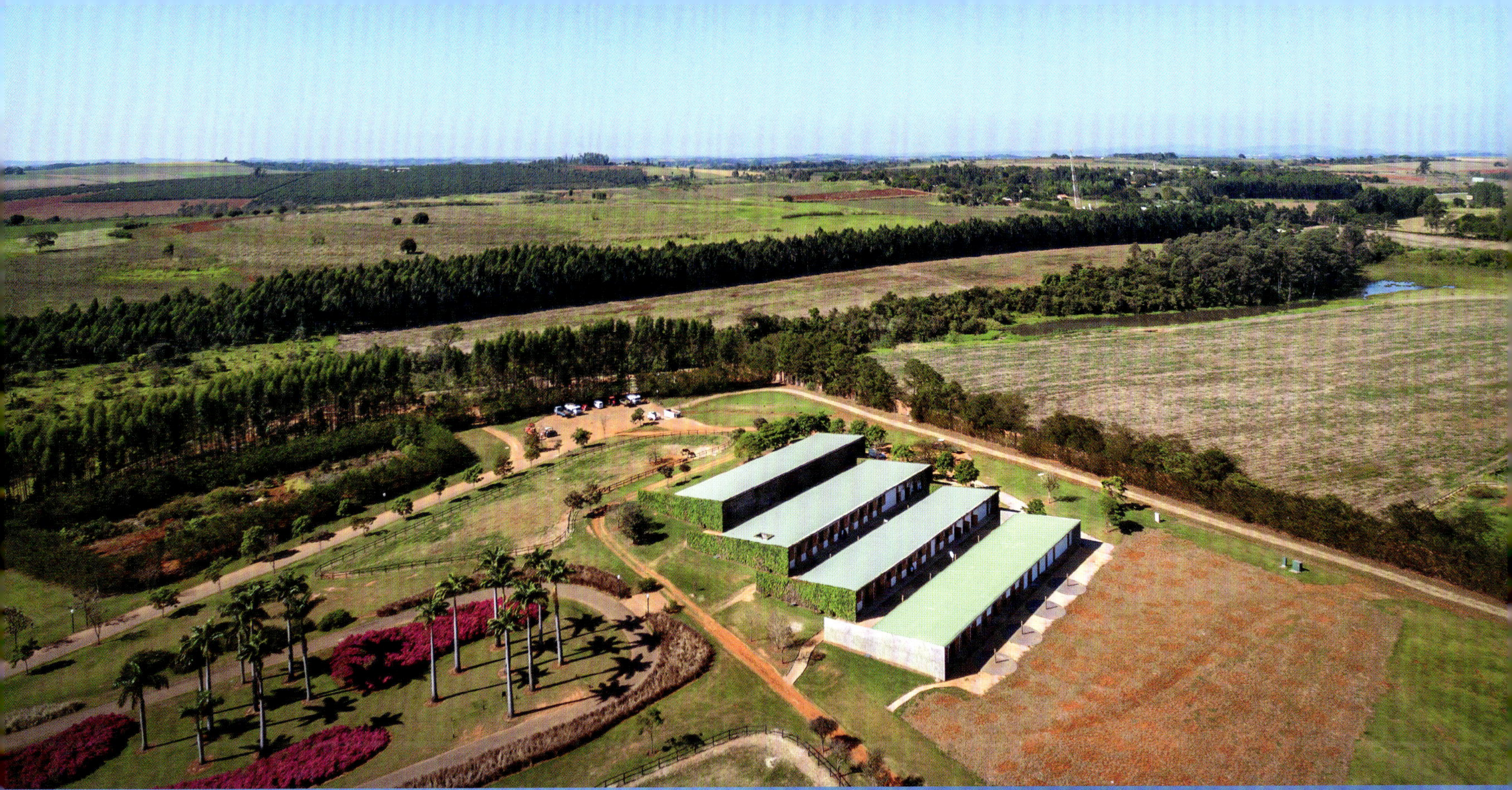

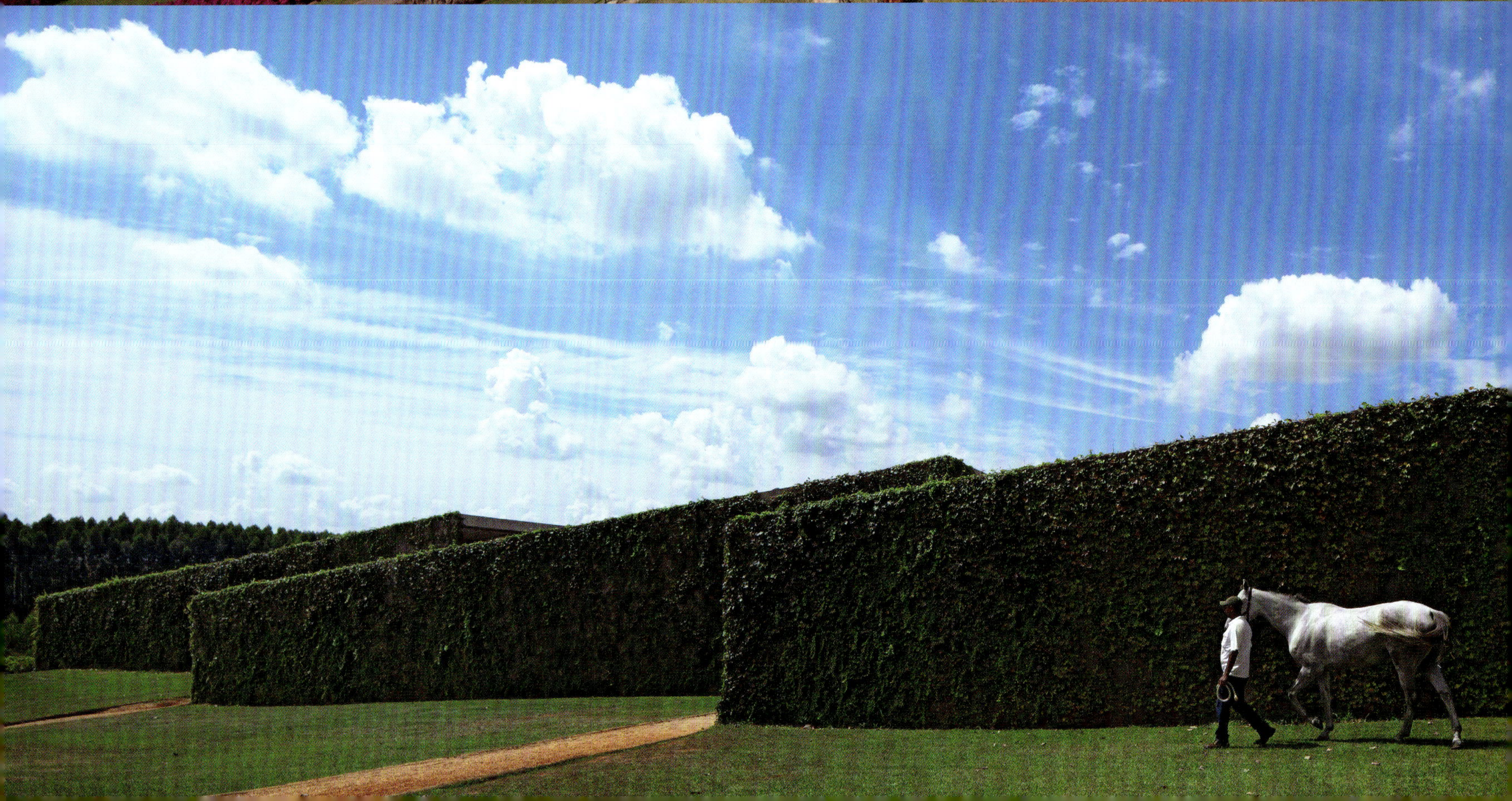

92 ISAY WEINFELD

FAZENDA BOA VISTA **93**

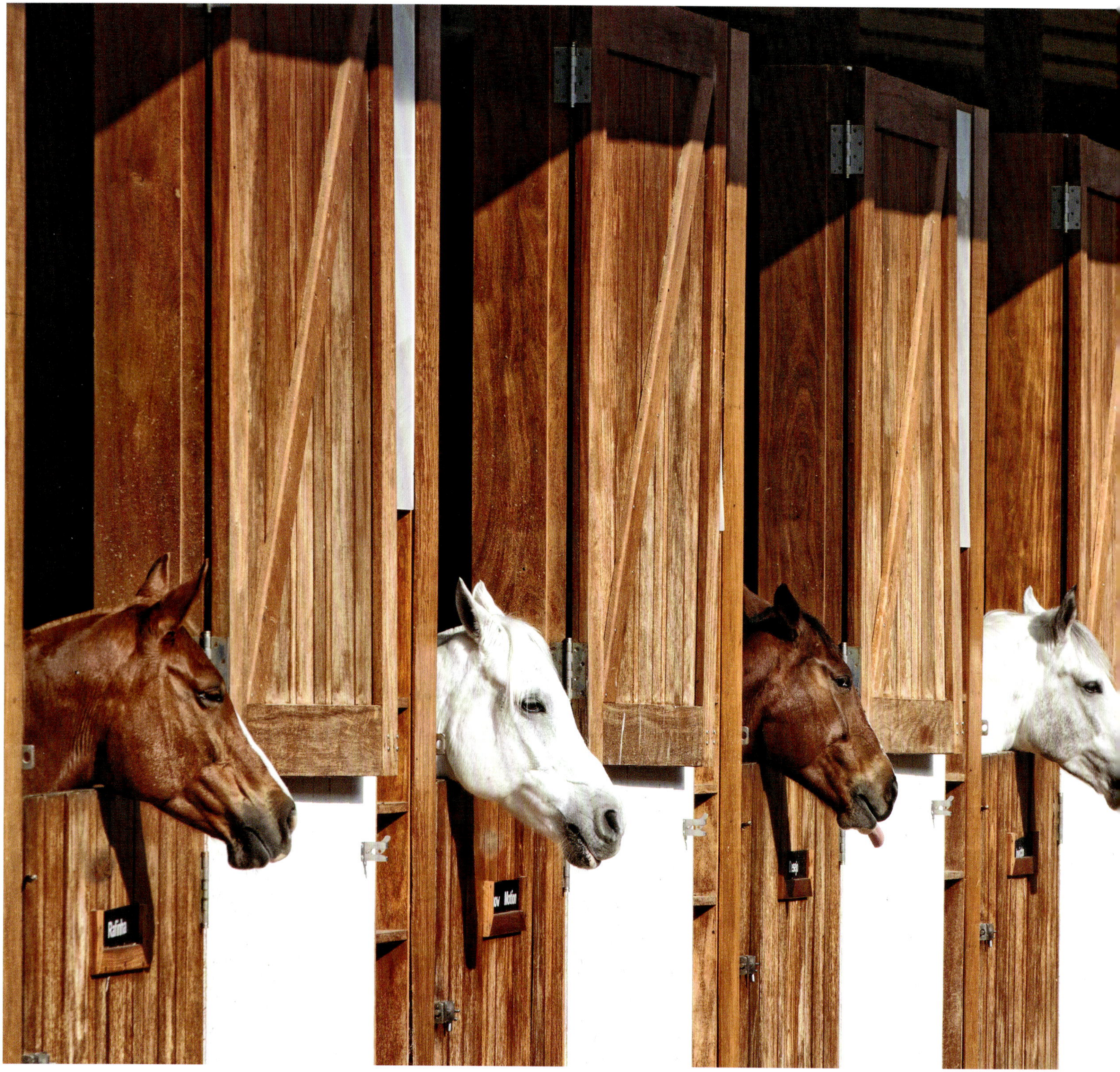

FAZENDA BOA VISTA **95**

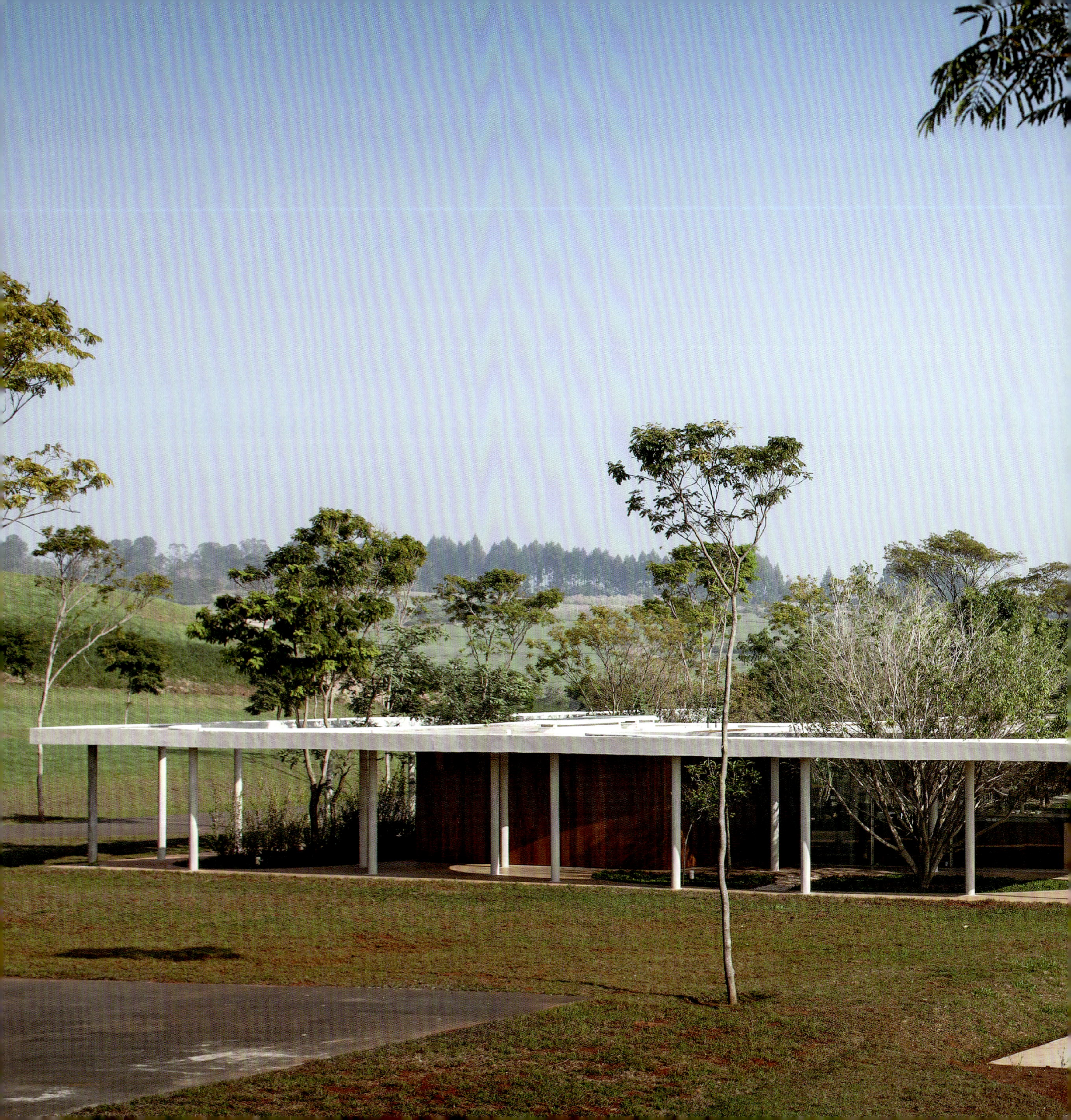

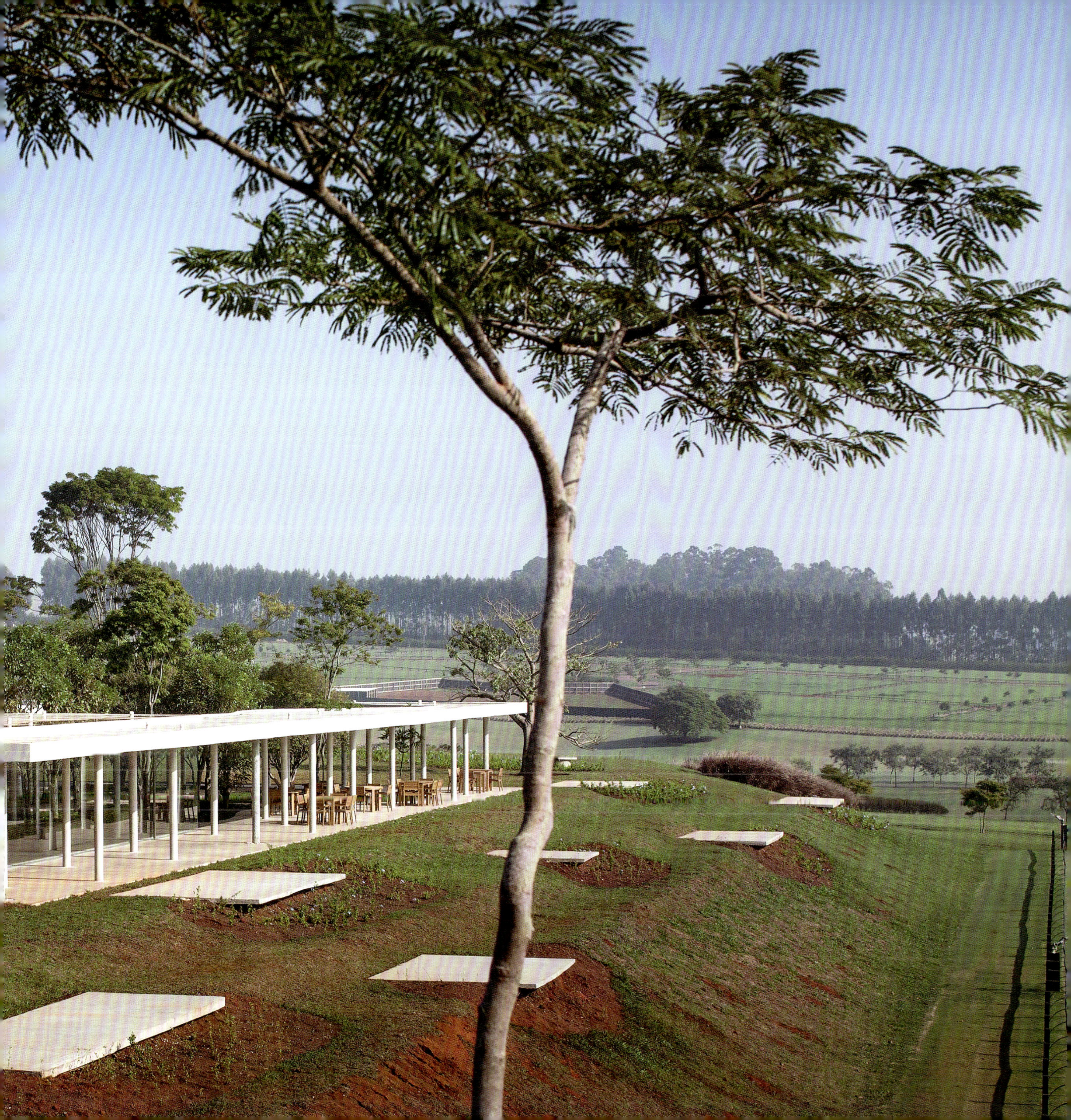

98 ISAY WEINFELD

FAZENDA BOA VISTA **99**

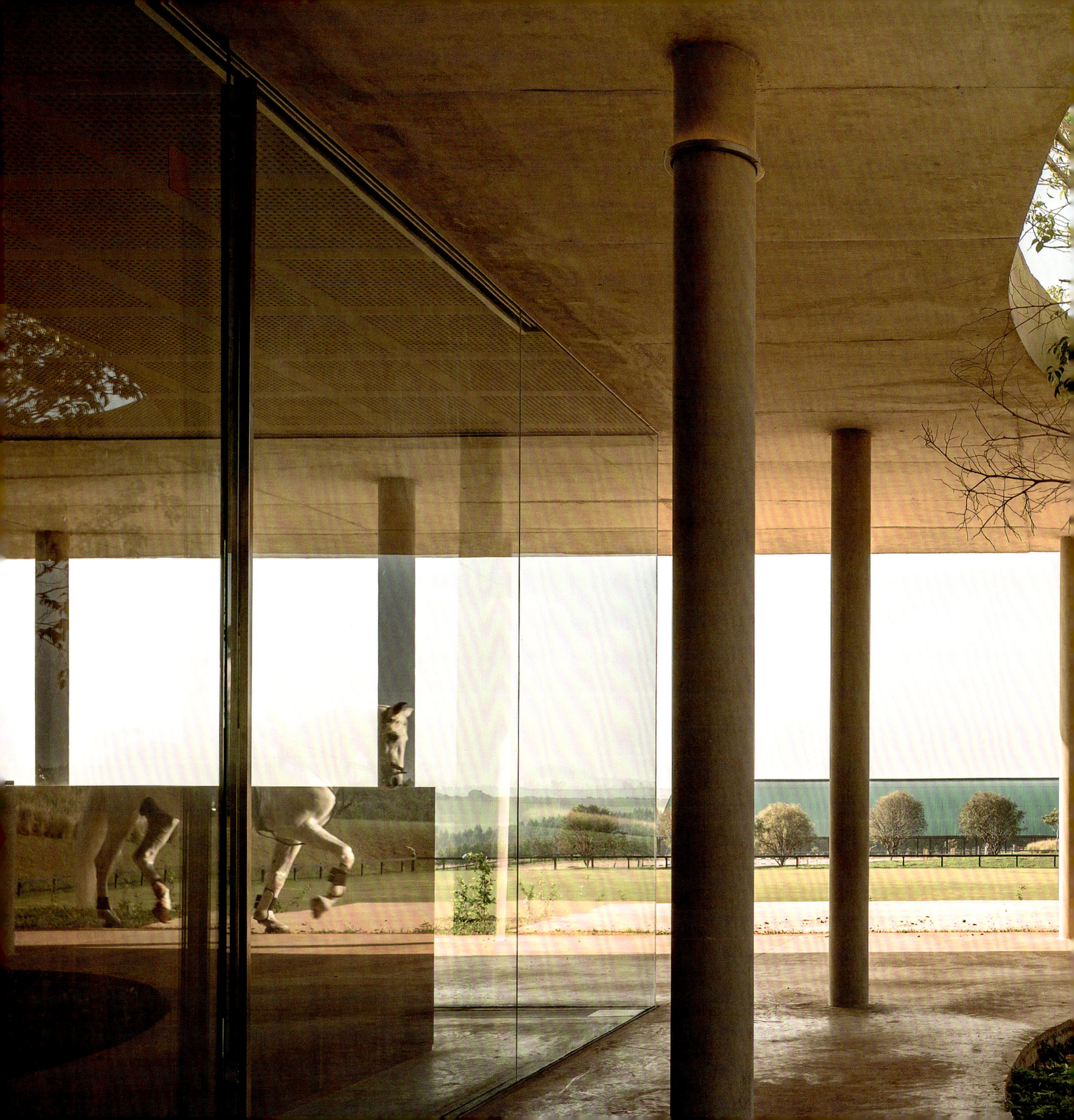

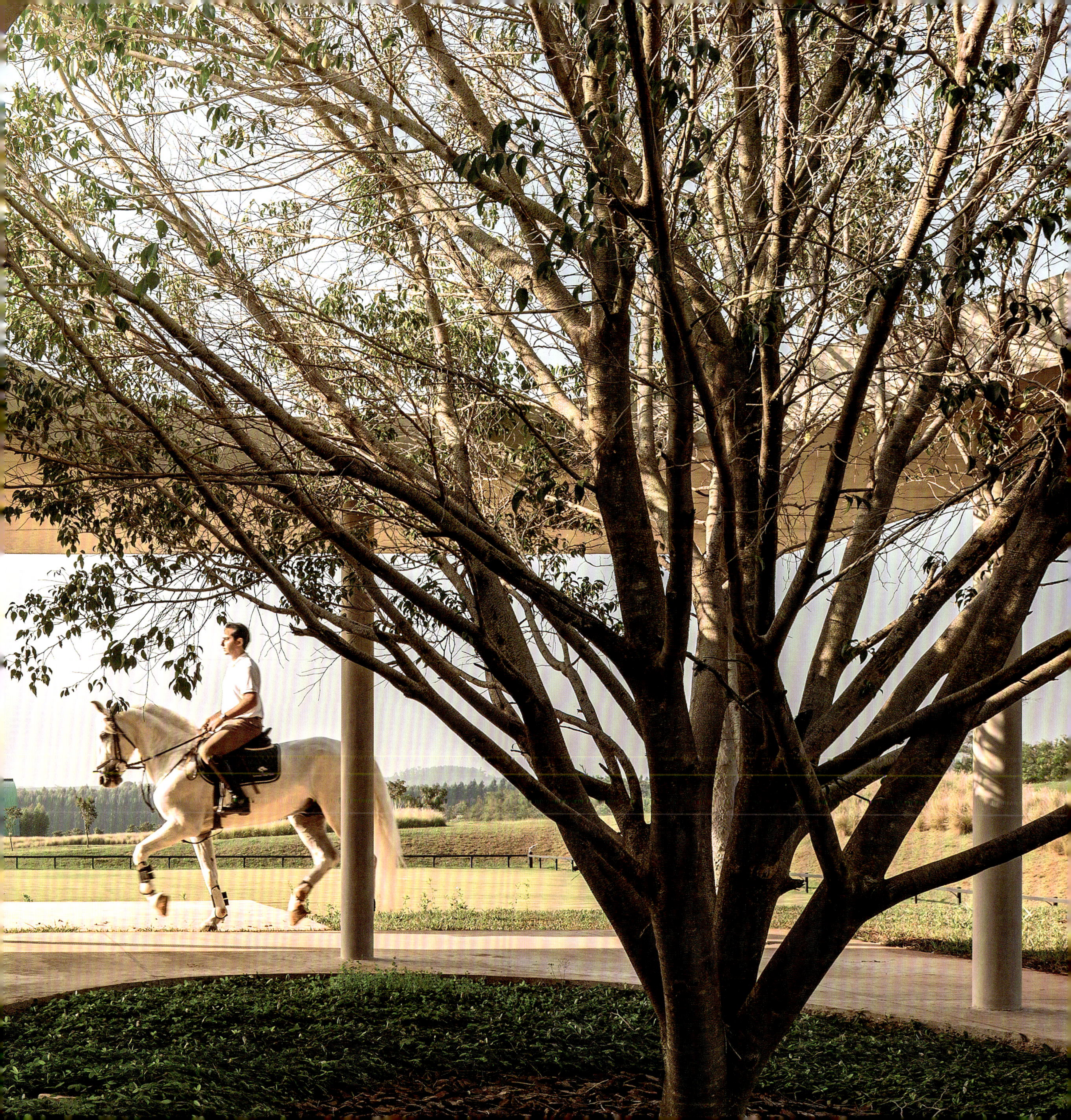

Air Barns
Lake|Flato

San Saba, Texas, United States

Building Area:
1,208 m² conditioned;
446 m² covered porch space

Architect in Charge:
David Lake, Ted Flato

Project Team:
Ted Flato, David Lake, John Grable,
Brian Korte, Joseph Benjamin.
Contractor: Truax Construction, Inc.
Structural Engineer: Reynolds,
Schlattner, Chetter and Row, Inc.
Equine Consultant: Luis Echezarreta

Photographer:
Dawn Laurel, Lake|Flato

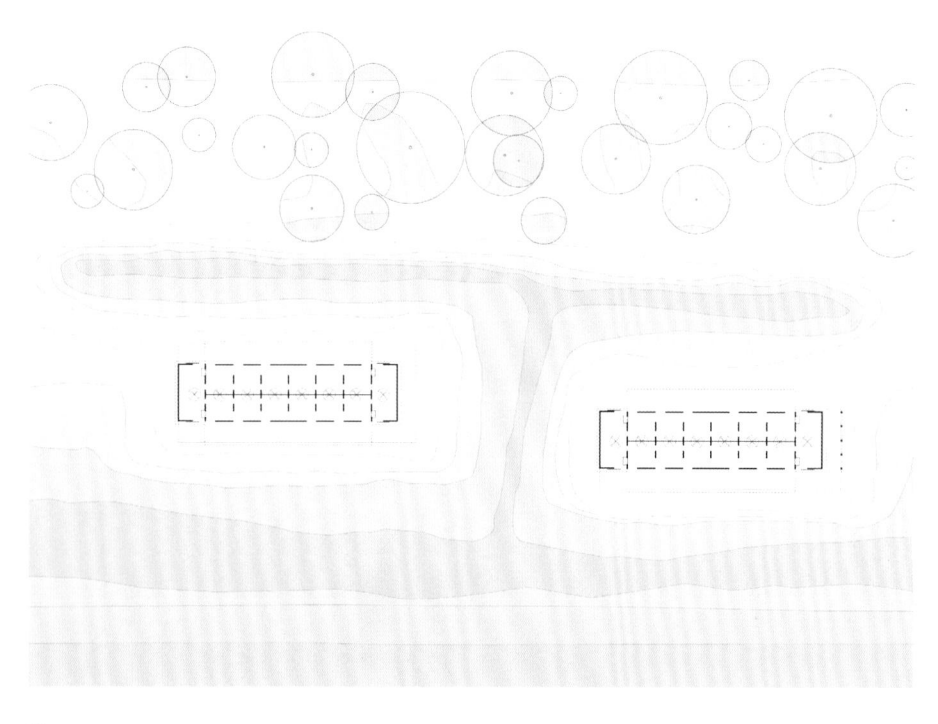

Plan

Located just outside of the city of San Saba in central Texas—about 100 miles northwest of Austin—the Air Barns are two industrial looking stable buildings designed to be functionally and environmentally responsive. The area is known for its farming industry, mostly growing pecans, and therefore the clients wanted a series of agricultural barns that would not only house their polo ponies comfortably, but also appear attractive within the landscape as they are situated along the edge of two open and sun-filled polo fields. In plan the two stable buildings are unusual in that there is no central corridor. In fact, the stalls are placed against each other in two rows—like a party wall system—and service is provided along the exterior under a generous overhanging roof. The two nearly identical barns create a shady, cool home for both the horses and their riders. Admirably built of locally salvaged rusted oil field pipes, with open, airy interiors, substantial eight-foot overhangs, and continuous ridge vents, the barns maximize shade while capturing the prevailing cool breezes. The partition system, with walls of wooden slats, provides each horse with individual space while maintaining a communal sense of the herd on the open range. Additional solid shed-roof forms, with rolling barn doors for access, flank both ends of the stalls. The east shed is the feed room (or kitchen) and the west shed contains the tack room (or closets) storing all the required equine gear. Resembling in profile the rolling hills just to the south of the stable complex, these symmetrical farm structures offer an excellent example of how industrial buildings can be sensitive to both their users and the natural environment, and yet appear extremely attractive. They are distinctly modern interpretations of stable buildings that at the same time still fall within the long tradition of North American agricultural barns.

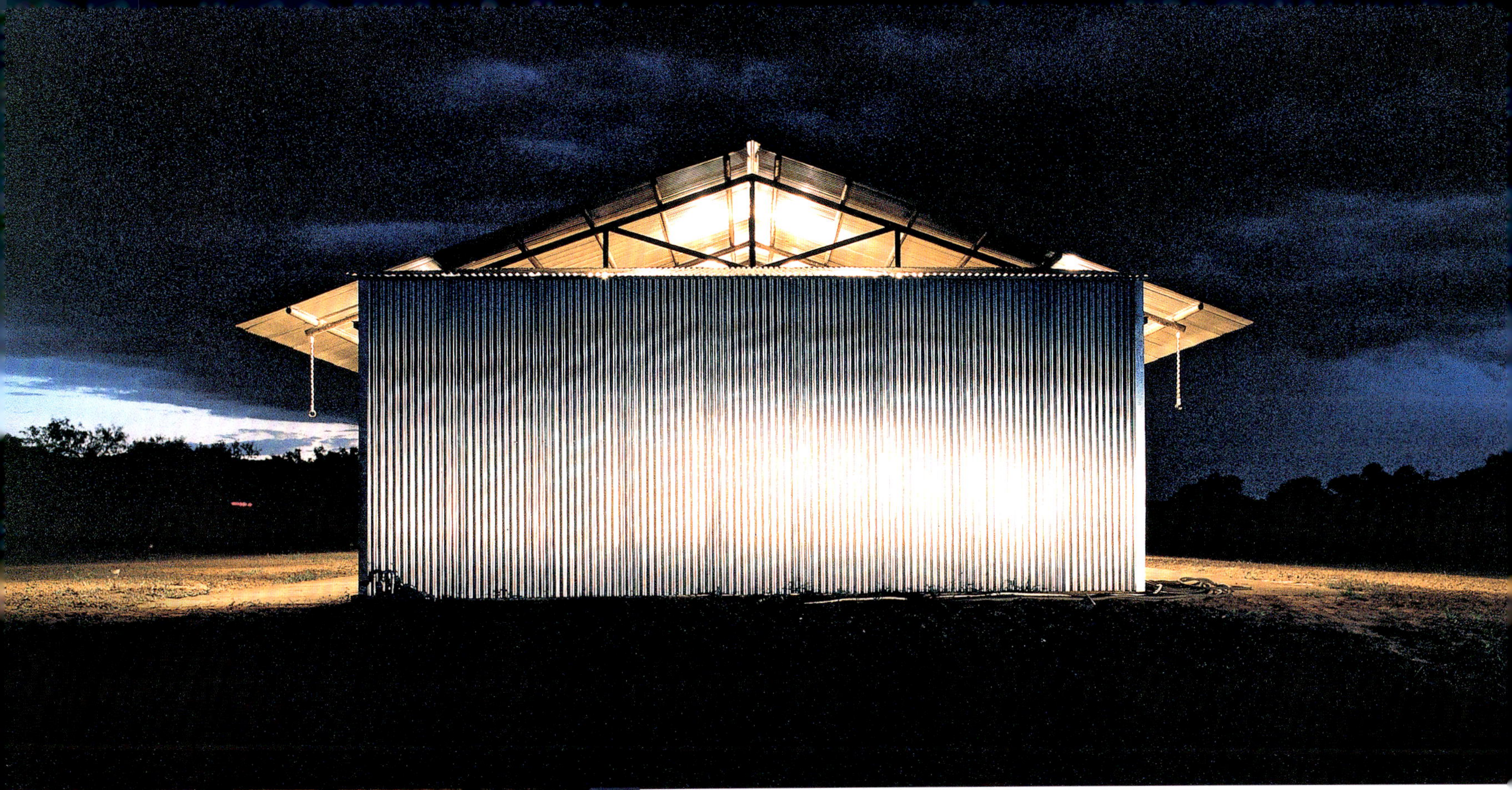

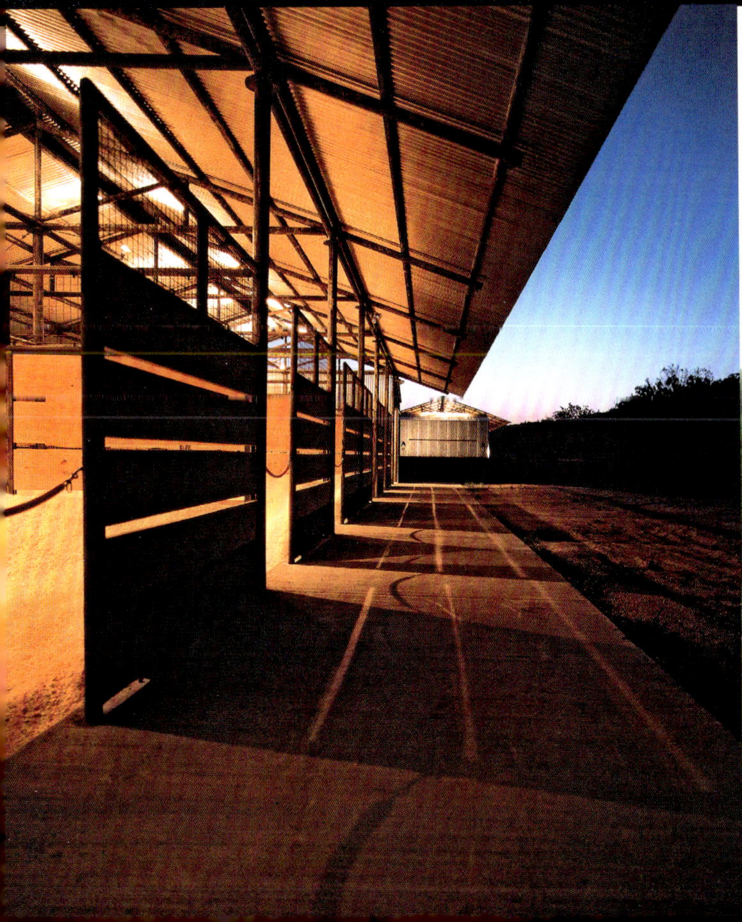

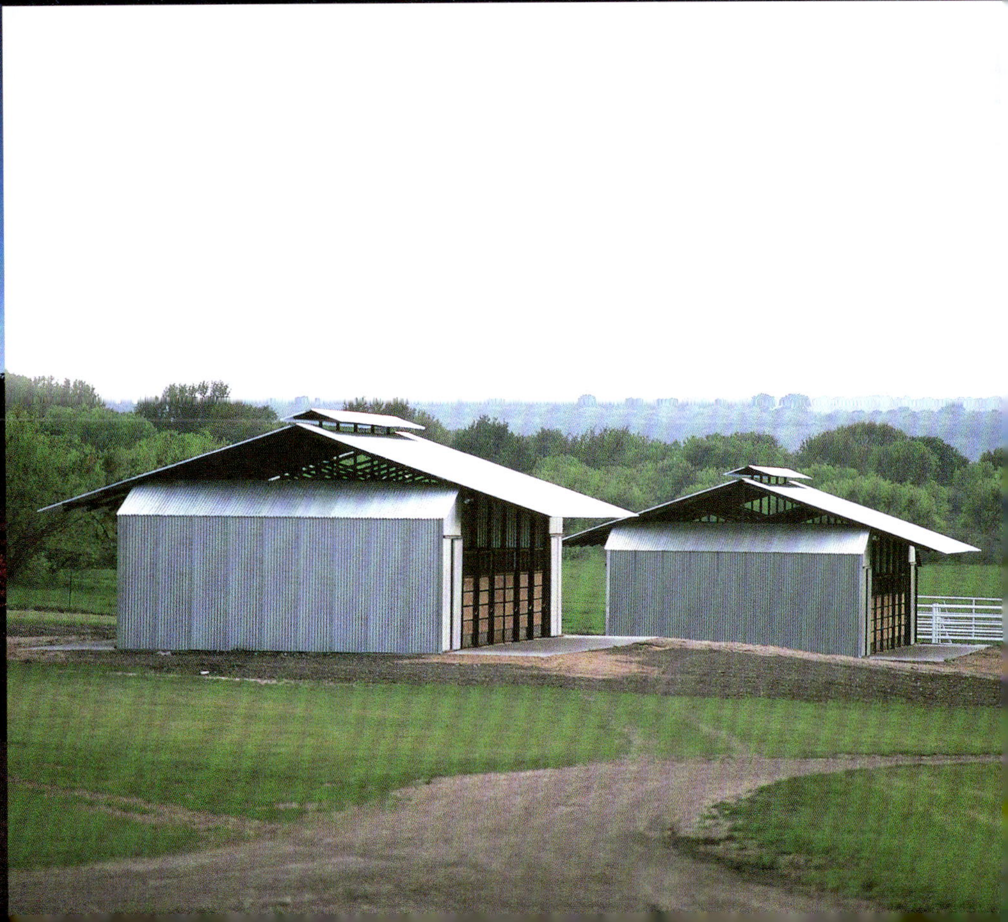

106 LAKE|FLATO

AIR BARNS 107

Hípico del Bosque
APT arquitectura para todos

Cuernavaca, Morelos, México

House Area:
844 m²

Plot Area:
19,289.50 m²

Architect in Charge:
Lilian Rebollo Uribe

Project Team:
Edgar Bahena Cruz, Víctor Escobar Lagunas (structural engineering)

Interior Designer:
APT arquitectura para todos / Lilian Rebollo

Landscape Designer:
APT arquitectura para todos / Lilian Rebollo

Photographer:
Luis Gordoa

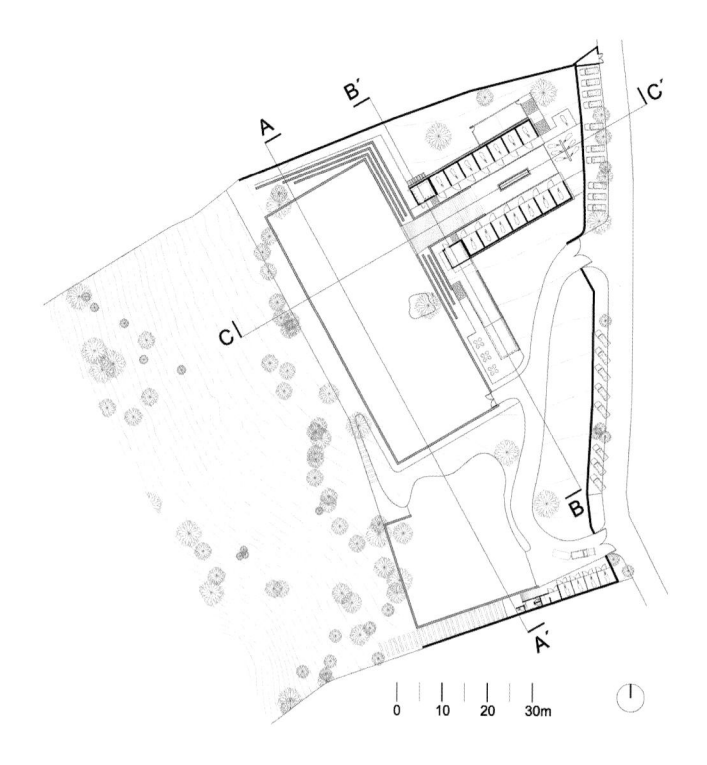

Plan

Situated at the highest part of the city of Cuernavaca, in the middle of a dense wooded area, the Hípico del Bosque horse club (the word "hípico" means equestrian in Spanish) covers an area of 7,000 square meters on land of almost two hectares. The majority of the club's site is a forest with pine trees on a downward slope extending to a natural reserve. The remaining area was determined as the site for the horse club. The design approach to the project combined the client's needs with the local scenery, respecting the natural topography, orientation, and landscape of the site. The project was developed on three levels that incorporated various buildings and terraces. At the highest part are two rows of stables with an open court in between, and water troughs running down the middle of the court and against the back wall. Storage rooms, harness rooms, and administrative offices complete the upper level. Through a series of massive stone retaining walls, ramps, and stairs, these uses are linked to the principal riding arena and public social areas with coffee shop, terraces, bathrooms, and changing rooms. At the lower part of the site is the service and grooming area next to the paddock and stables for competitions. The main aim of this configuration was to highlight the purity of the elements that shape it, synthesizing their utility with the simplicity of materials, and using constructive techniques to conserve the site's natural aspects. The principle materials used on the exterior are stone, concrete, and wood recovered from the formwork used during construction. The wood was converted into a protective surface, unifying the different parts of the project. Inside, the walls were coated using mortar and paint made from the local soil. The project also has rainwater harvesting, biological filters (in order to use clean and sewage water for the watering of green areas), lighting using LED lights, and solar cells. The rustic wooden volumes and stone clad retaining walls contrast with the flat concrete slab roofs held aloft by thin columns painted in black, that allow for maximum natural light and ventilation throughout.

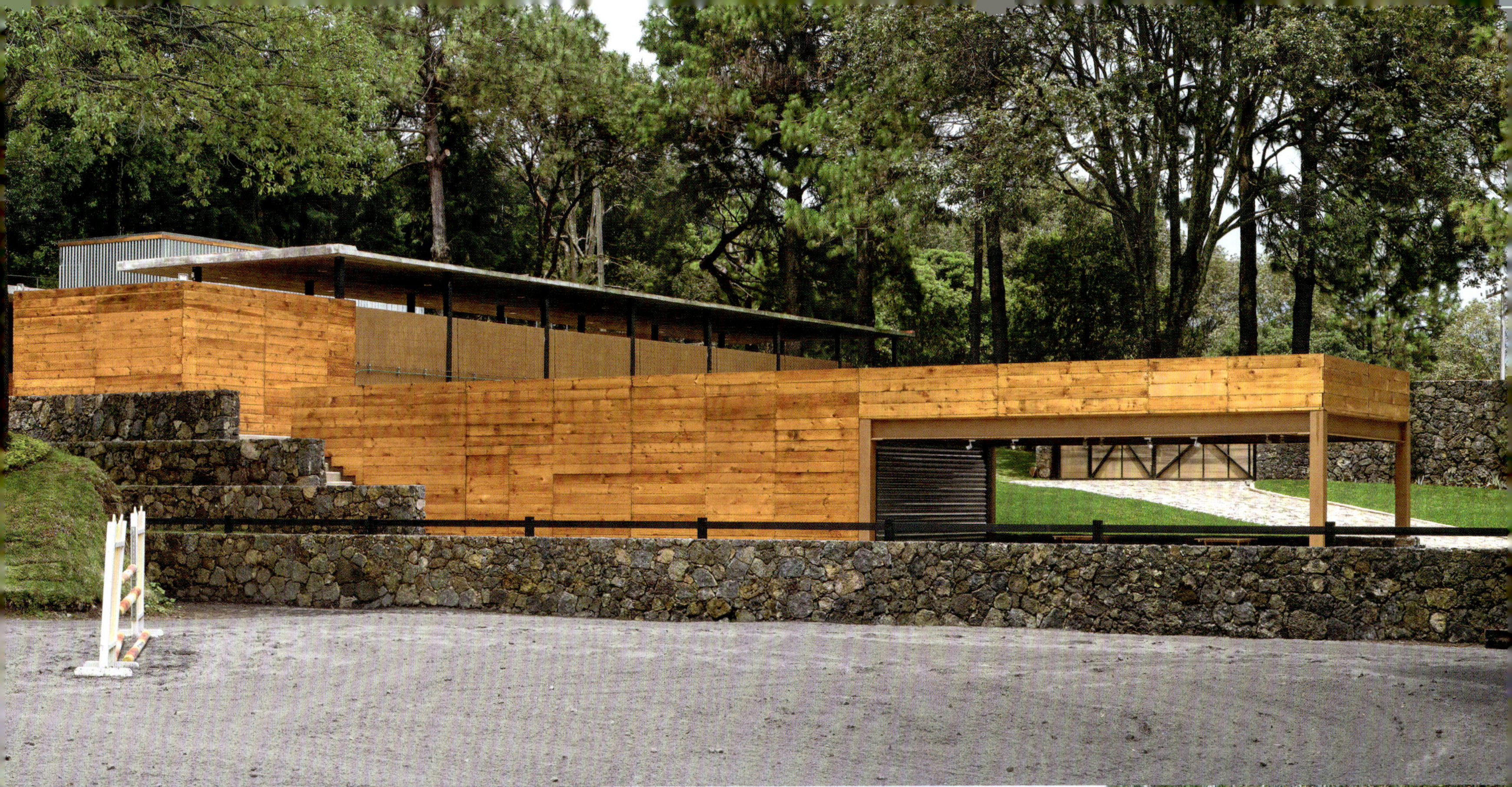

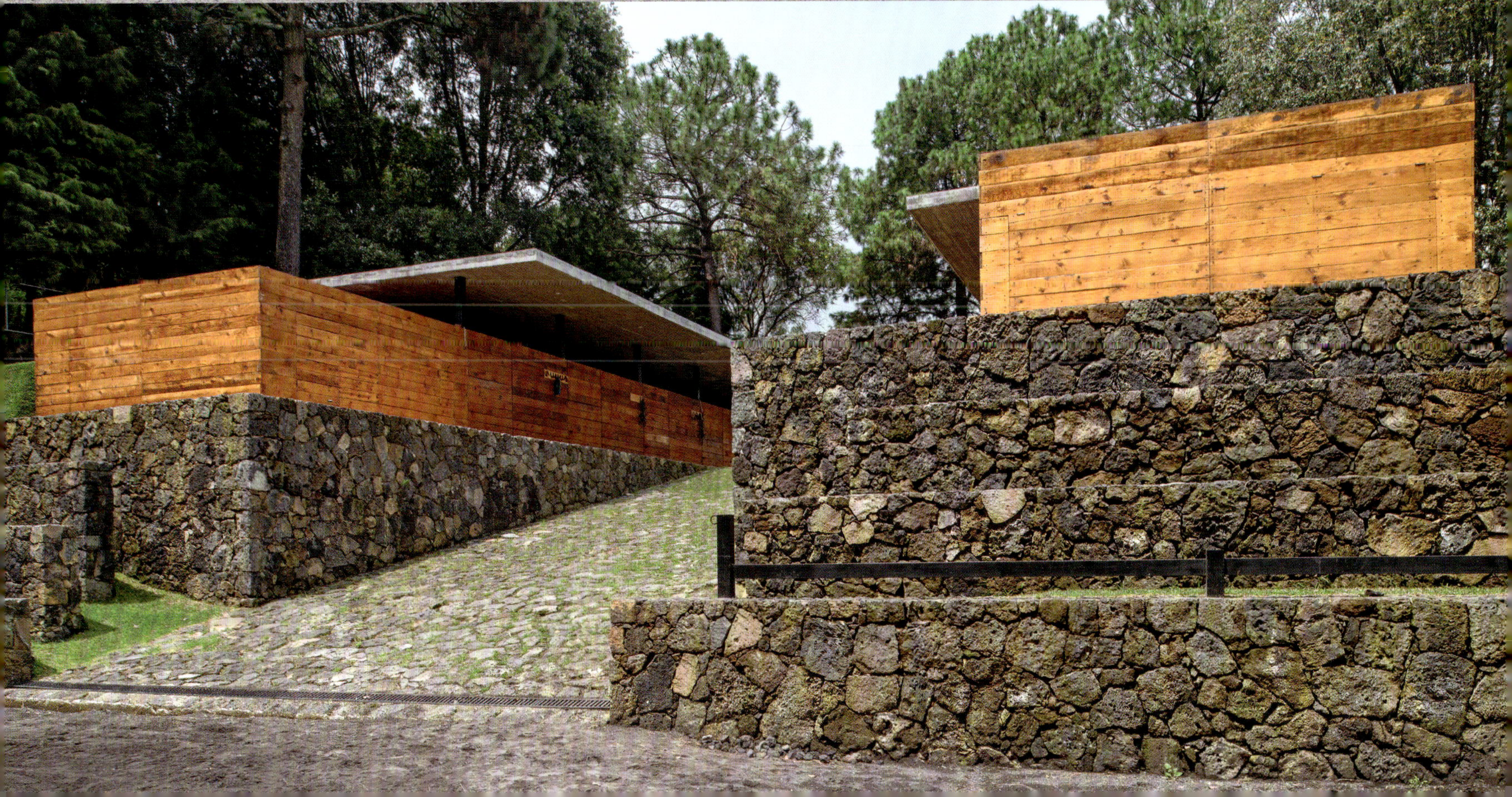

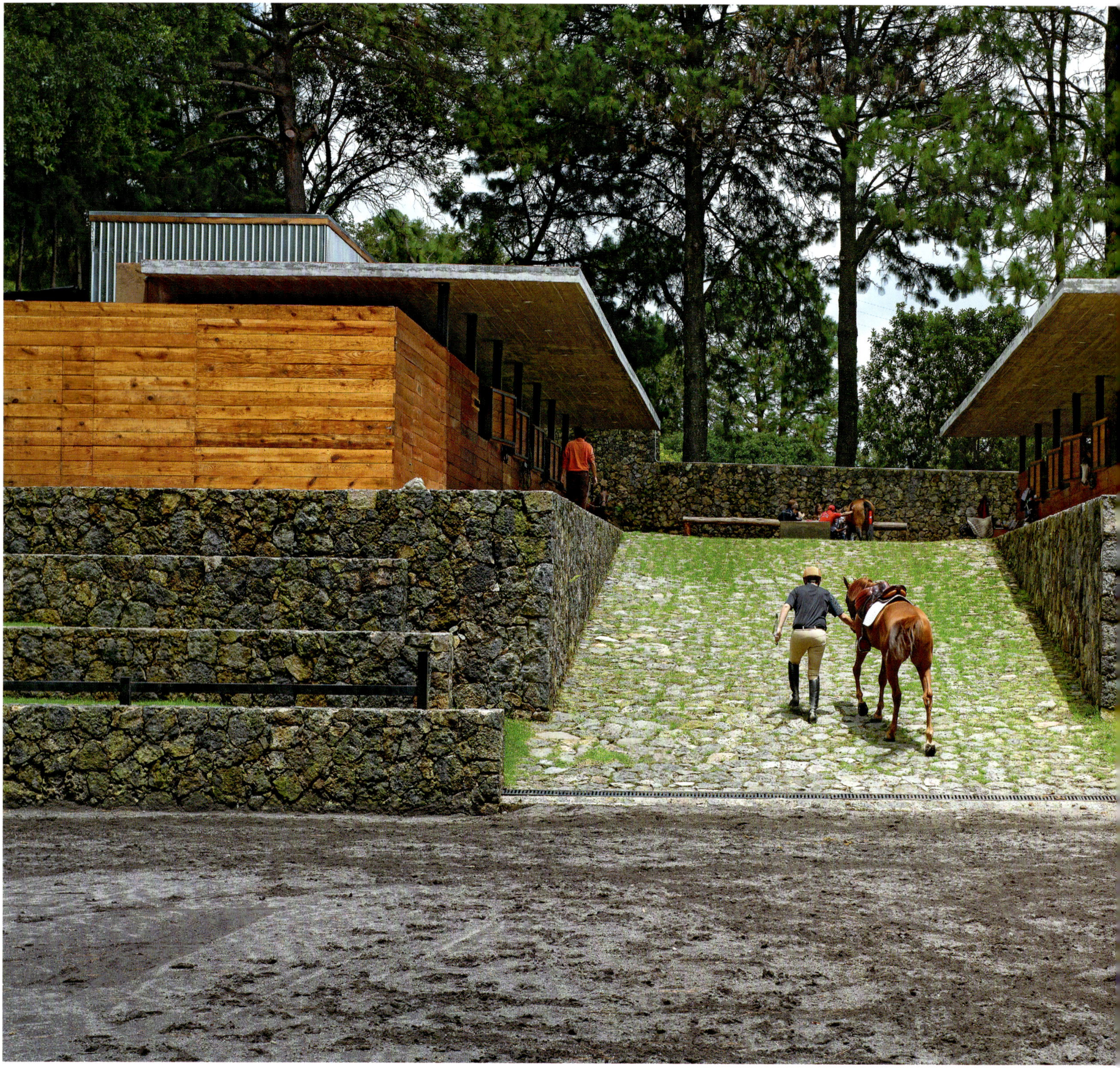

HÍPICO DEL BOSQUE 113

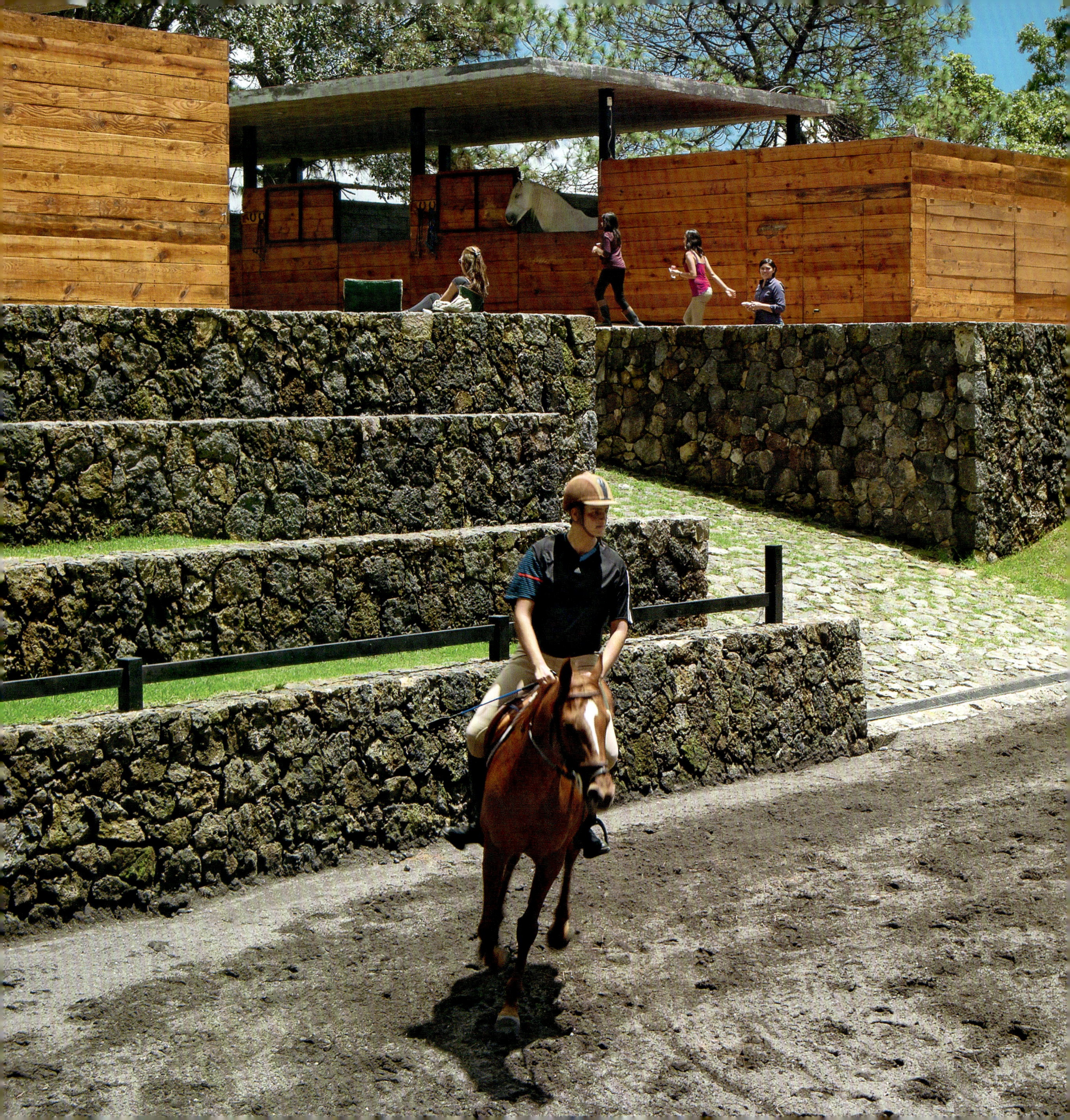

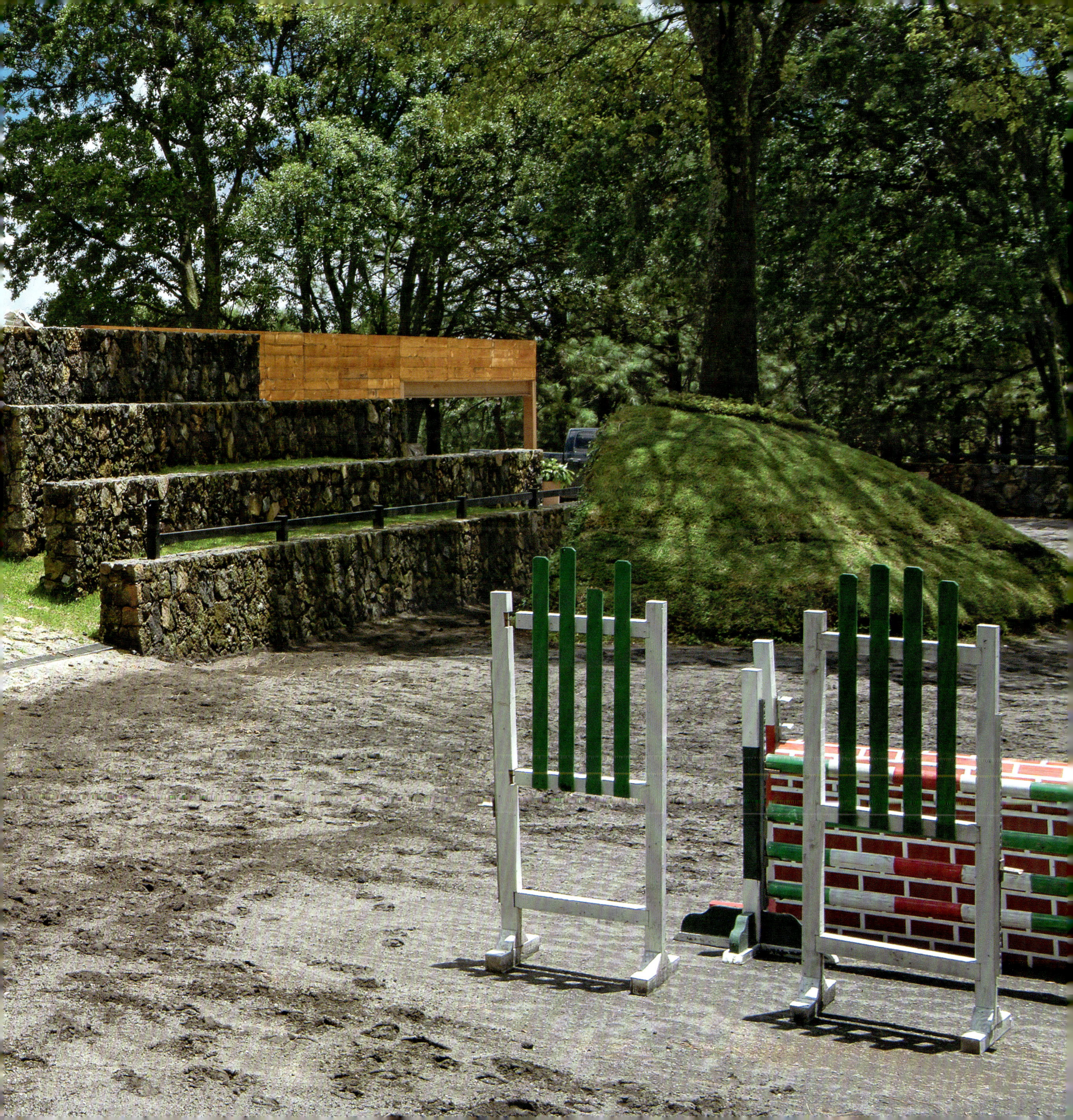

116　APT ARQUITECTURA PARA TODOS

HÍPICO DEL BOSQUE

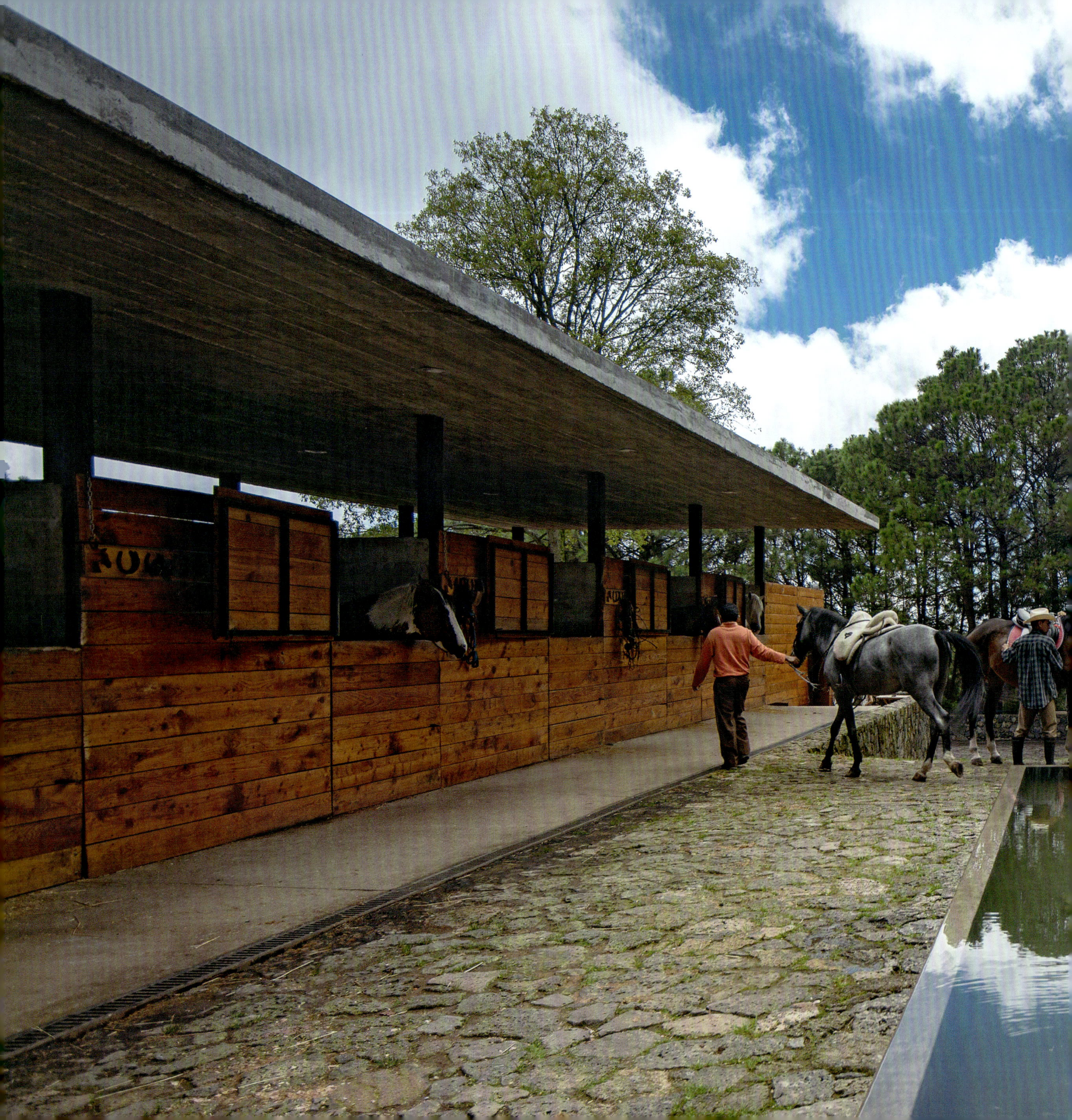

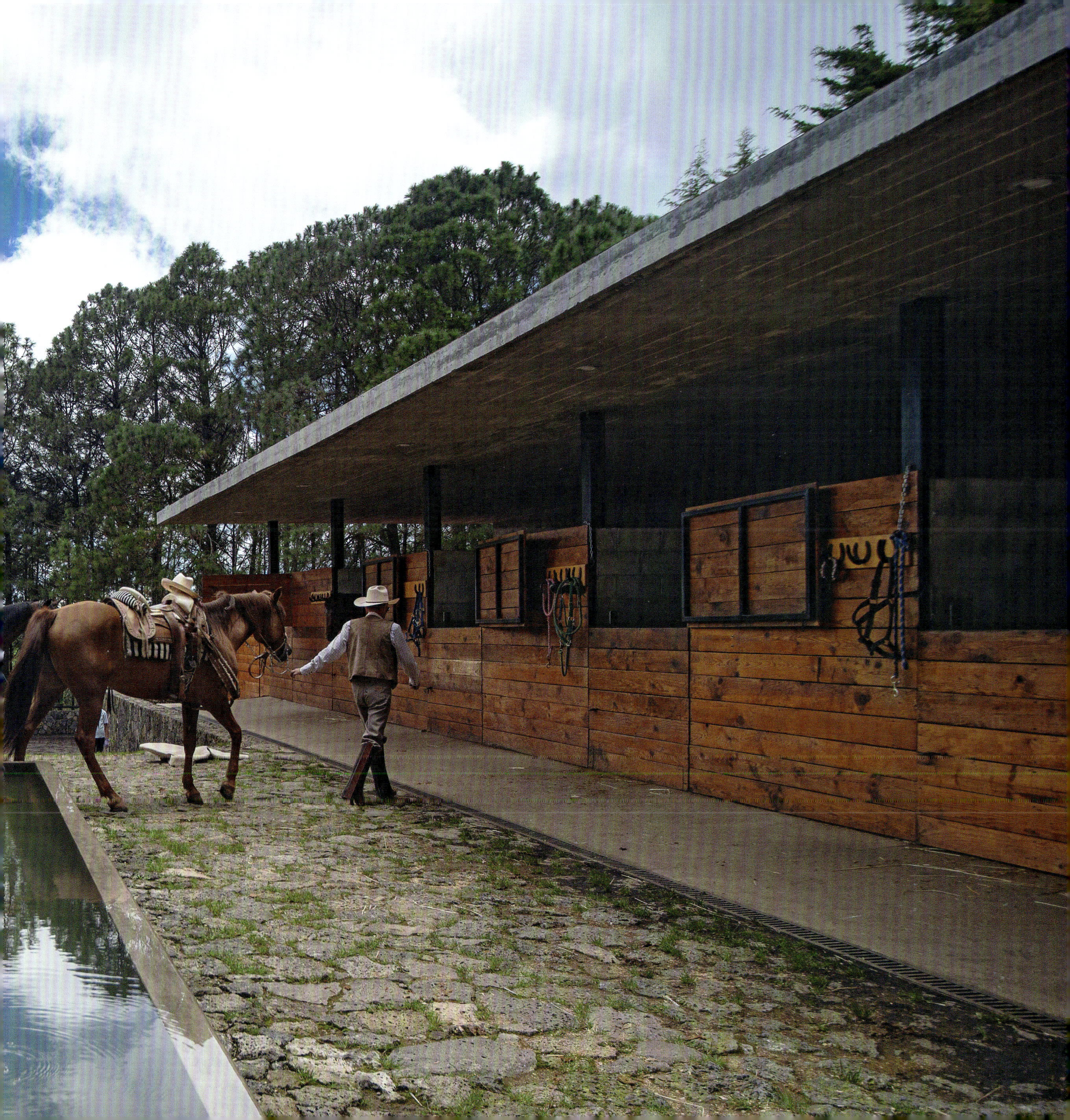

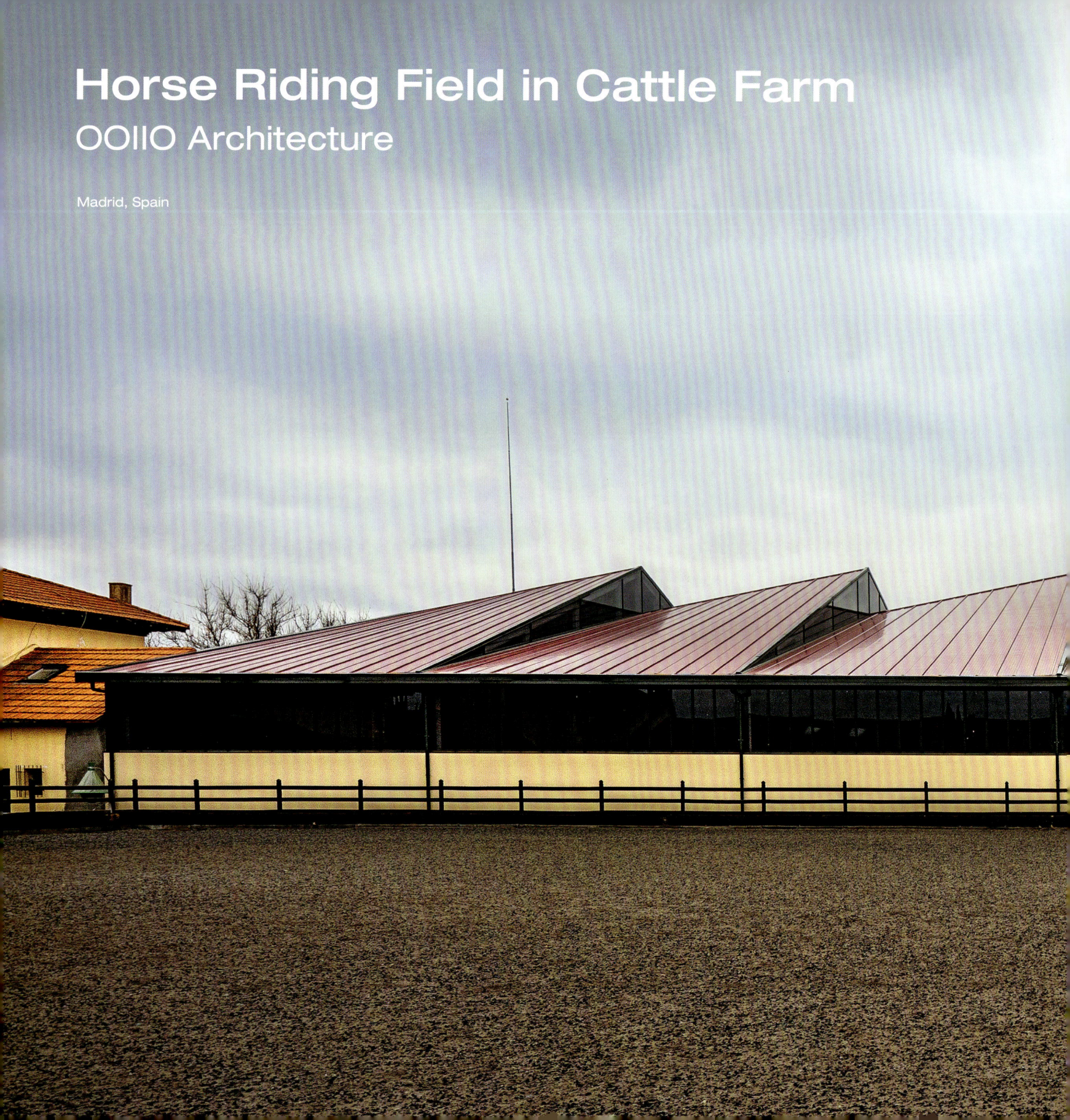

Horse Riding Field in Cattle Farm
OOIIO Architecture

Madrid, Spain

Building Area:
2,350 m²

Site Area:
120 hectares

Architect in Charge:
Joaquín Millán Villamuelas

Project Team:
Joaquín Millán Villamuelas, Manuel Fernández Corral, Natalia Garmendia Cobo

Photographer:
Josefotoinmo

Plan

Located in a beautiful landscape in the Province of Castile, Spain, OOIIO Architecture transformed an existing cattle farm into a sports facility for the care and training of show jumping horses. The challenge was to integrate a new horse-riding arena into a large traditional country house, bringing the old stables up to date, and making the new group of buildings a first-class riding facility. Moreover, as competition horses are the real protagonists of this project, every detail was designed so that they would feel as comfortable as possible. A horse-riding arena is ultimately a large quadrangular space, bounded by four walls, with soft ground where riders and horses are trained. Show jumping is an equestrian event that consists of completing a set course of several jumping obstacles in an allotted period, without accumulating any faults or toppling over the obstacle bars. The original building was in the form of a rectangular block, with a central courtyard that acted as an outdoor arena. In order to train in inclement weather, it was decided to build a new covered riding arena, demolishing one of the arms of the block and integrating the new construction with the rest of the country house, therefore allowing for both indoor and outdoor riding. The new building also had to have good neutral lighting as the owners did not want shadows to distract or confuse the horses when jumping. Therefore, the arena was conceived as a series of six large 30-meter bays, with open triangular trusses that make up a saw-tooth roof of ridges with dual pitches and a succession of north-facing skylights to shield the horses from direct sunlight. When seen from a distance, the new roof formed by the repetition of skylights appears as a repetition of frozen waves in the middle of a vast expanse of landscape. The arena is integrated into the traditional pre-existing building making a new composite whole. The color of the walls encircling the riding arena—made from large pieces of prefabricated concrete—the doors and carpentry, the roof, in short, all the external aspects of the new structure are integrated into what was already there. The stable blocks that surround the new arena were refurbished and adapted to become fully equipped sports facilities, so the riders, caregivers, and horses could enjoy, train, and rest comfortably.

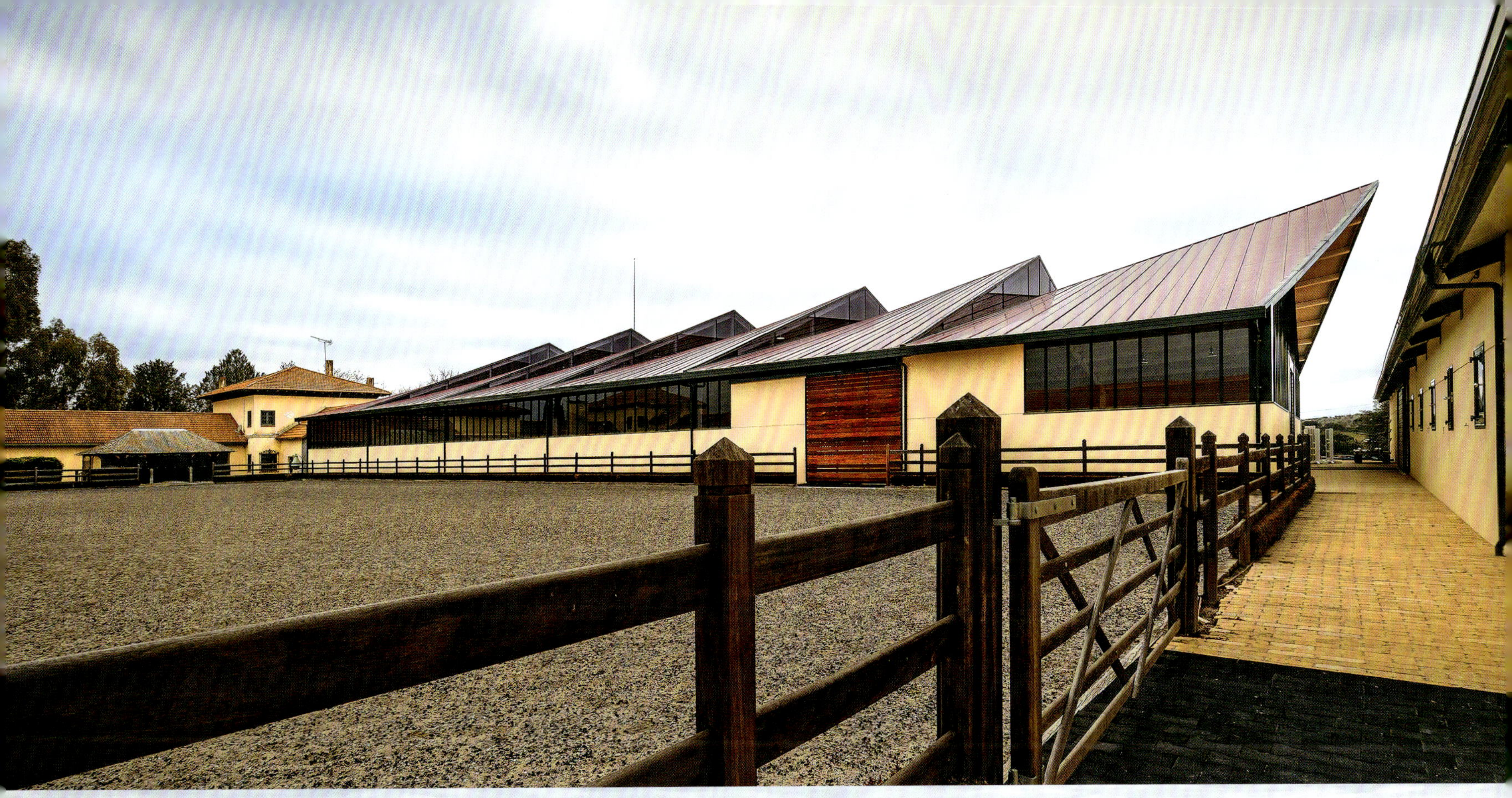

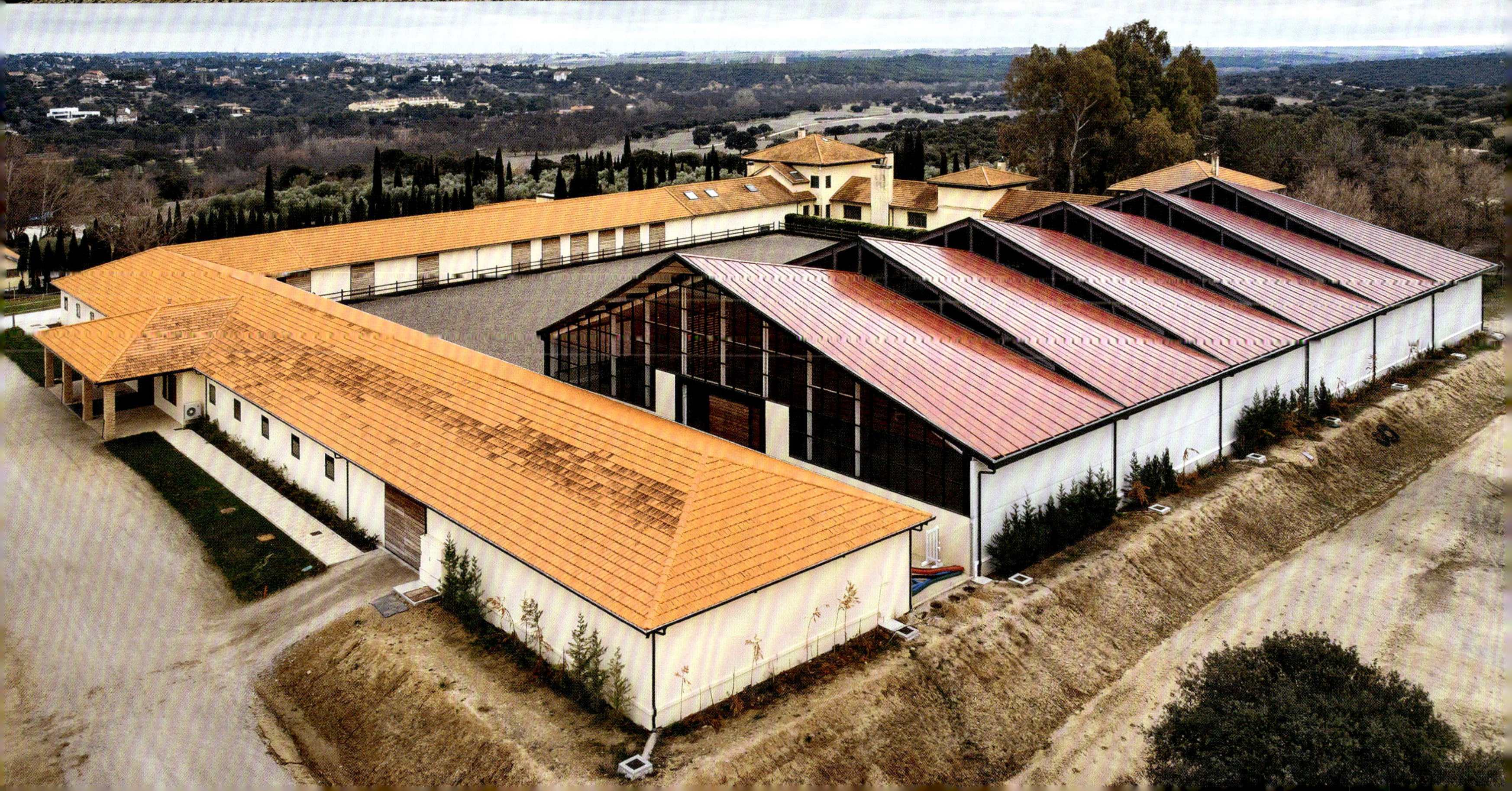

124 OOIIO ARCHITECTURE

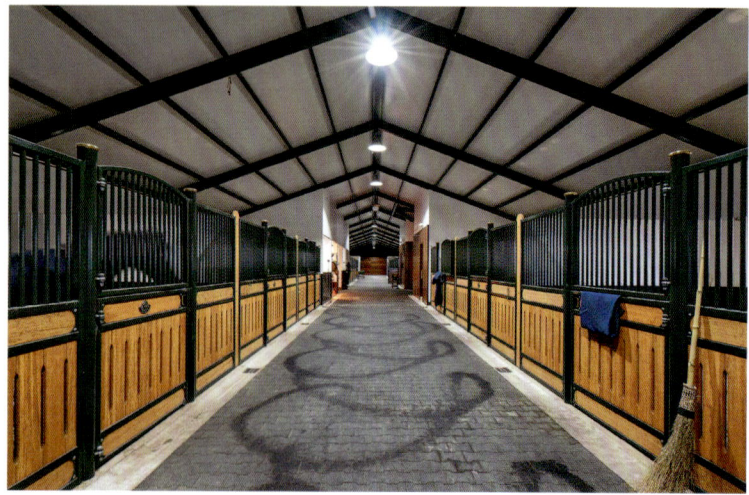

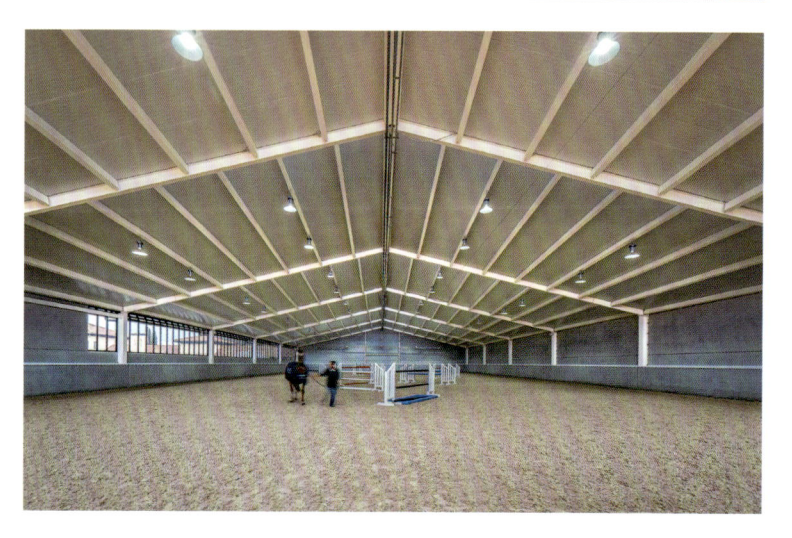

HORSE RIDING FIELD IN CATTLE FARM

House In Cerro Gordo
LEGORRETA®

Cerro Gordo, Estado de México, México

Building Area:
2,247 m²

Site Area:
19,000 m²

Architect in Charge:
Ricardo Legorreta, Víctor Legorreta

Architecture and Interior Design Team:
Ricardo Legorreta, Víctor Legorreta, Miguel Almaraz, Adriana Ciklik, Carlos Vargas, Miguel Alatriste, Daniel Reyes, Carlos Sánchez, Juan Antonio Moreno, Hugo Acosta, Samuel Aguilar, Jesús Suárez, Alberto Ramírez, Roberto López, Angélica Mendívil, Michelle Garmendia, Maggy Carral

Landscape Designer:
Espacios Verdes SA de CV

Photographer:
Lourdes Legorreta, James Silverman, Dolores Robles-Martínez

Plan

1. ACCESS
2. STABLE
3. TENNIS COURT
4. PARKING
5. FOUNTAIN
6. GUEST HOUSE
7. MAIN HOUSE
8. POOL
9. LAKE
10. HELIPORT

The project is located in the mountains of Cerro Gordo in the center of Mexico, about 100 miles west of Mexico City. The site has approximately 2 million square feet, with large areas of forest within the boundaries of the property. From its highest point, the terrain descends 100 feet downhill, generating a dramatic view of the surrounding hills. The concept of the house includes several buildings, located at different points on the site, connected by several landscape routes that converge on a large circular water basin that serves as the distributor to each of the buildings. Access to the site, both pedestrian and vehicular, is arrived at through a depression in a great stone wall that covers the entire front of the property, highlighting the fundamental concept of a "tecorral," or dry-stone wall. The property includes a gatehouse, guest house, main house, a stables court and riding arena, and several gardens, terraces, a pool, lake, and heliport. All the buildings are made of stone walls, timber, and tile, giving the impression of a modern rustic farm. The stables are located at the terminus of an allée of trees that extend from the circular water basin and consist of two rectangular buildings with a formal garden and open service space in between, and a riding arena behind. Another circular riding arena is located at one end of the stables block, with the garden (where the covered walk ends) and a tennis court at the other. A covered loggia connects the two wings where the stables meet the allée and garden, creating a social space for resting after a day of playing tennis or horseback riding. This project, perhaps more than any other in this book, recalls Hadrian's imperial villa at Tivoli, just outside of Rome, with its rich combination of residential, entertainment, social, and athletic functions all connected via a complex series of outdoor gardens and paths. However, the materials employed and the simplicity of forms throughout remind us that the project is indeed in Mexico and that it is very much of today.

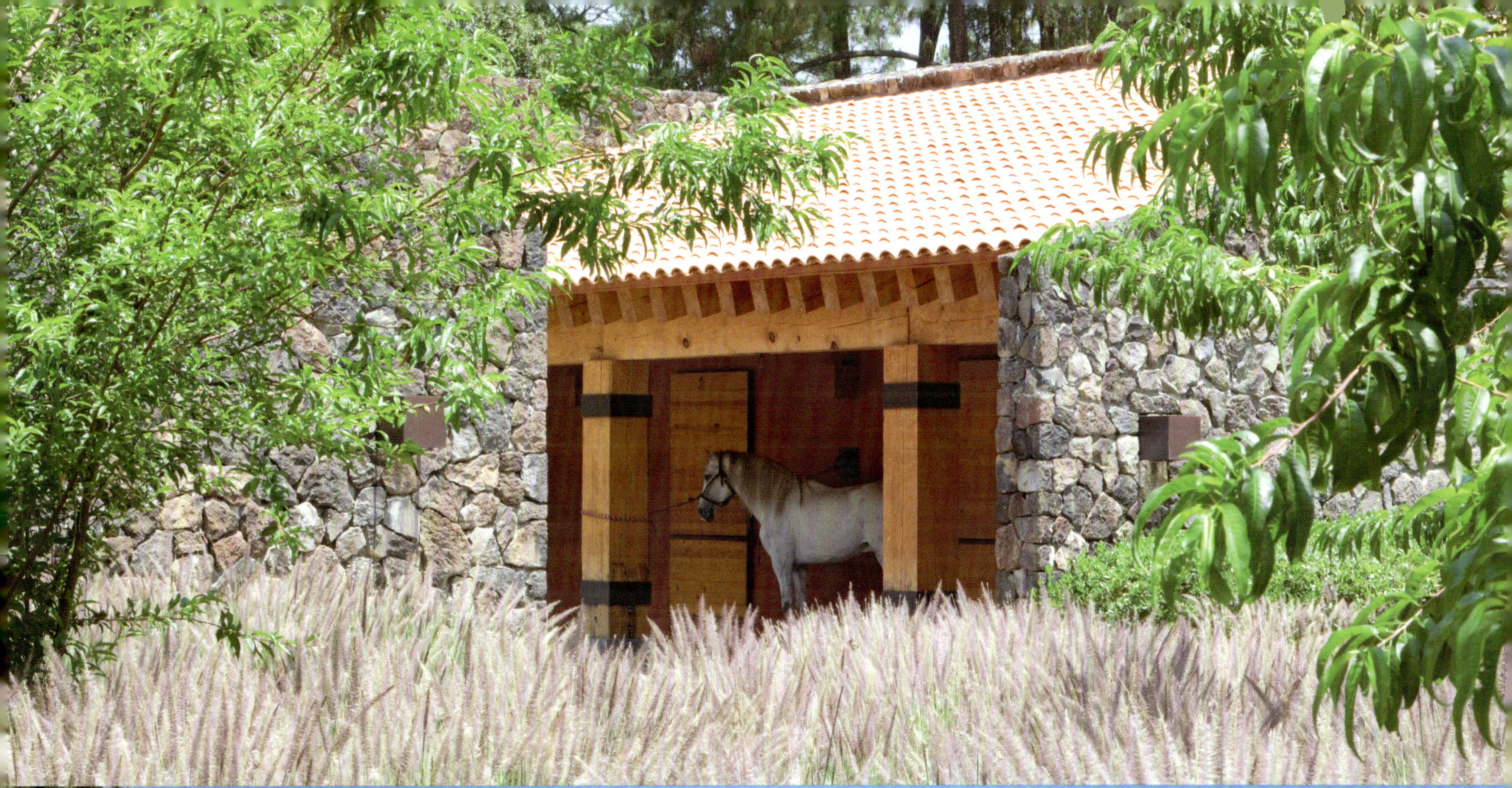

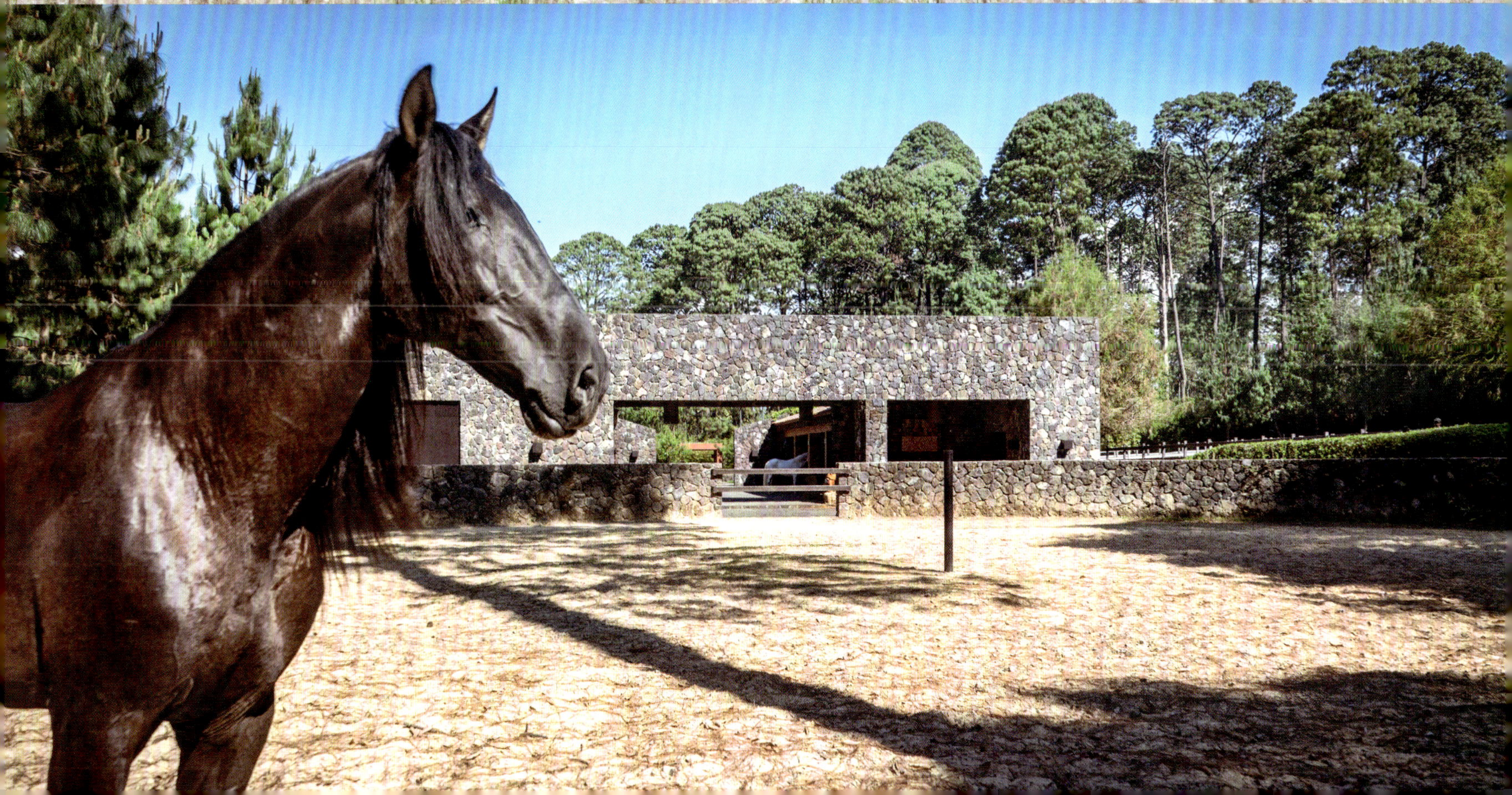

130 LEGORRETA®

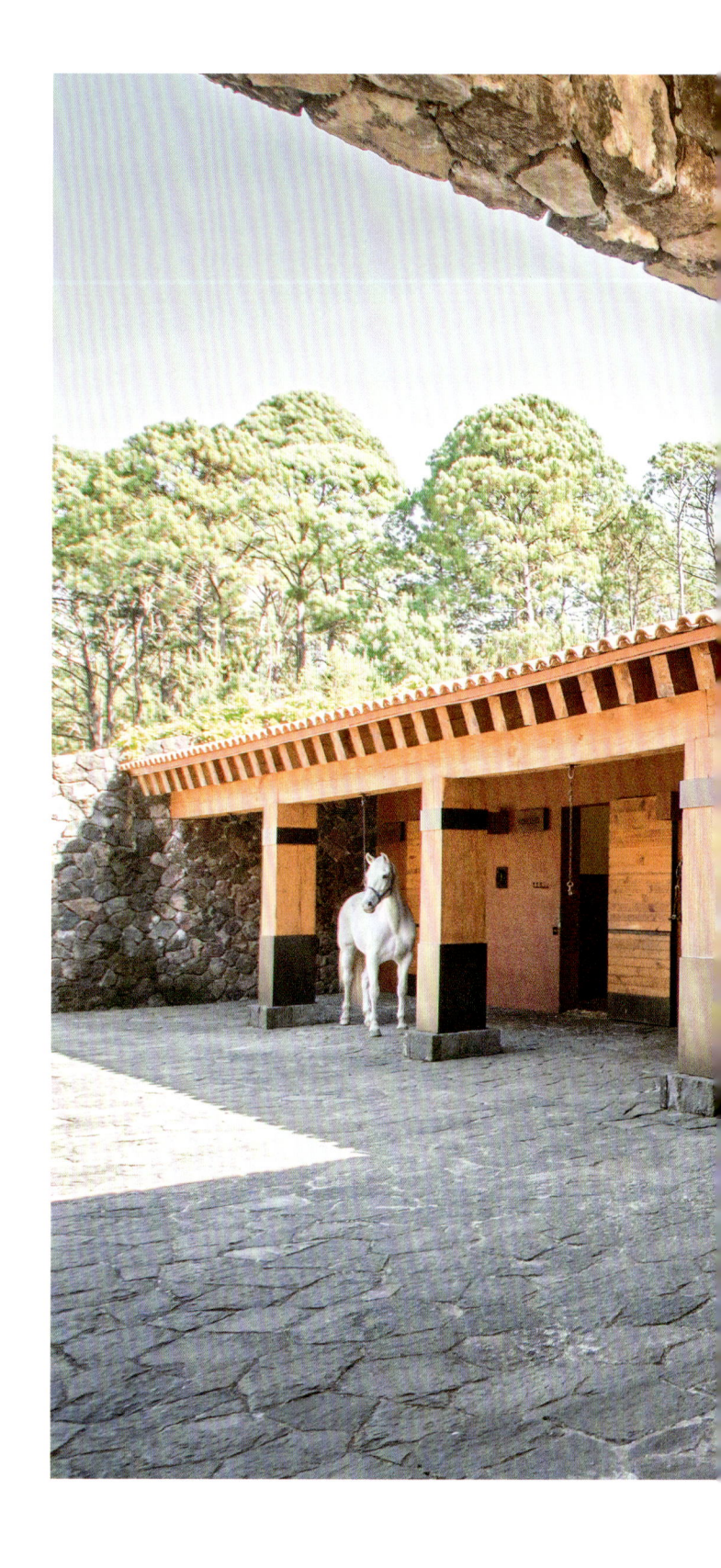

HOUSE IN CERRO GORDO

132 LEGORRETA®

HOUSE IN CERRO GORDO   **133**

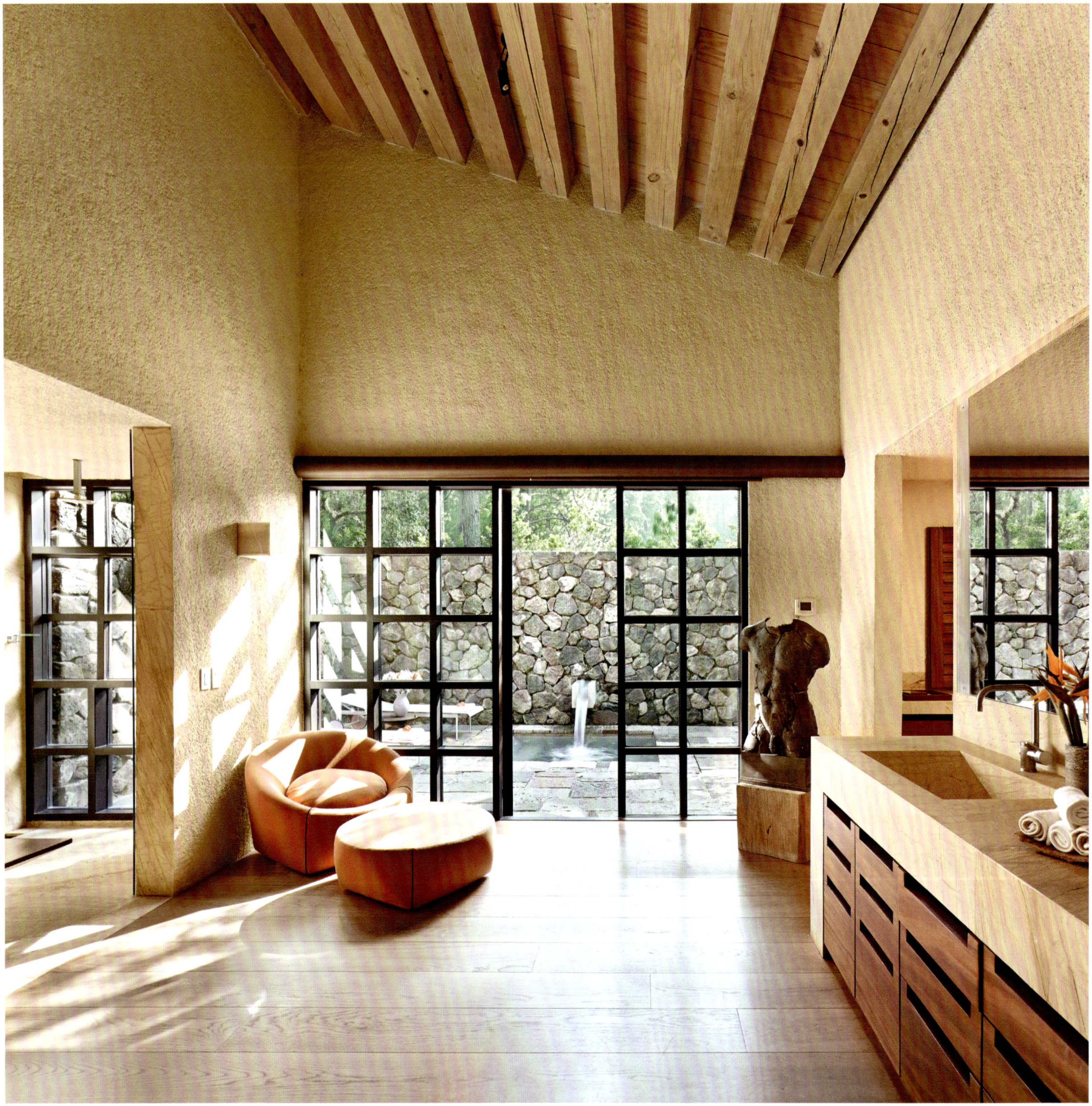

HOUSE IN CERRO GORDO 135

Beechwood Stables
Blackburn Architects with Marcus Gleysteen Architects

Weston, Massachusetts, United States

Building Area:
Total Barn: 772.5 m^2
Total Arena: 2,104 m^2

Site Area:
29,746 m^2

Architect in Charge:
Blackburn Architects with
Marcus Gleysteen Architects

Project Team:
Ian Kelly (Project Manager),
Kenneth Vona Construction Inc
(Builder)

Interior Designer:
SLC Interiors

Landscape Designer:
Gregory Lombardi Design

Photographers:
Kenneth M. Wyner Photography
Inc., Marcus Gleysteen, Richard
Mandelkorn

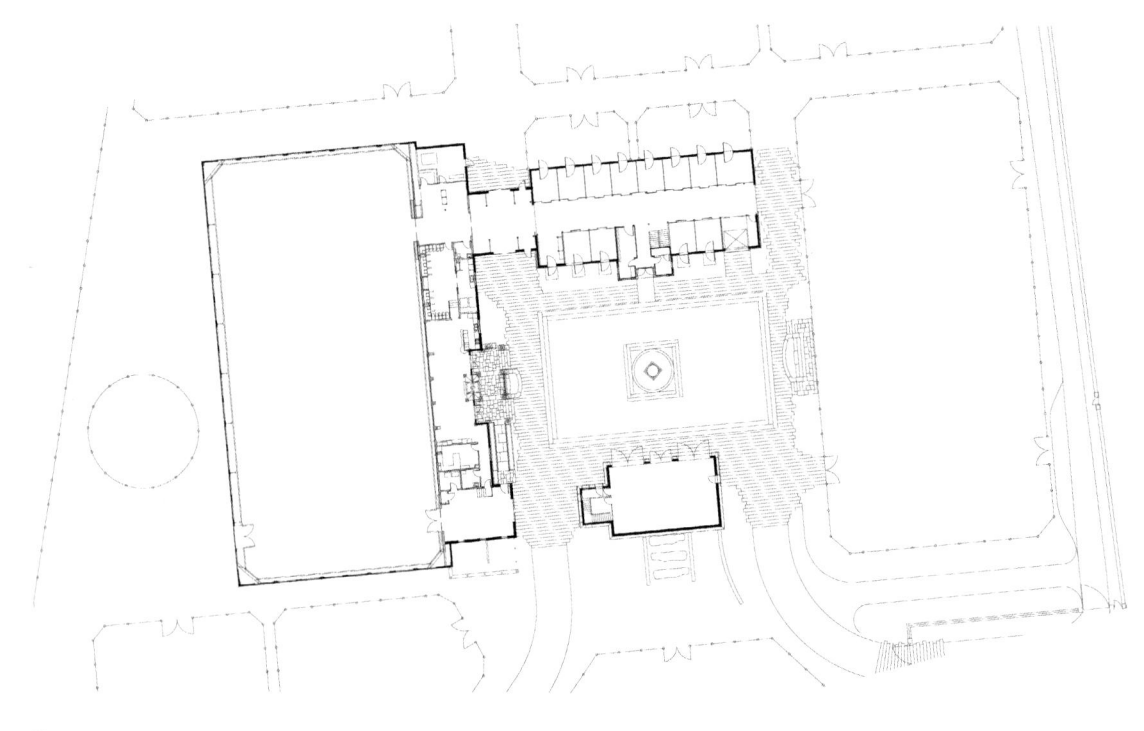

Plan

This unique ten-acre site in Weston, Massachusetts, just outside of Boston, is bordered by 200 acres of conservation land, creating an intimate, private setting for a family-owned farm. The project consists of three different sized barn buildings around an open central service court. The twelve-stall barn on the northern edge of the court is equipped with a half bath, wash/groom stall, feed room, tool and equipment storage, and a partial hayloft. Behind the stall barn are several fenced in fields for riding, and a picturesque New England pond. Opposite the stall barn, a new "bank barn" provides storage for vehicles and equipment on the ground floor while the first floor and loft above serve as a two-bedroom apartment with two-and-a-half baths, a kitchen, dining room, and living room. A large 180 x 90-foot enclosed riding arena forms the third side of the composition to the west, and includes a mounting area, an observation lounge with a small kitchen, an office, tack room, and laundry. The large structure framed in steel is clad in wood with continuous ribbon windows along three sides. A small arched pavilion connects the indoor riding arena with the stall barn providing covered access between the two, and a direct pathway from the courtyard to the fields at the back. The open courtyard between the three volumes overlooks a large outdoor riding arena and offers an inviting atmosphere for the owners and their family and friends to enjoy the beautiful landscape. The architecture of the complex reflects the local New England vernacular, using heavy timber and steel-frame construction, wood cladding throughout the exterior and interior, brick and stone paving around the buildings and court, and large metal roof coverings for the various barn structures. Picket fences, sliding barn doors, dormer windows, and wooden brackets further enhance the rustic character of the complex. Only the inconspicuous skylights above the stall barn and indoor riding arena remind us that the project is a work of thoroughly contemporary design.

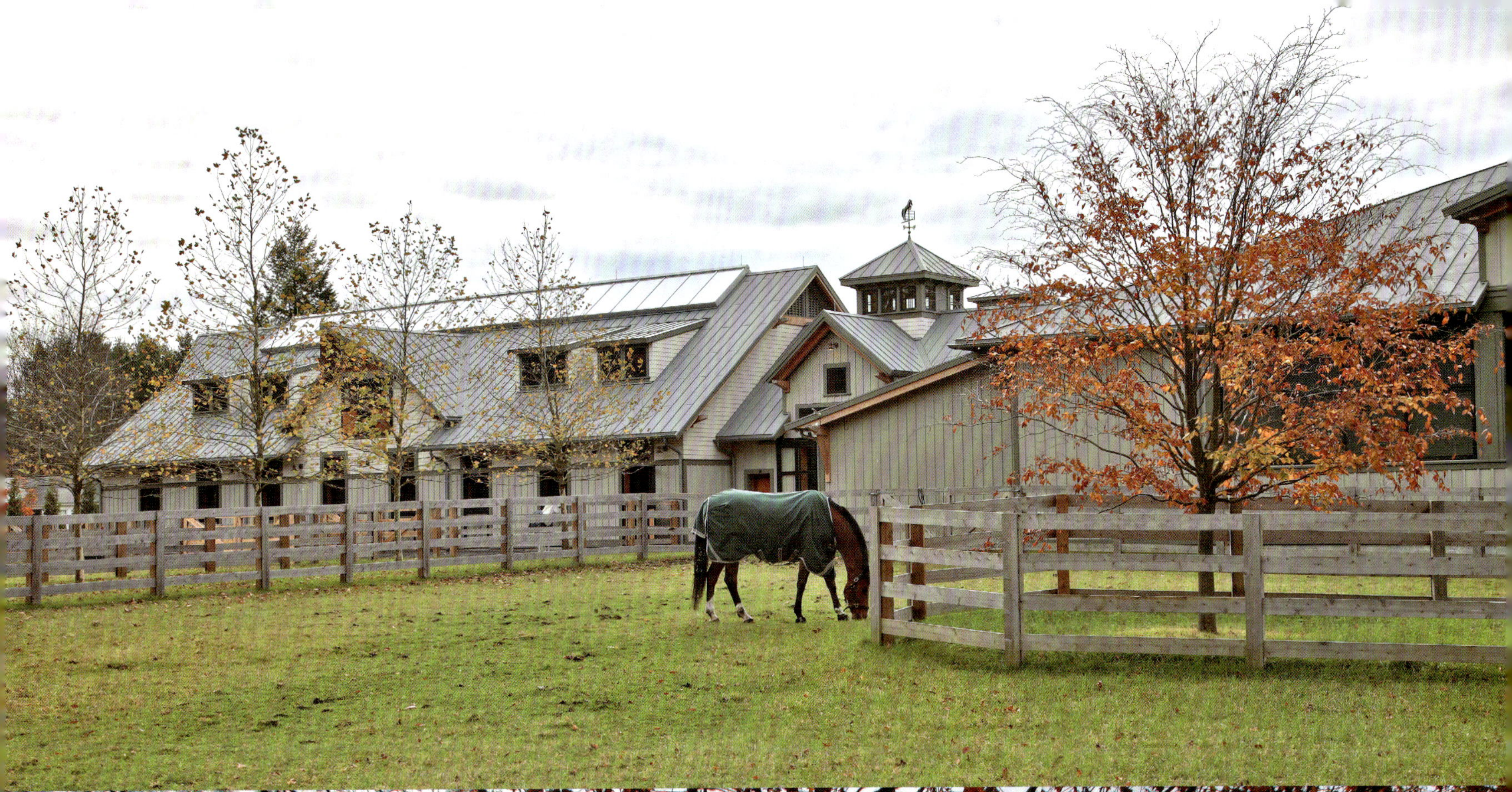
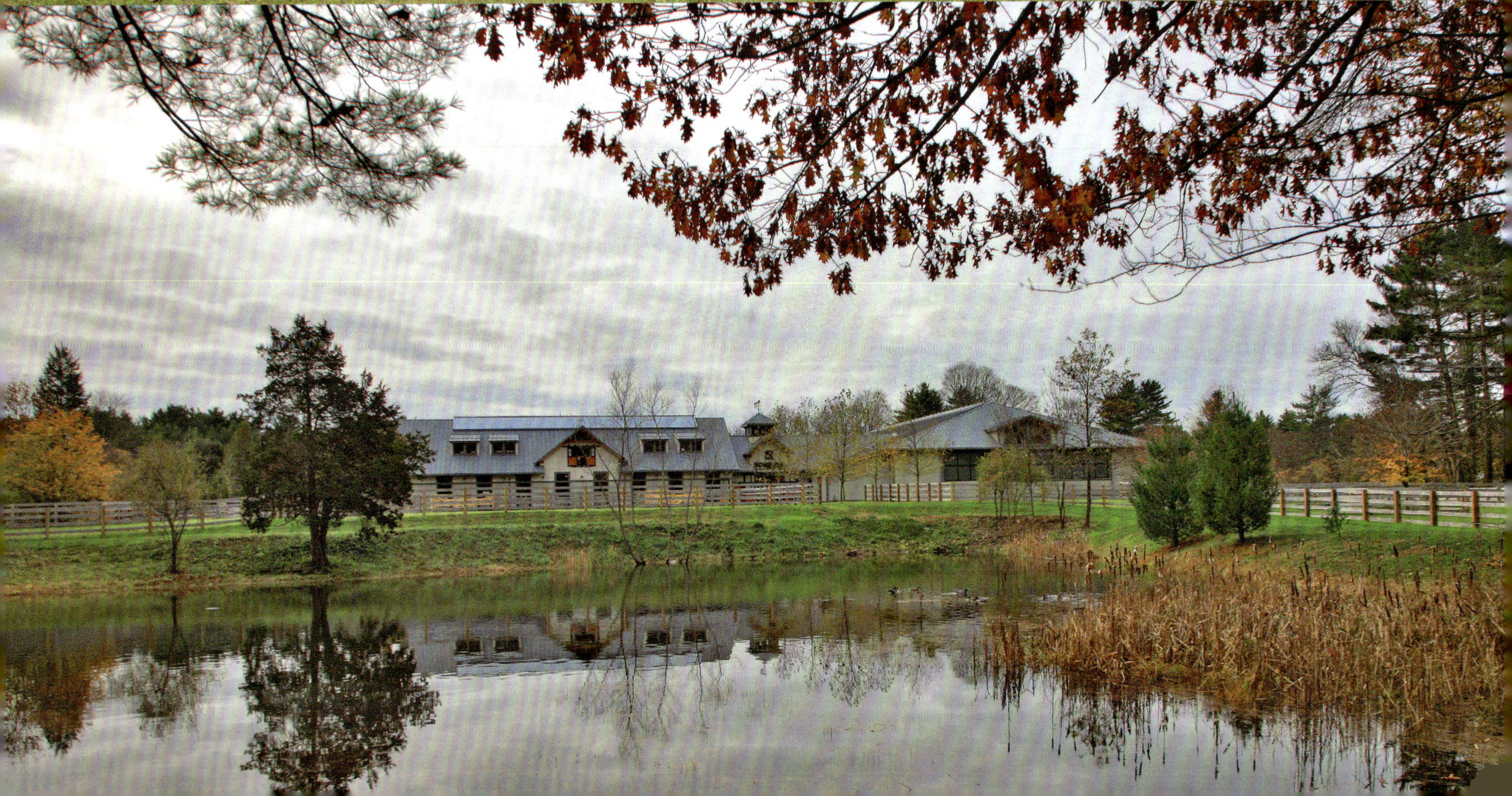

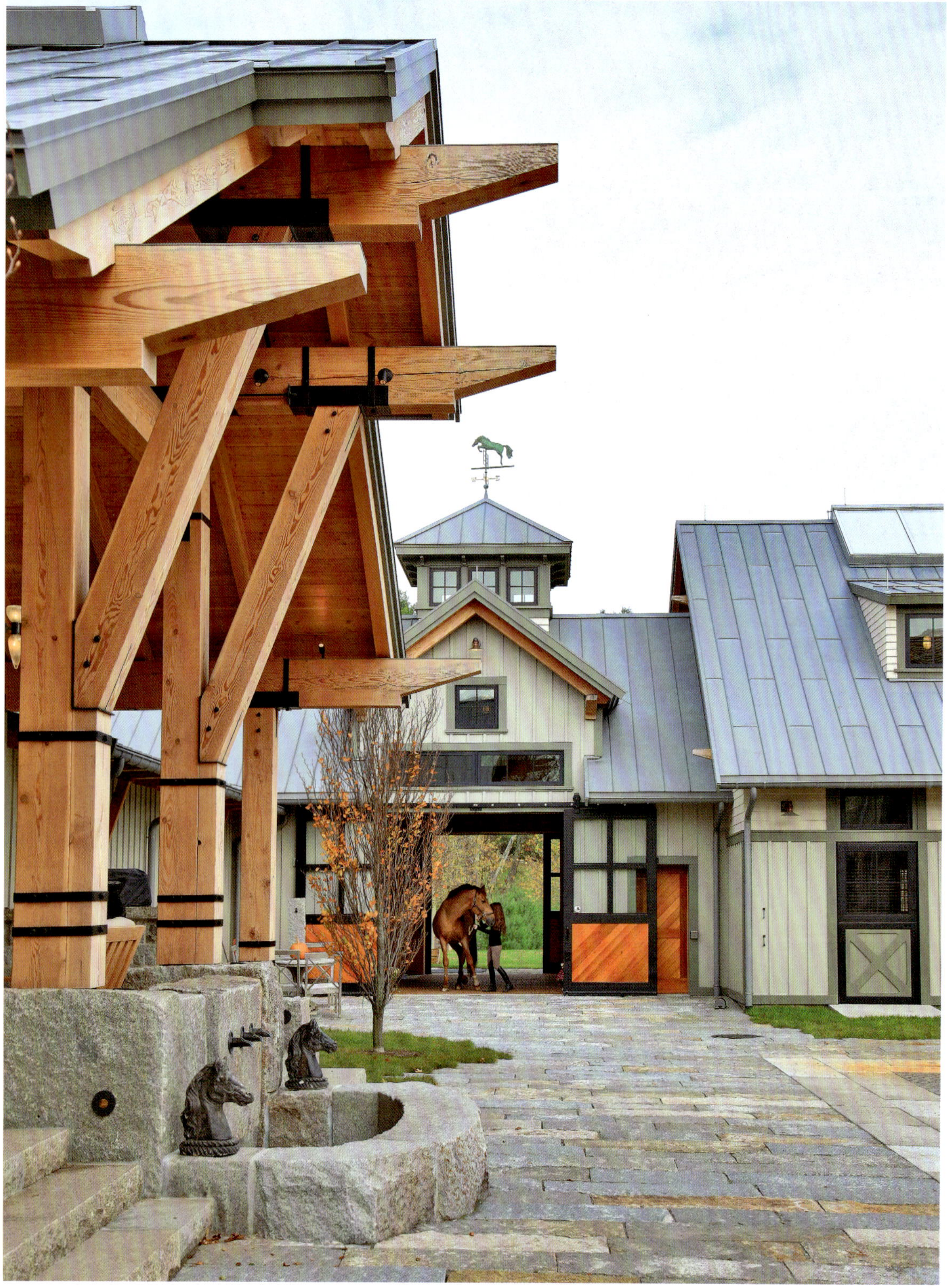

BEECHWOOD STABLES

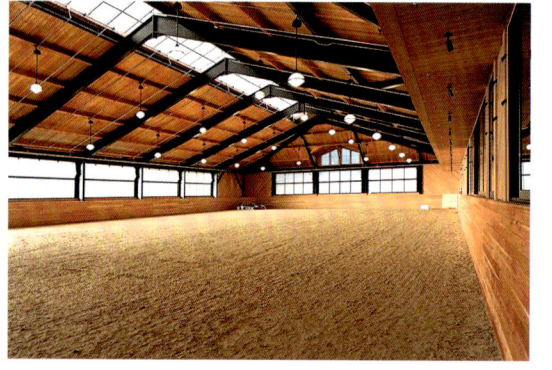

142 BLACKBURN ARCHITECTS & MARCUS GLEYSTEEN ARCHITECTS

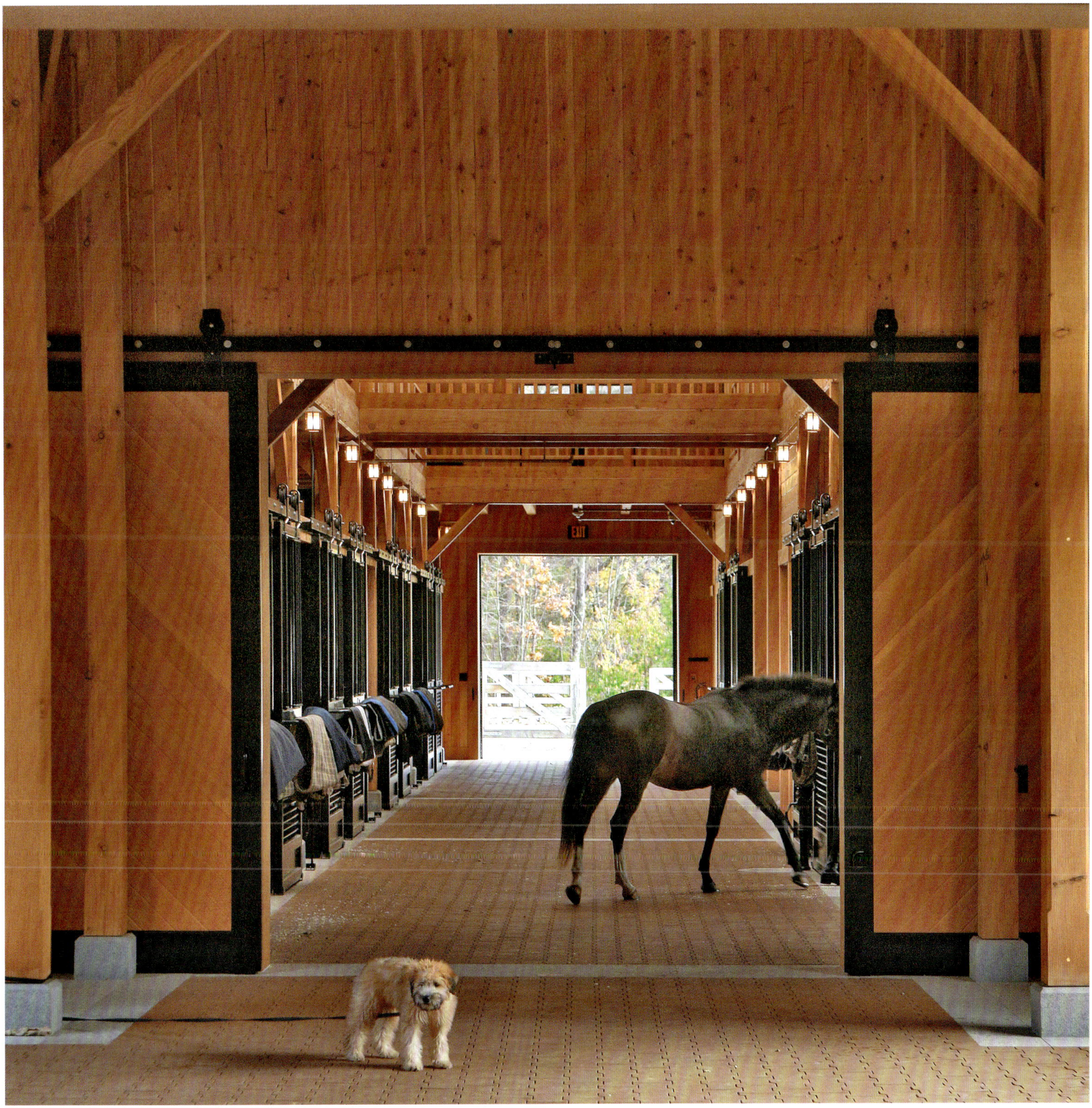

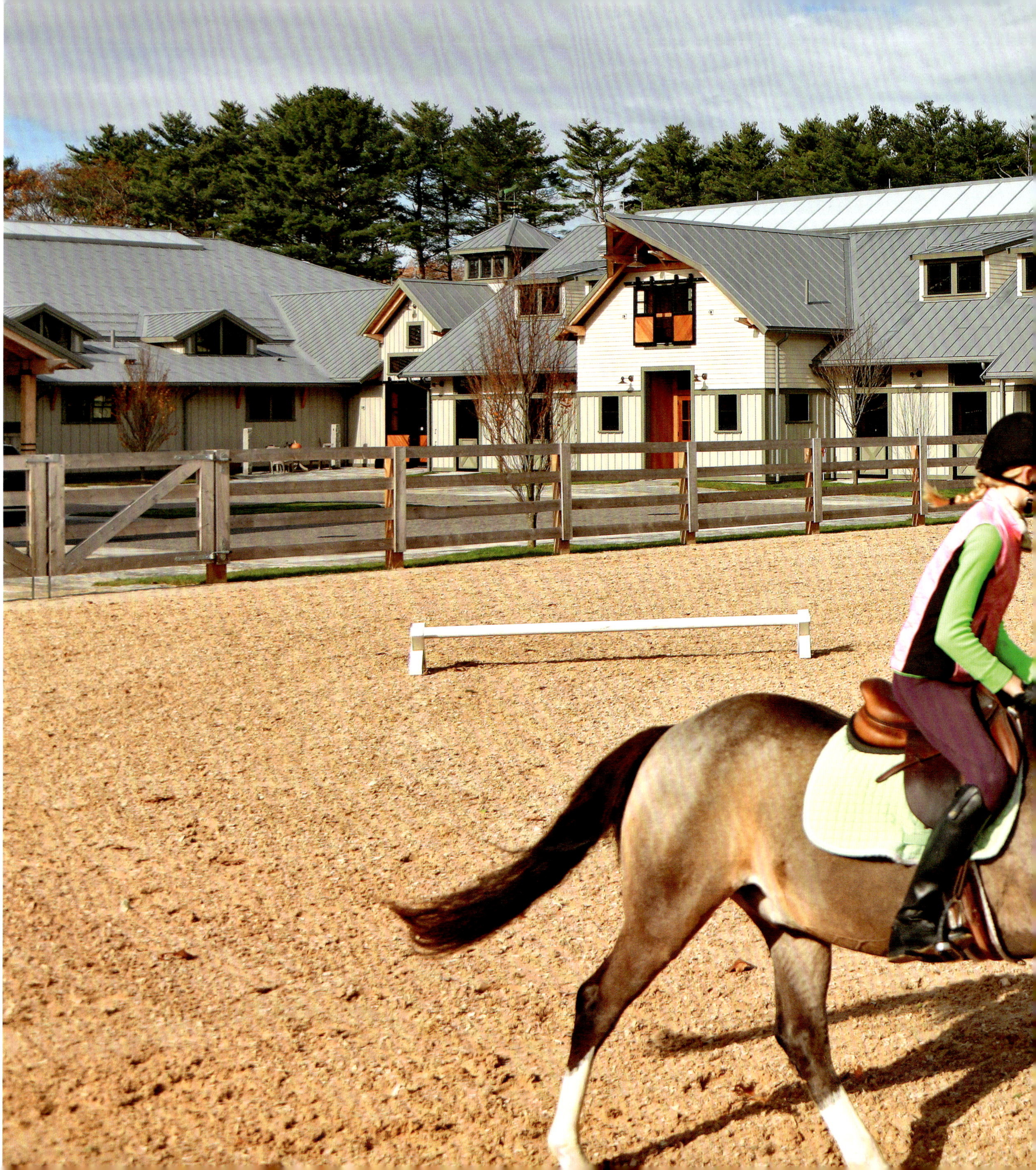

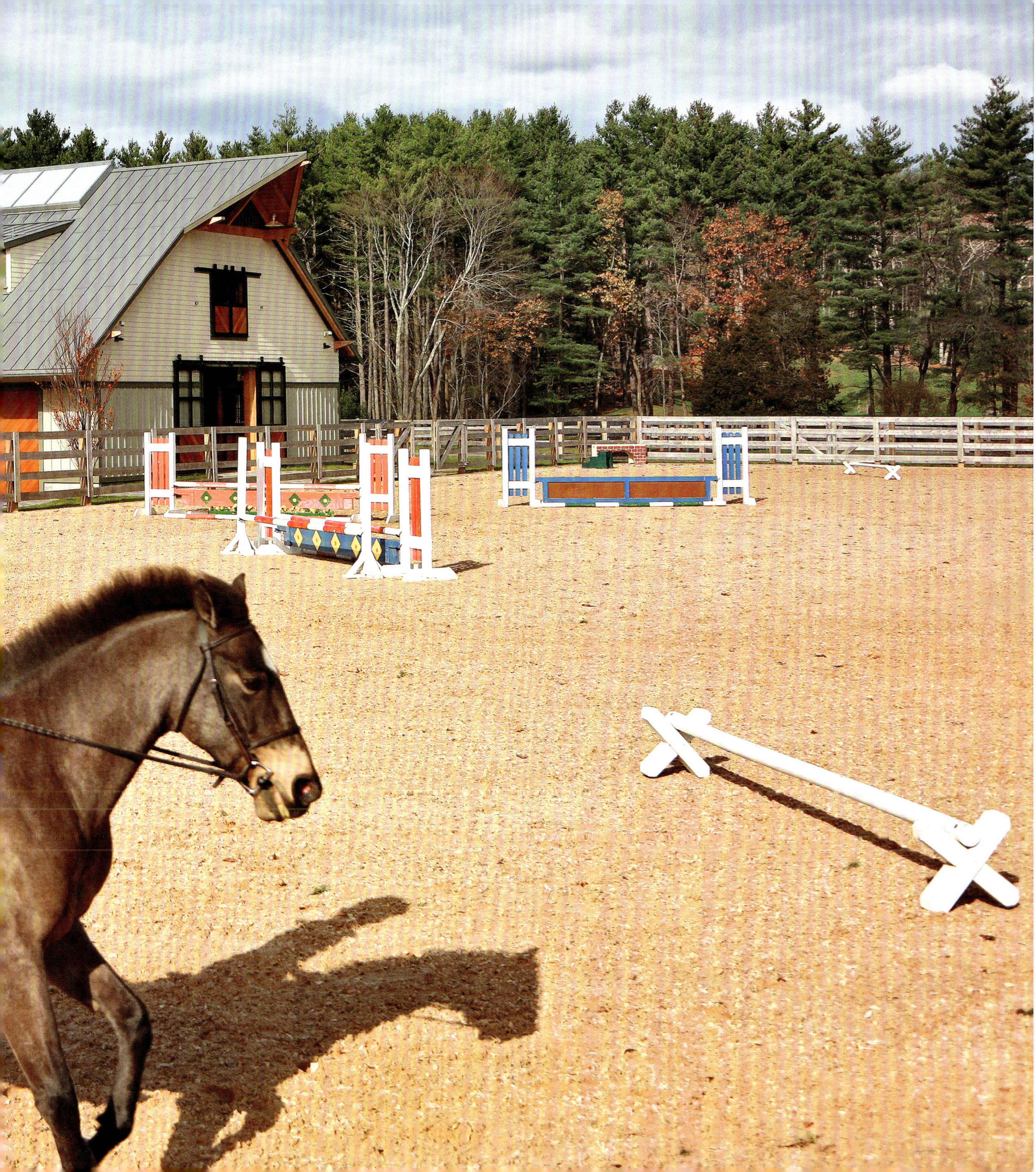

146 BLACKBURN ARCHITECTS & MARCUS GLEYSTEEN ARCHITECTS

BEECHWOOD STABLES 147

Klagshamn Equestrian Center
FOJAB architects

Klagshamn, Malmö, Sweden

Building Area:
4,600 m²

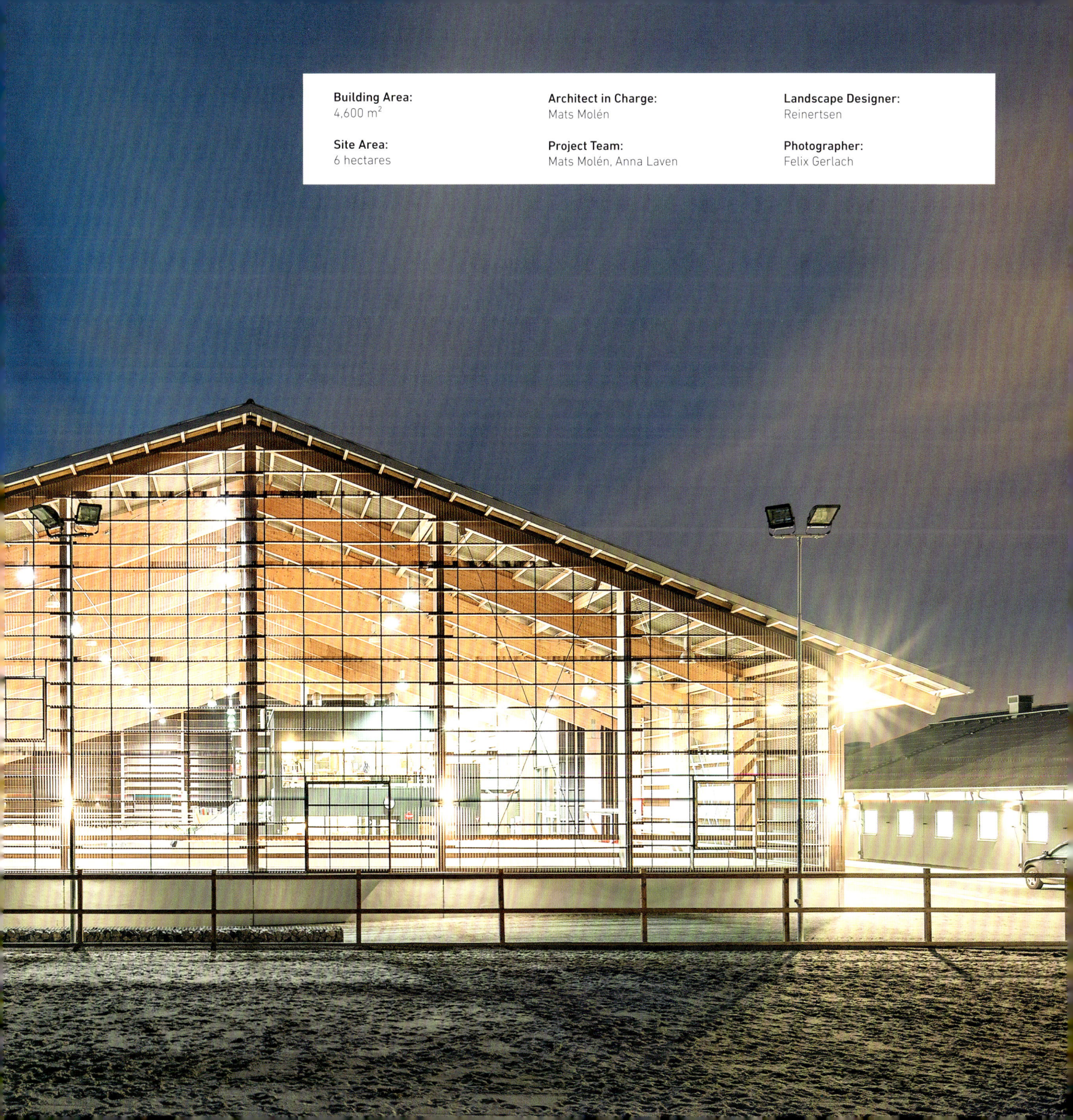

Site Area:
6 hectares

Architect in Charge:
Mats Molén

Project Team:
Mats Molén, Anna Laven

Landscape Designer:
Reinertsen

Photographer:
Felix Gerlach

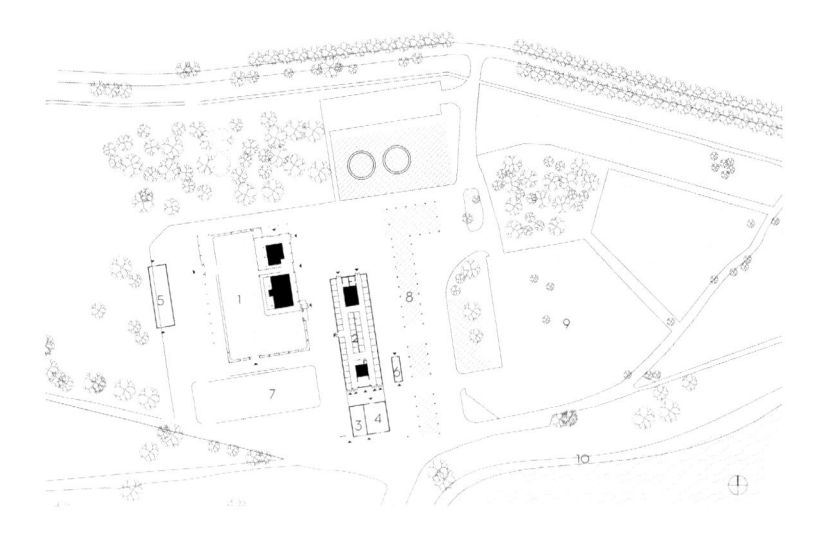

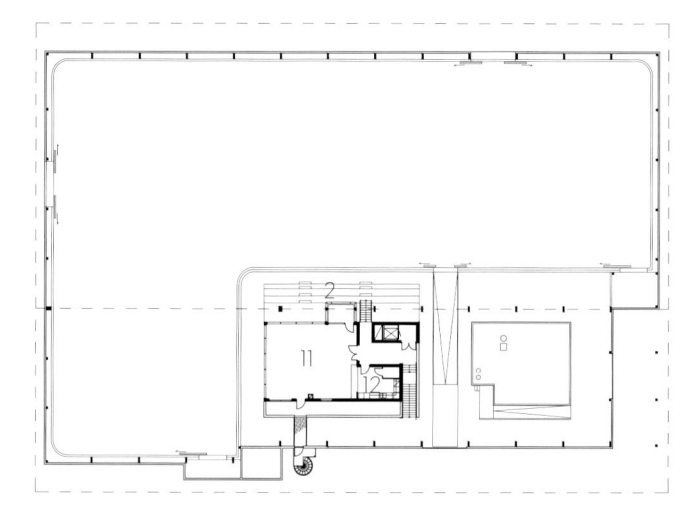

Site Plan

Plan

Klagshamn's Point is a peninsula that extends into the strait of Öresund, about 10 km south of Malmö, Sweden. The southern edge of the peninsula contains long sandy beaches that are excellent for horseback riding. Until recently, Klagshamn's Riding Club was located in a former concrete plant. When the city planned for a new equestrian center, it was natural to build in the same place as the concrete plant with its proximity to sandy beaches and ridges along the water. The city also chose to make the ruins of the demolished concrete plant into a park. The siting of the project runs parallel to the remains of the concrete factory, with the paddocks located east of the ruins. The two main buildings, stable, and riding center have distinctive, connected roof surfaces that bridge the different functions of the facility. The buildings have been positioned so that a variety of spaces are created in and around the ruins, the entrance courtyard, farm, and riding track. The buildings also provide nice views of the nearby Öresund strait. The character of the buildings is that of industrial open shells with clearly demarcated spaces (buildings within buildings), depending on temperature and functional requirements. Working with horses means that movements in and out of the buildings must feel natural, without a sharp border between indoors and outdoors. Wall and ceiling materials are simple and directly linked to function and structure. The concrete elements closest to the ground in the plinth and the wall are resistant to machines, horses, snow, rain, and wind. The wall and ceiling are lattice constructions in the form of columns and beams that clearly reflect the building's supporting structure. Perforated sheet metal in the facade provides several concurrent effects—natural ventilation, daylight, views in and out, and sound absorption. In addition, the perforated sheet metal is cost-effective, as it ensures that the moisture balance is guaranteed by natural air exchange. Robust building materials such as concrete, glue-laminated wood, and brick are resistant to the challenging environment in which the facility is located and will age in a natural and beautiful way. Bricks from former buildings on the site were recycled in parts of the stable and the riding center. Besides the gravel surfaces, the ground and floor coverings are also made of wooden bricks, concrete, and paving stones, both inside and out, which further enhance the blurred meeting of interior and exterior.

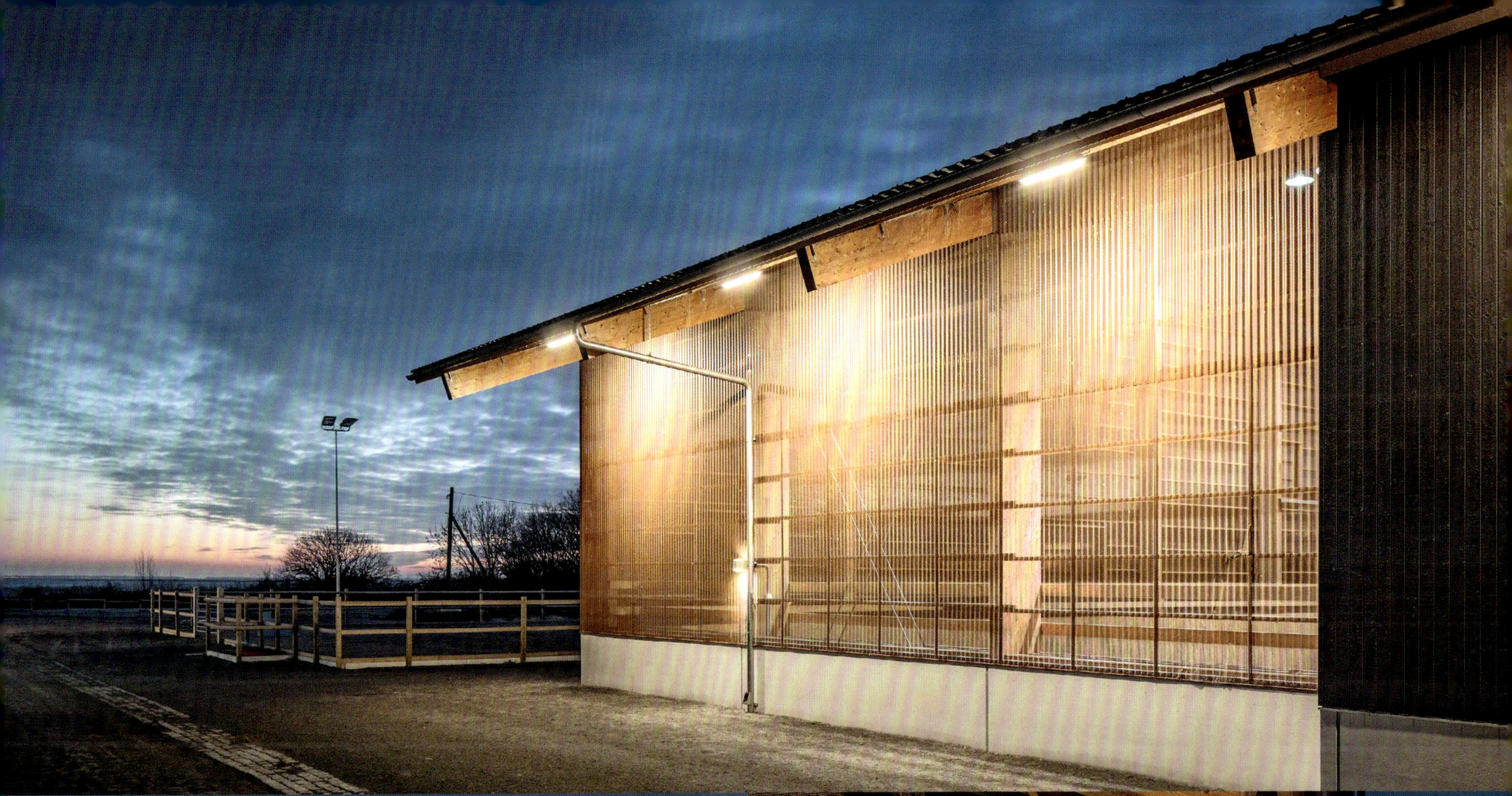
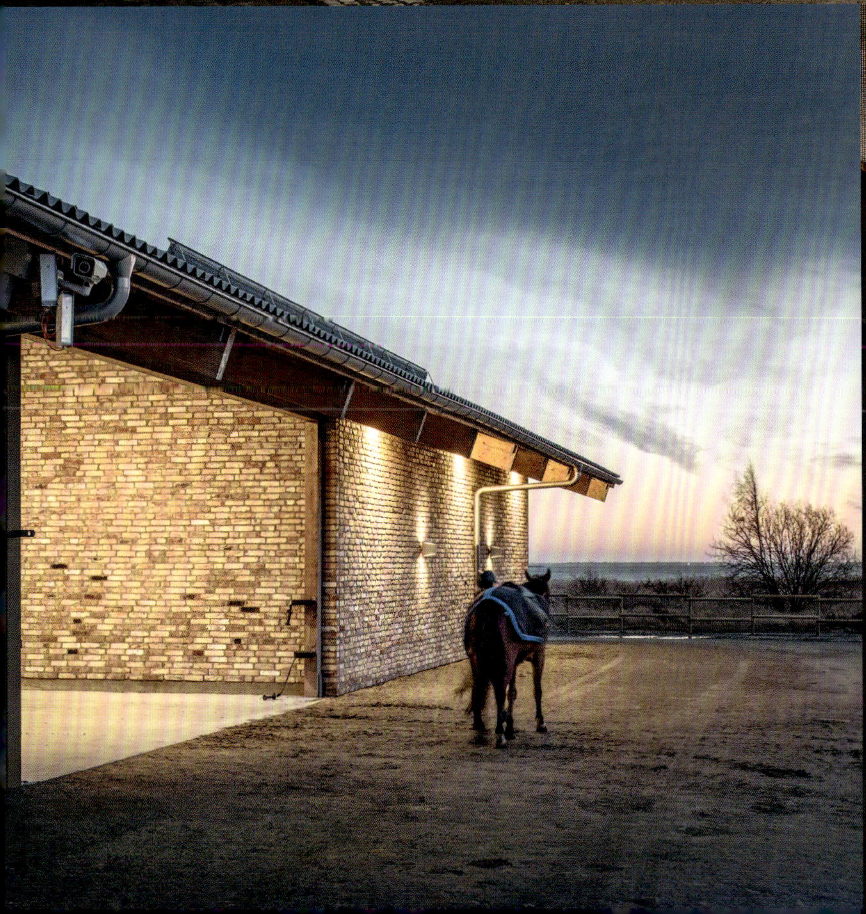
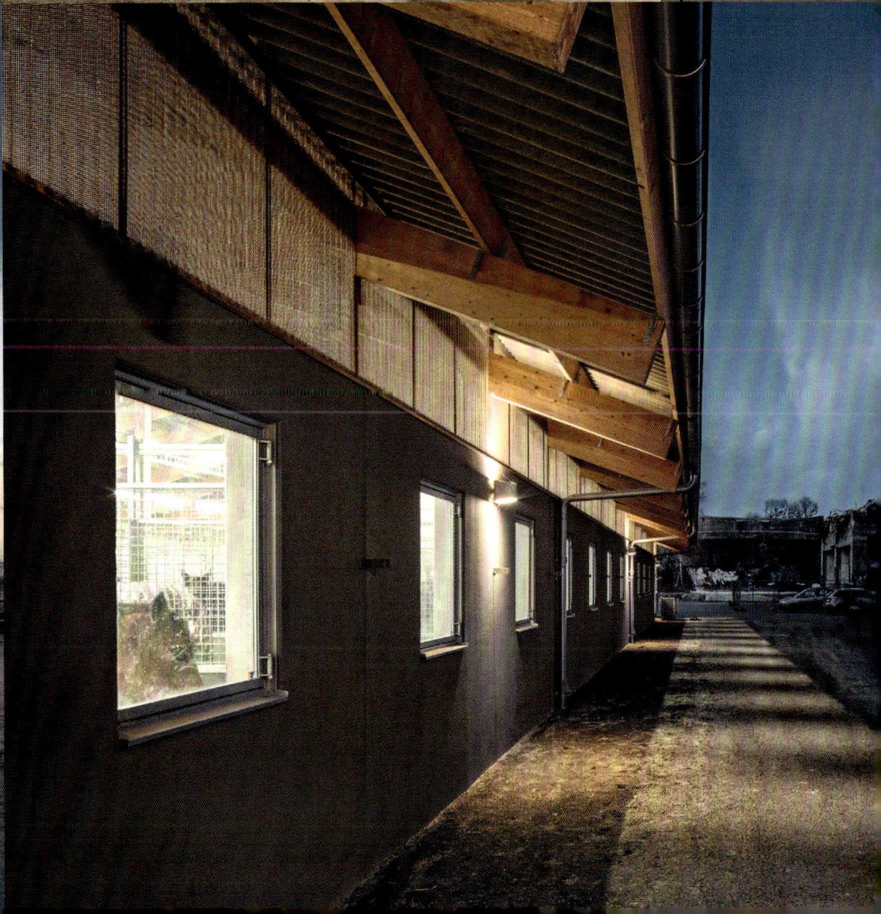

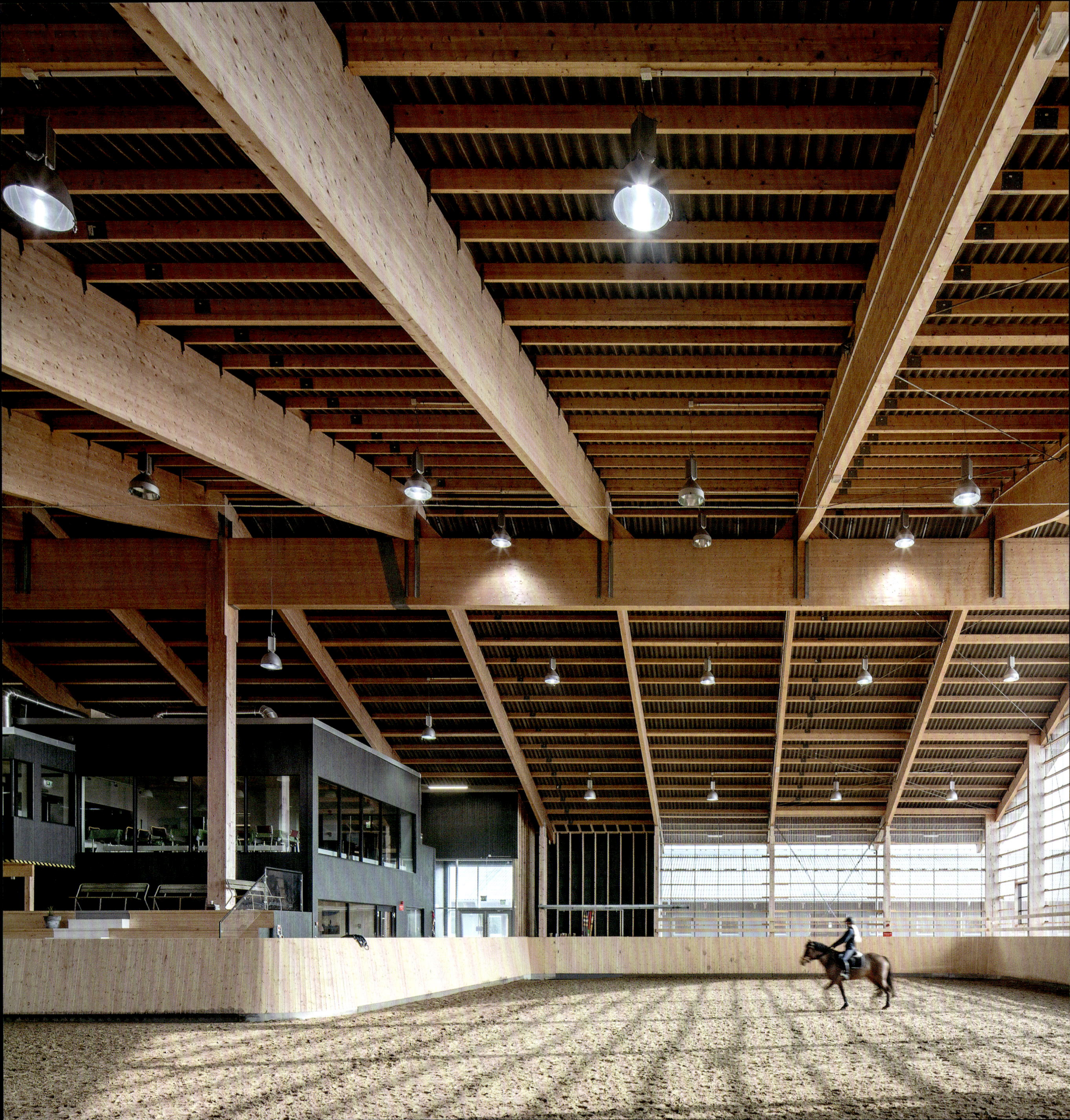

KLAGSHAMN EQUESTRIAN CENTER **153**

MSporthorses
Matias Zegers Arquitectos

Fundo el Durazno, Lo Barnechea, Santiago, Chile

Building Area:
576 m²

Site Area:
30,000 m²

Architect in Charge:
Matias Zegers

Project Team:
Andrés Gayangos (Project manager)
Diego Terán, Marianne Weber,
Nina Vidic Invancic, Pedro Coello

Landscape Designer:
Jacinta Errázuriz

Photographer:
© Cristóbal Palma

Plan

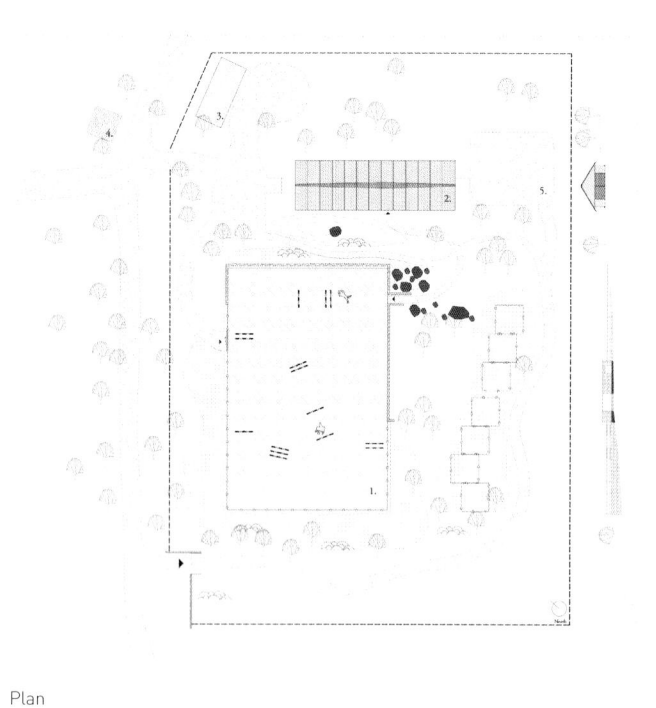

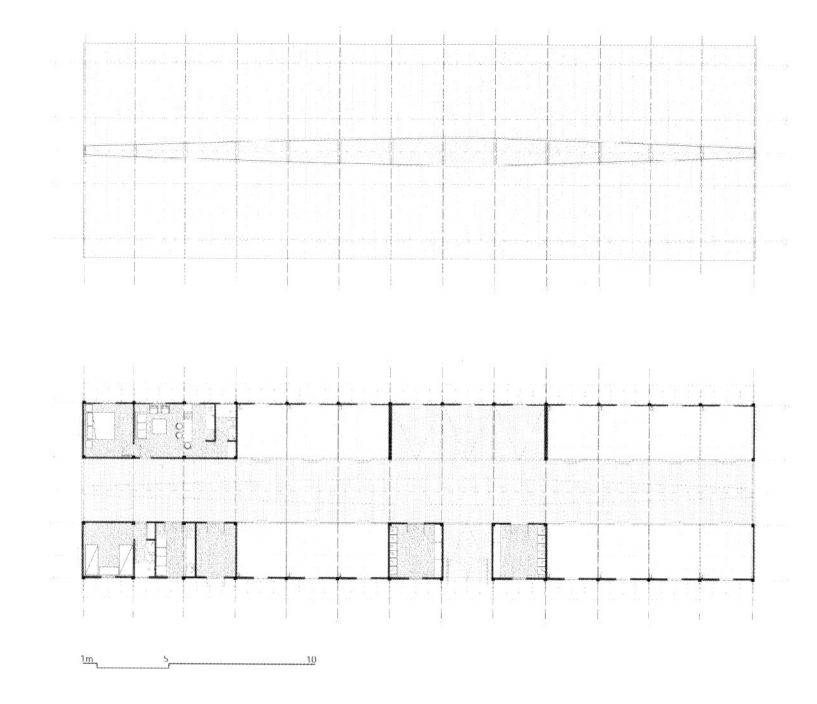

The MSporthorses barn is part of a group of vernacular structures scattered on five acres on the outskirts of Santiago, Chile, in the foothills of the Andes. It stands amidst the presence of an old group of "Quillayes," a native tree in central Chile. The site has the outdoor training arena at its center, perfectly level and surrounded by an exercise ring, an equipment barn, and a terrace where one can relax after a long day of riding. The terrain is contained by retaining walls that are four to five feet tall and made of local stone. The main barn is a long structure with a central aisle and stalls on either side, and service functions on either end. A great skylight runs along the ridge of the structure allowing for neutral light to enter year-round. The bulk of light is concentrated in the center, a spacious area in which grooms perform their duties. The skylight tapers towards both ends reducing light for the horses to rest in their stalls. A curved ceiling prevents backlighting effect, while a double layer of whitened glass generates an undifferentiated blur or light halo with no contrast, as if the suspended air had been lit. When seen from a distance, both the shape and texture of the barn make it disappear not only to the eye but also from memory. The interior remains secret, and when the gates are open, the visitor is surprised, as there is no transitional space between the exterior and interior. The roof geometry is unnoticeably complex. A subtle variation in the ridge width generates an asymmetrical curve on the roof surface, changing the pitch angle along its length. The outer layer of metallic tiles appears as a kind of textile negotiating the geometry of the structure with little trouble. Daylight reflects off this skin displaying different hues on the "satin bronze" color of the tiles. This project was built out of laminated timber, with the structure and enclosure prefabricated and computationally mechanized in a factory in Los Angeles, Chile. The assembly took 45 days, and yet despite the industrially produced nature of the design, the barn could easily be mistaken for a historic vernacular structure.

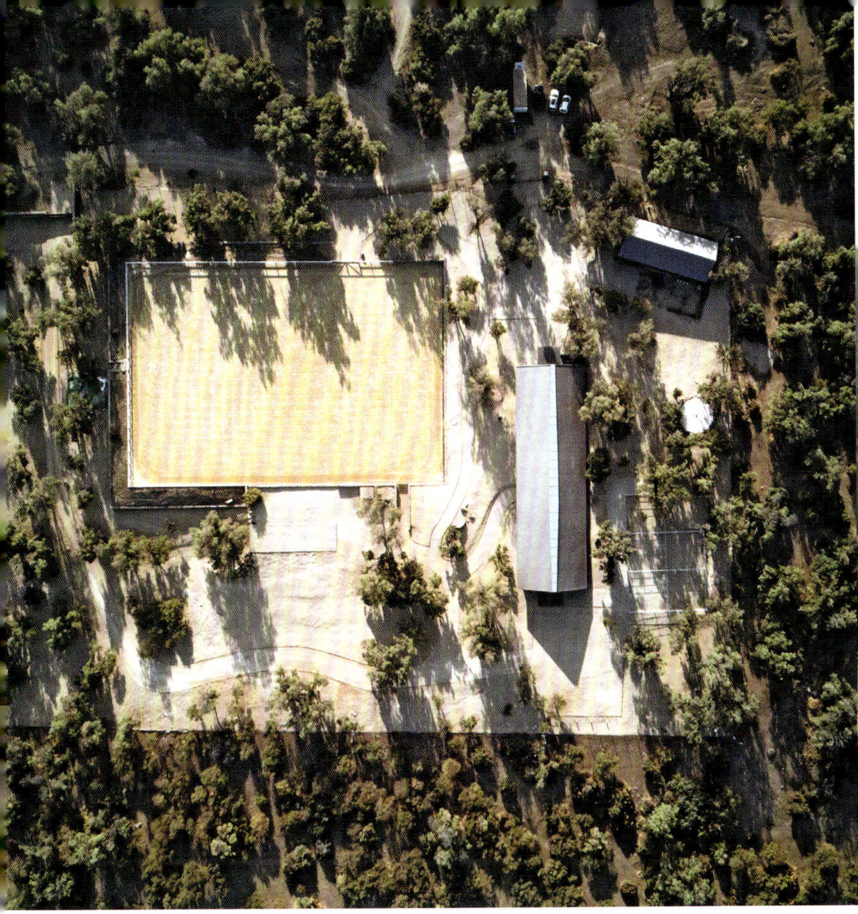
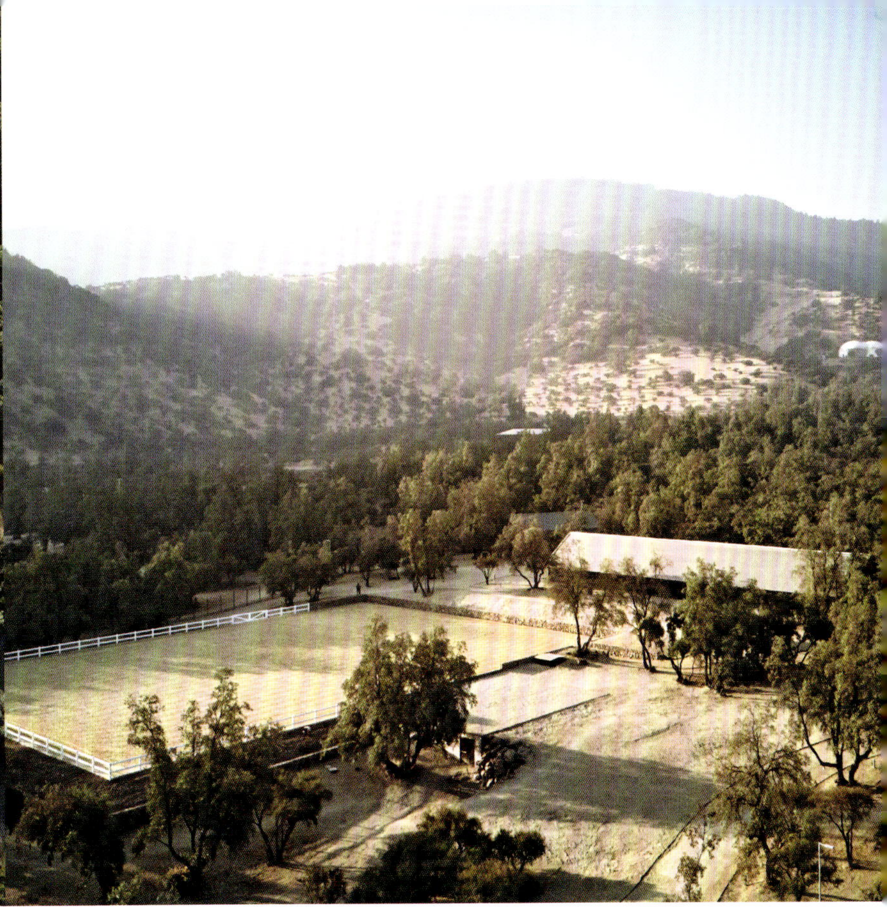
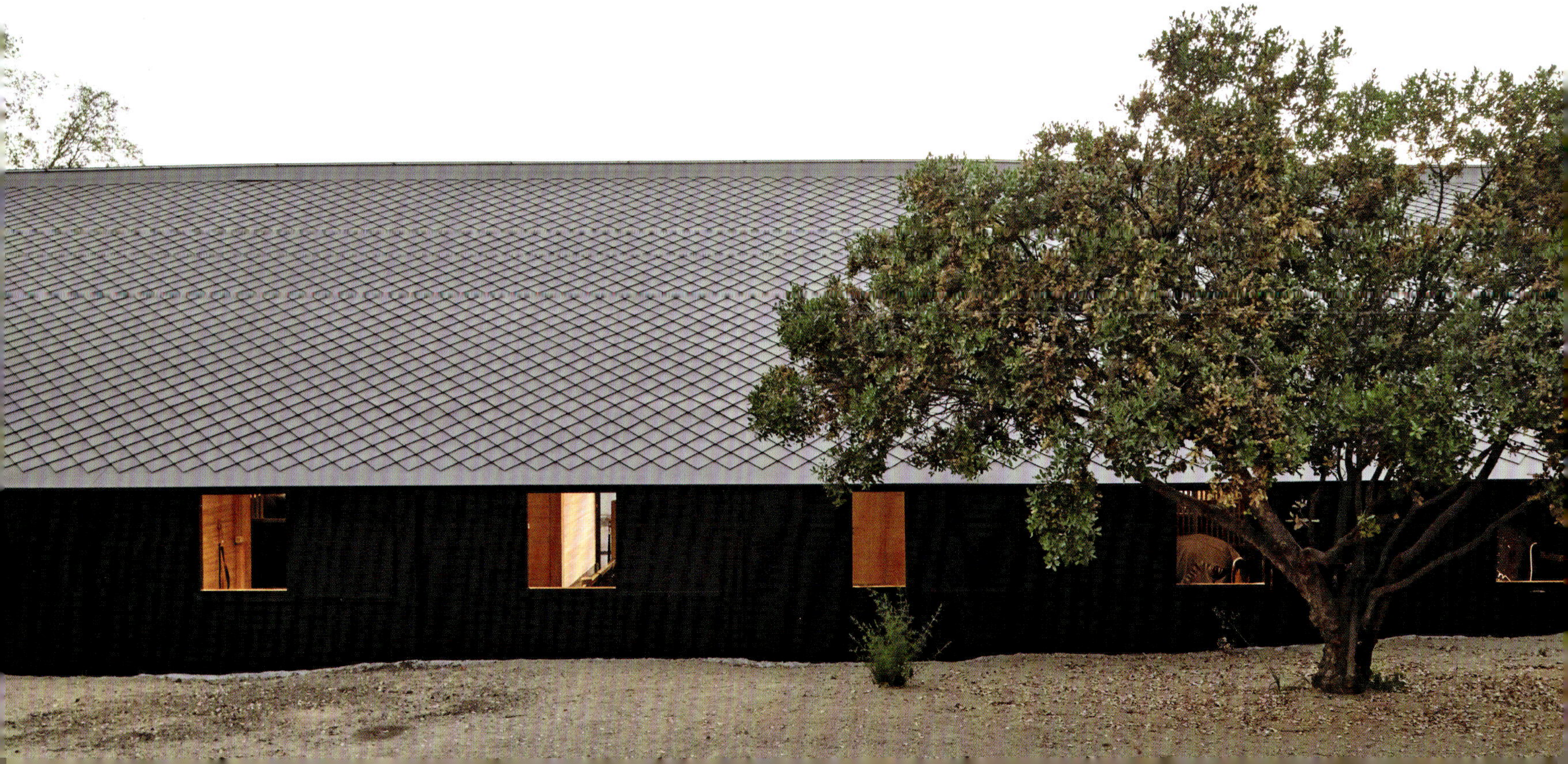

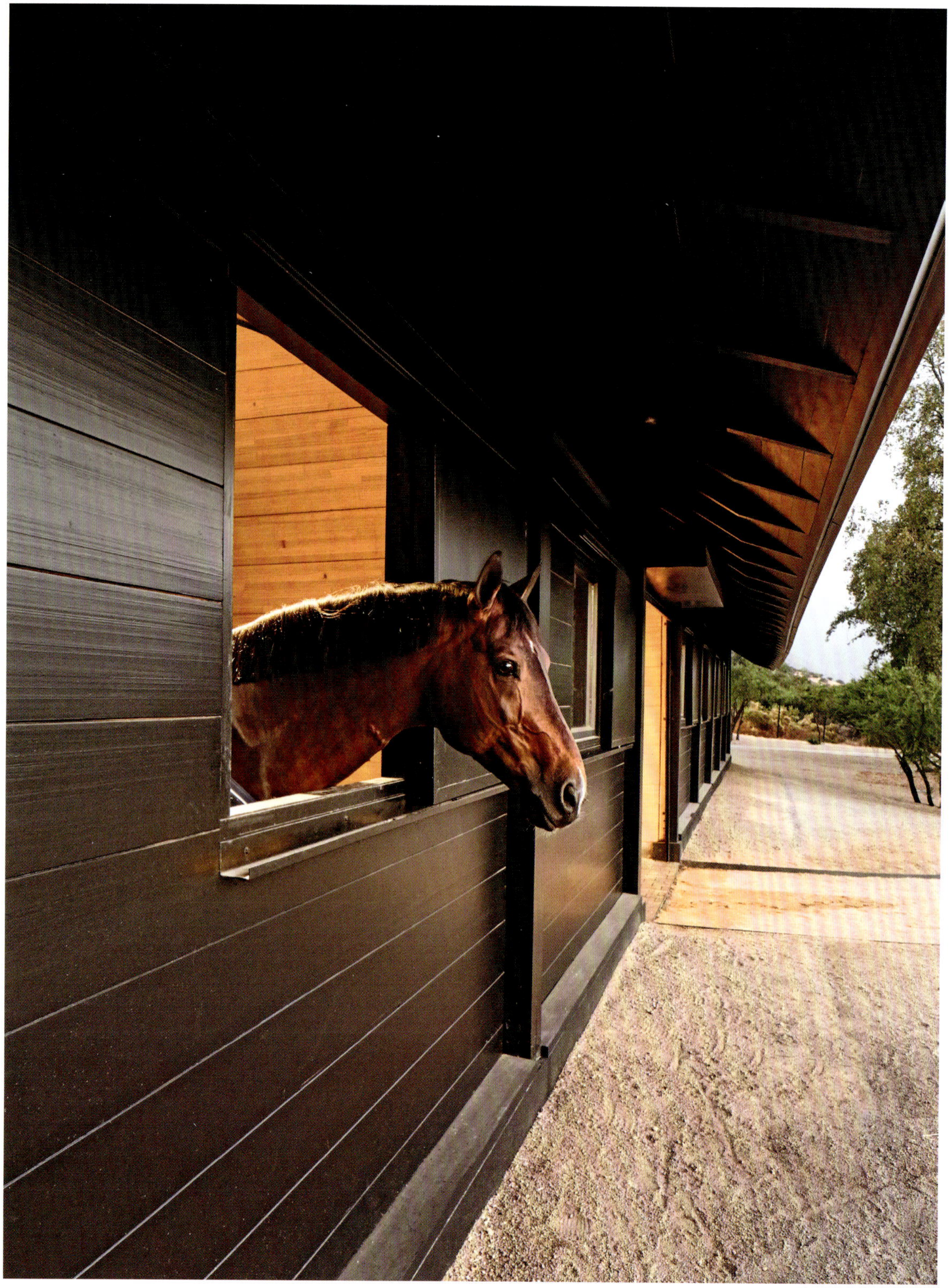

MSPORTHORSES 159

MATIAS ZEGERS ARQUITECTOS

MSPORTHORSES

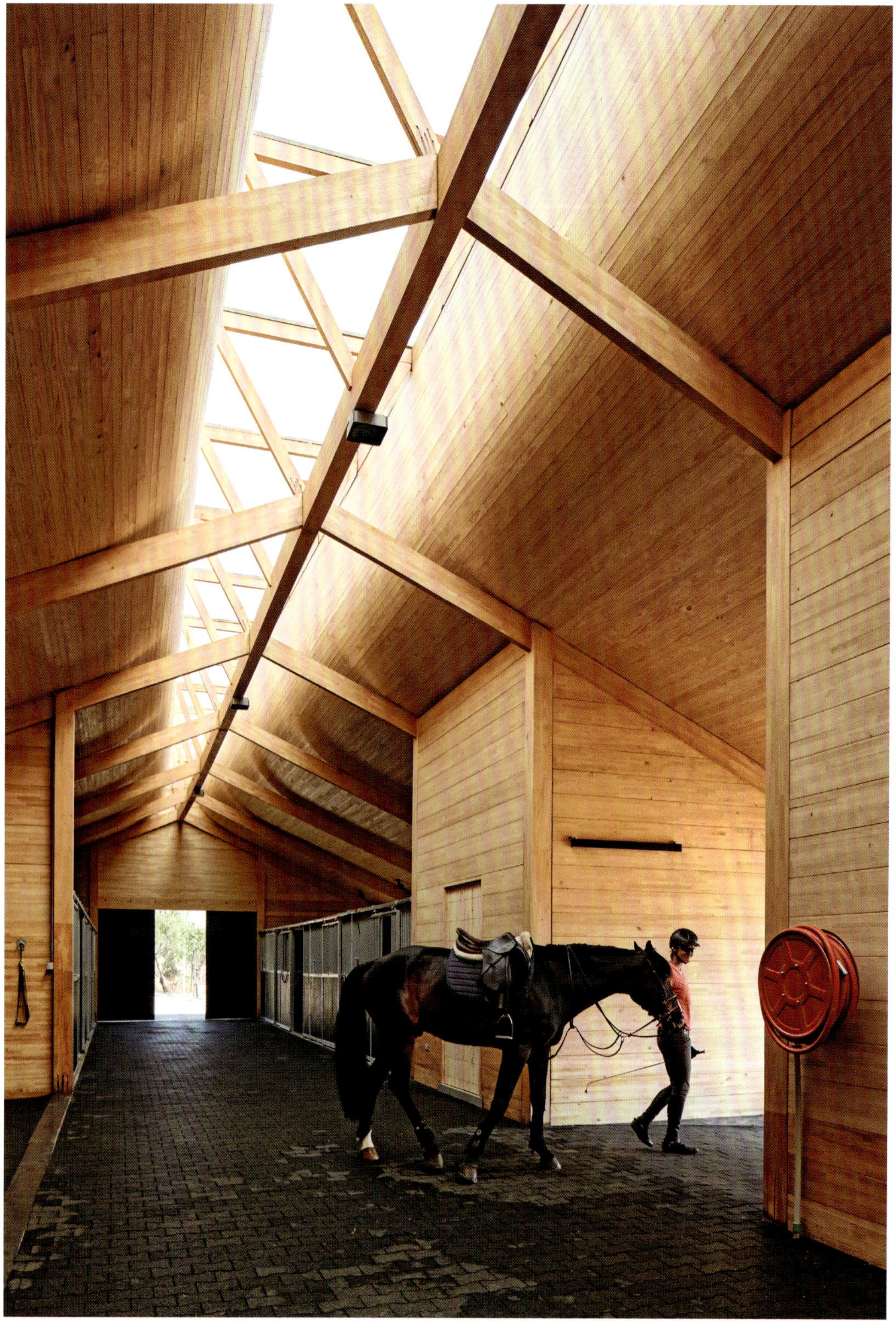

MSPORTHORSES **163**

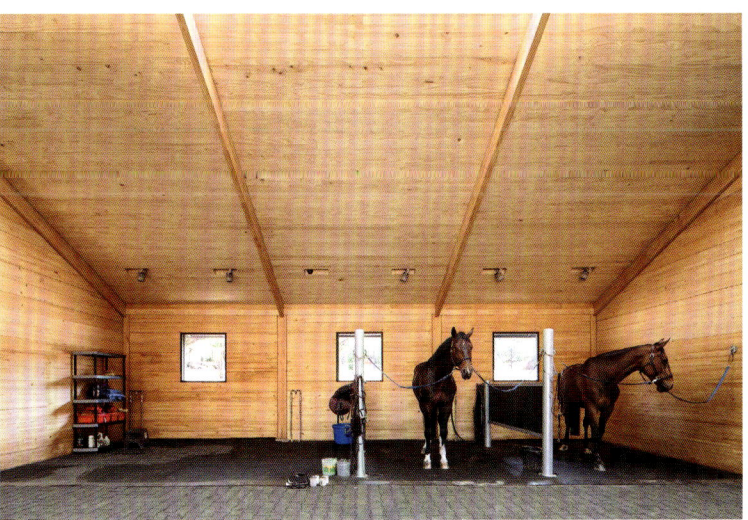

Cannery Barn

Archer & Buchanan Architecture

Coatesville, Pennsylvania, United States

Building Area: 161 m²	**Architect in Charge:** Richard Buchanan	**Landscape Designer:** Elliott Templeton
Site Area: 25 acres	**Project Team:** Lily Summers	**Photographer:** Jim Graham Photography

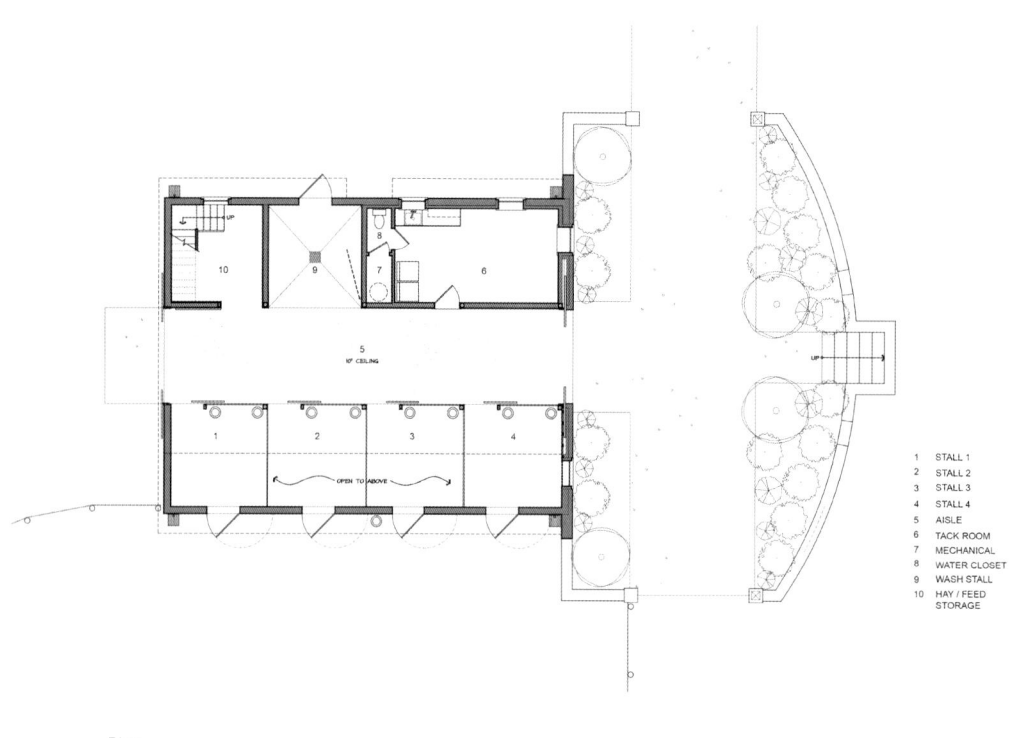

Plan

1. STALL 1
2. STALL 2
3. STALL 3
4. STALL 4
5. AISLE
6. TACK ROOM
7. MECHANICAL
8. WATER CLOSET
9. WASH STALL
10. HAY / FEED STORAGE

This modest four-horse stall barn on Cannery Road in Chester County, Pennsylvania, not far from Philadelphia, brings together diverse needs and functions within one simple building. The 25-acre property was initially developed as a rural retreat with only a home carved out of the wilderness of the rare "Serpentine Barrens" landscape. However, the decision to add horses to the domestic life of the family required several other considerations. Being a professor of equine reproduction at the University of Pennsylvania, the client was keenly interested in the creation of an environment that was safe, healthy, and eminently practical for both her horses and her daughters. Conversely, her husband was focused on the landscape of their home and required that the inclusion of horses on the property would deliver a net gain to the gardens and landscape design. The new barn was situated near the home with a strong axial relationship between the primary living spaces of the house and the stables. This connection gave a sense of hierarchy to the formerly untamed landscape surrounding the house while leaving as much of the property open for pasture, woodlands, and nature. The barn is in the form of a traditional shed structure made of heavy timber construction and clad in indigenous fieldstone. As such, it serves as a backdrop for a walled forecourt that is cut into the slope of the lawn below the house providing access to the residence. The traditional form of the barn and hard-wearing materials is both an understated companion to the house and timeless in style. Through massive pocket sliding doors, a broad aisle running from front to back organizes four stalls that open directly onto a turn out yard. The feed room, wash stall and club-like tack room line the other side, providing designated functional spaces for the efficient management of the barn. At the loft level above, hay and bedding are stored and easily sent down into the stalls with minimal handling. This modest project demonstrates how a relatively small traditional building can have a major impact on a rural site.

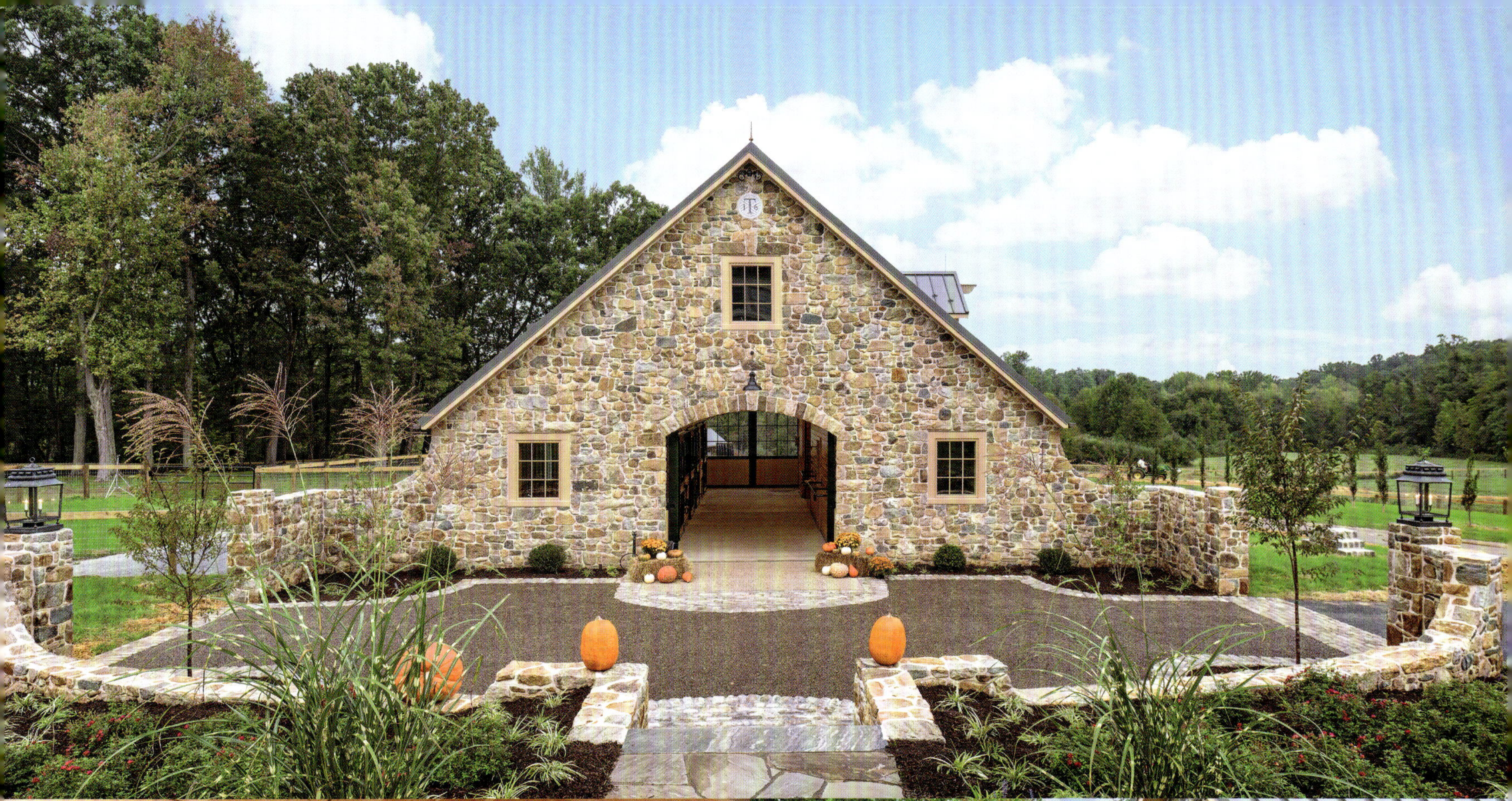
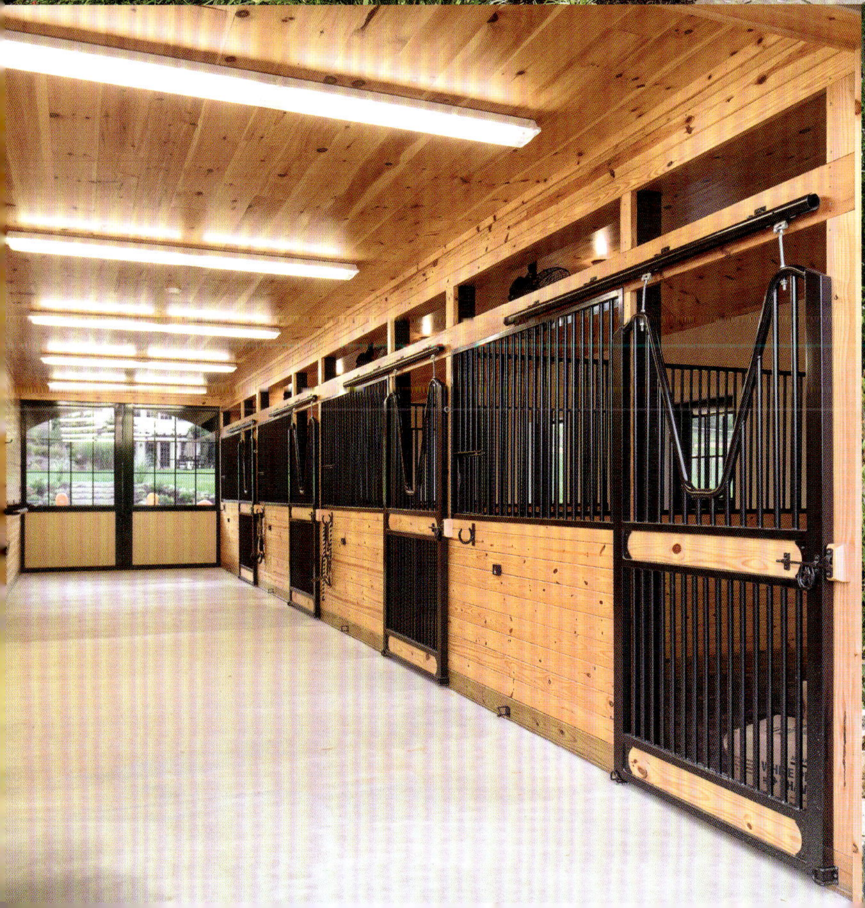
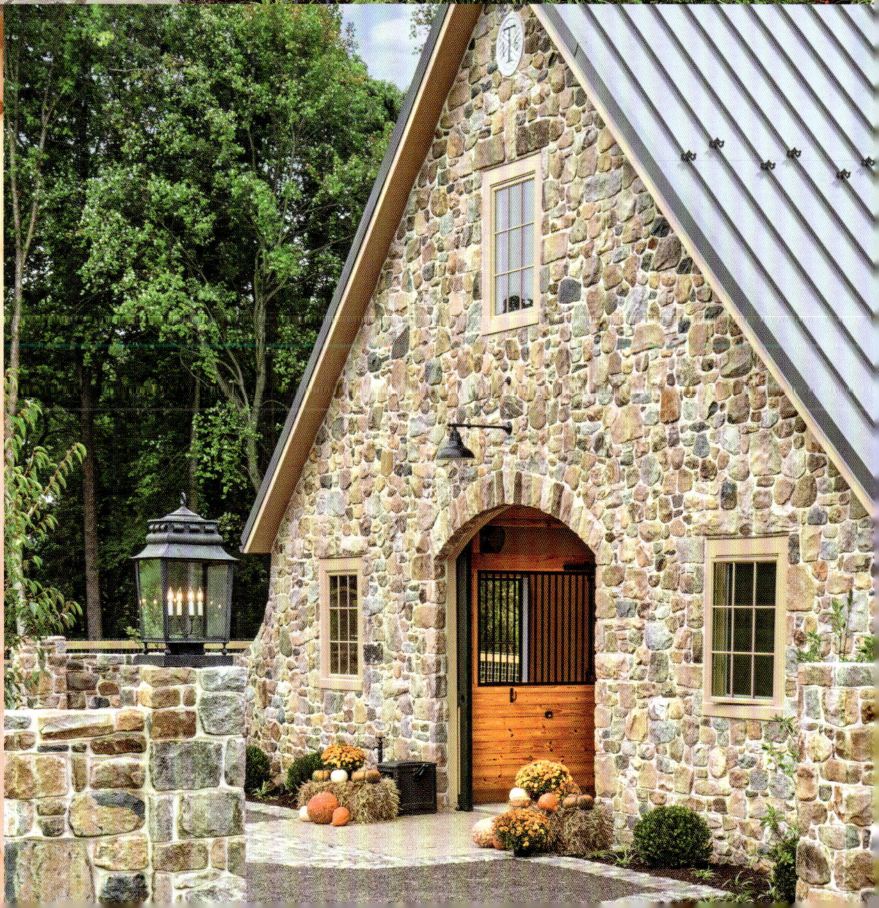

Pegaso Farm
Blackburn Architects

Mettawa, Illinois, United States

Building Area:
557 m^2

Site Area:
24 acres

Architect in Charge:
Blackburn Architects

Project Team:
Civil Engineer: SpaceCo Inc, Structural Engineer: Pease Borst & Associates, Septic Engineer: Ayres Associates

Photographer:
Cesar Lujan

Plan

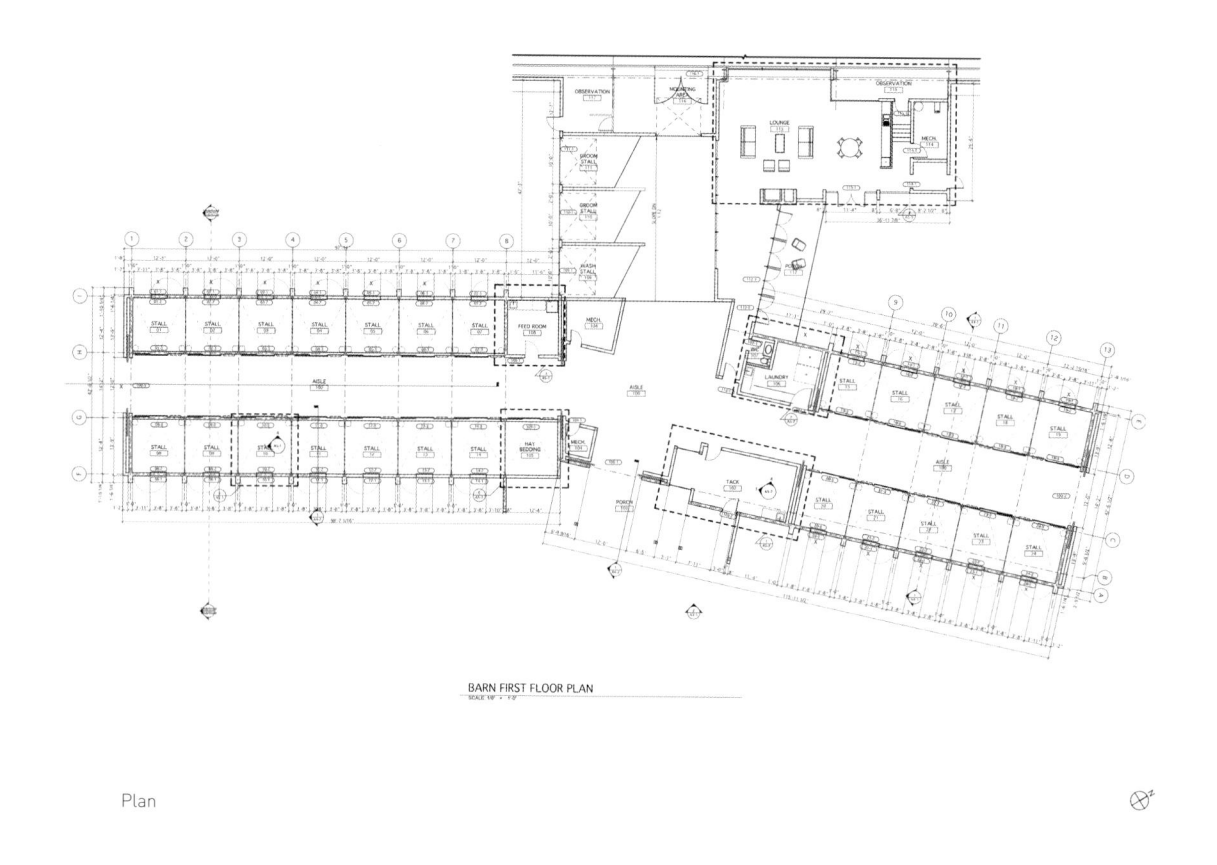

Pegaso Farm is a private equestrian farm located on a 24-acre site in the village of Mettawa, Illinois, just north of Chicago, on a flat property surrounded by various existing wetlands and tree species. The site was developed into a modern equestrian center that includes a 24-stall barn with lounge, a large indoor dressage arena, and other service buildings that are influenced by the design concepts and details of Chicago modernist and Prairie School architecture, a favorite building tradition of the owner. In plan the complex consists of two stall buildings out front connected by a central entrance hall. The two buildings are skewed around the central hall to respond to the various outdoor fenced in riding fields that extend in a radial pattern from the main entrance. The two stable wings consist of a central aisle with ten stalls in one, and fourteen in the other, with various service functions on either side of the entry hall. Behind the entry, a corridor with further service facilities leads to a large indoor riding arena, and a generous social lounge with direct views to the arena extends from the corridor. Thoroughly modern in its use of heavy-wood, steel, and concrete framing, block walls, glass and metal panels, the project is unapologetically industrial in appearance yet extremely sensitive with respect to animal safety and user experience, especially in the stall buildings. Moreover, with mono-sloped roofs, long overhanging eaves, continuous horizontal clerestory windows, and dark stained wood cladding throughout the exterior surfaces and stalls, the horse complex could also easily be mistaken for a house—or a school—both of which coincidentally it is. More than anything, though, the Pegaso Farm demonstrates how robust the Chicago Prairie School architecture really is, in that it can adapt to an architectural program that initially was never envisioned by its pioneer founders.

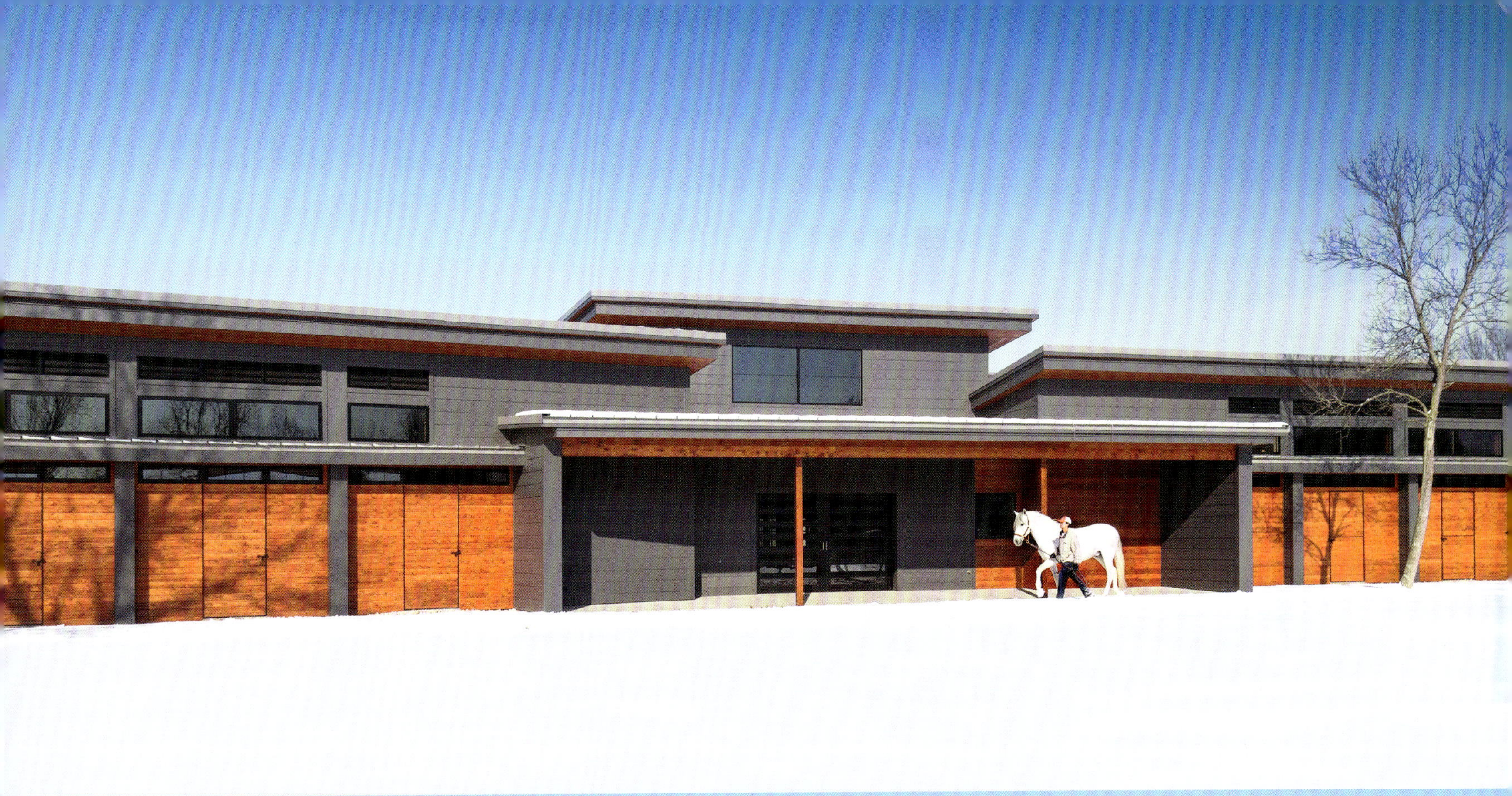

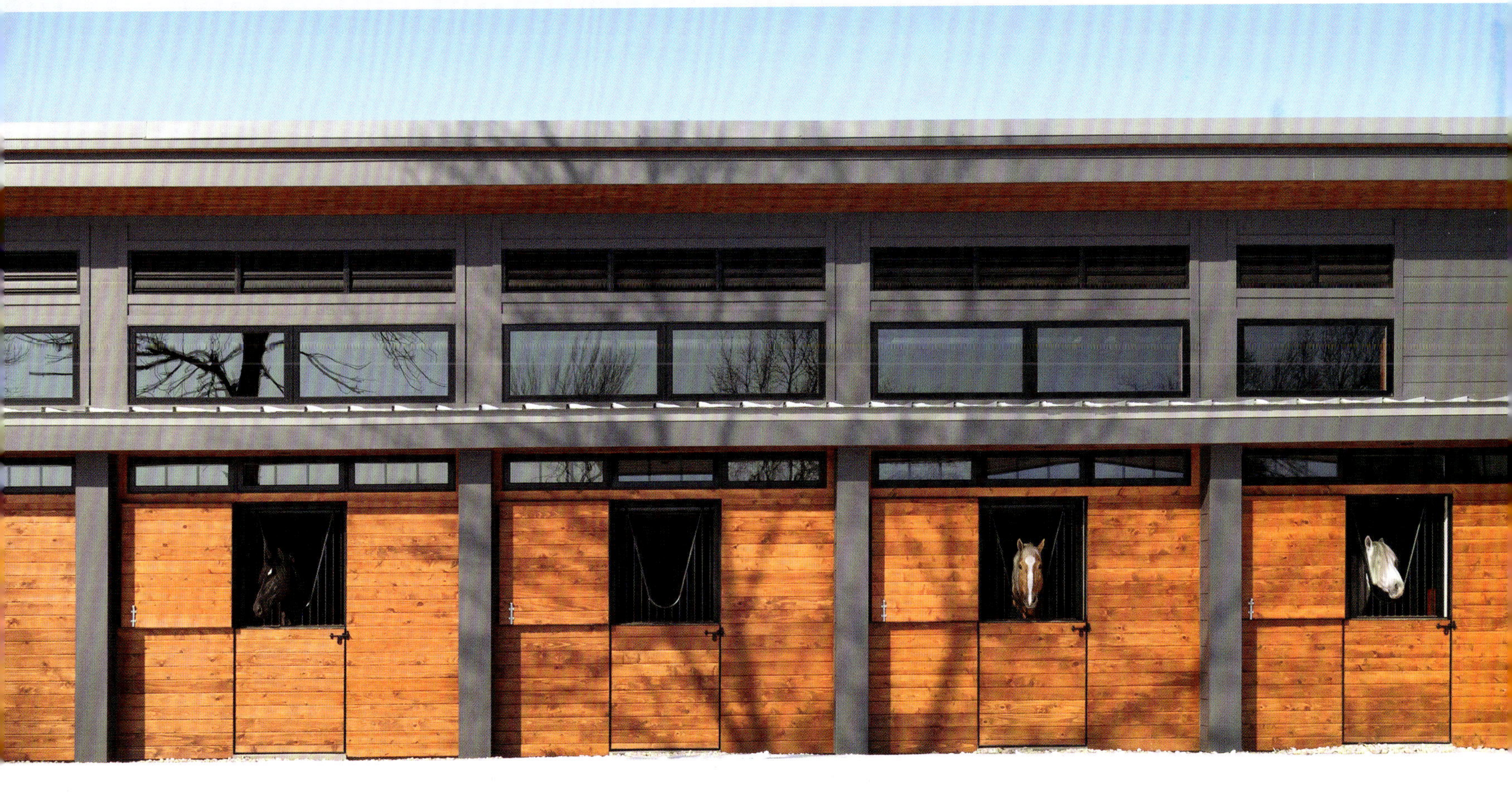

172 BLACKBURN ARCHITECTS

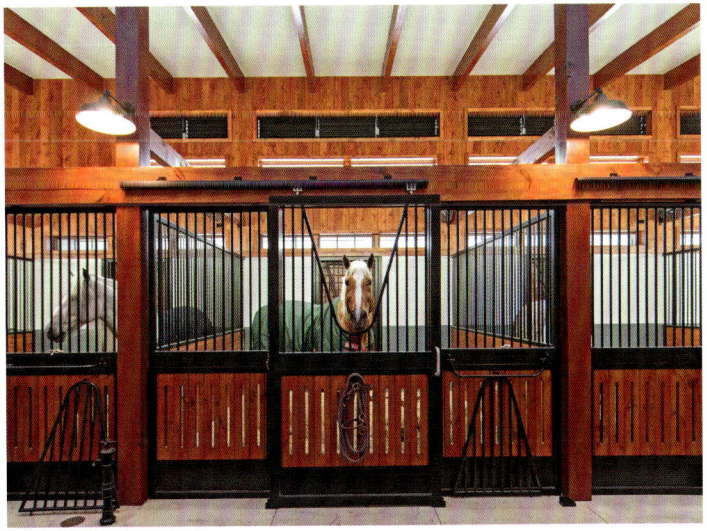

PEGASO FARM 173

174 BLACKBURN ARCHITECTS

PEGASO FARM **175**

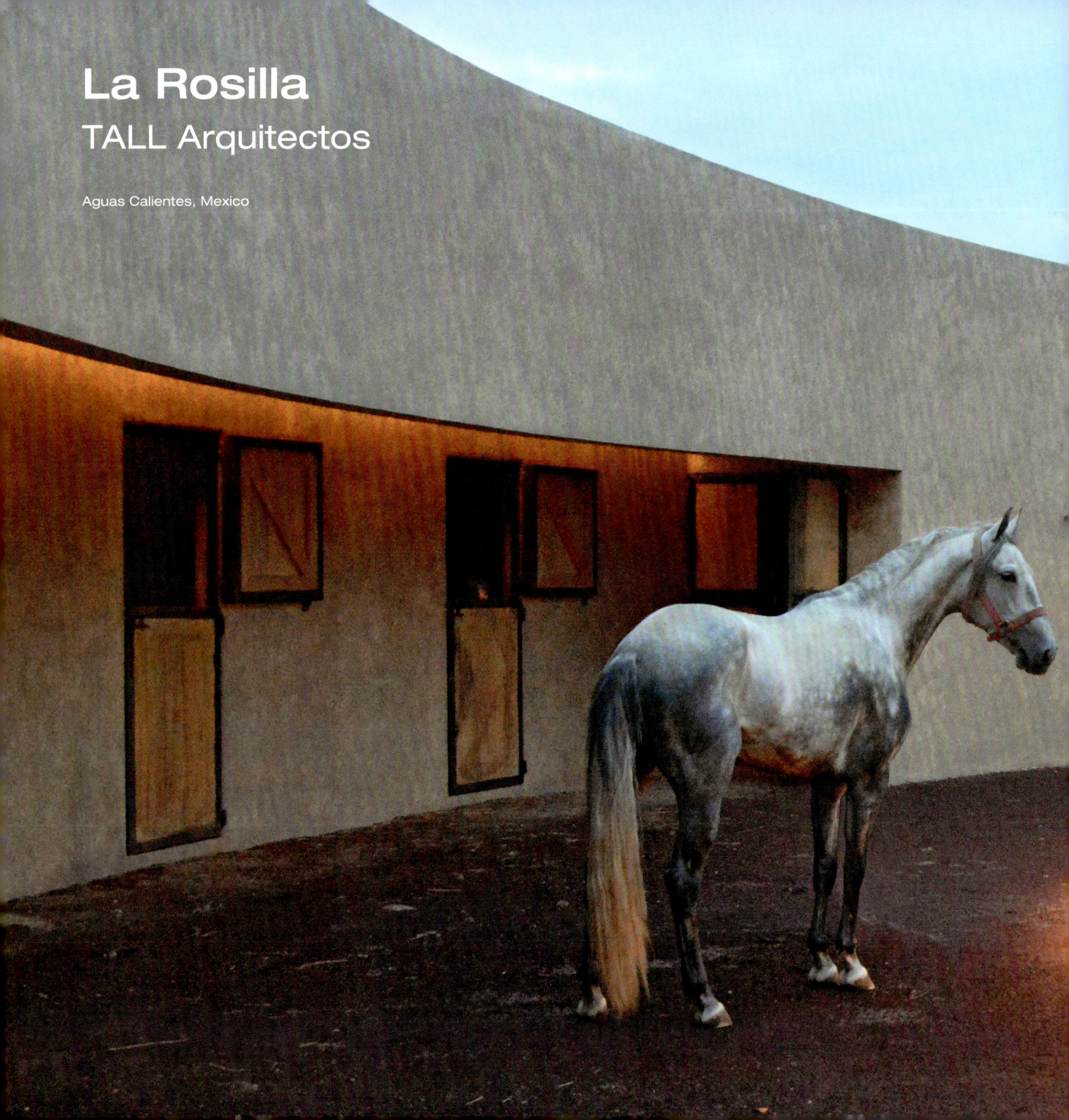

La Rosilla
TALL Arquitectos

Aguas Calientes, Mexico

Building Area:
250 m² stables, 1,000 m² house and public spaces, 500 m² future growth

Site Area:
200 acres

Architect in Charge:
Sebastián Gutiérrez Cortina Sainz,
Lazaro Gutiérrez Cortina Sainz,
Leonardo Montero Tello

Project Team:
Constructor Jaime Pio del Conde Gutiérrez

Interior Designer:
Sebastián Gutiérrez Cortina Sainz,
Lazaro Gutiérrez Cortina Sainz,
Leonardo Montero Tello

Landscape Designer:
Sebastián Gutiérrez Cortina Sainz,
Lazaro Gutiérrez Cortina Sainz,
Leonardo Montero Tello

Photographer:
Sebastián Gutiérrez Cortina Sainz,
Lazaro Gutiérrez Cortina Sainz,
Leonardo Montero Tello,
Rocio Gutiérrez Cortina

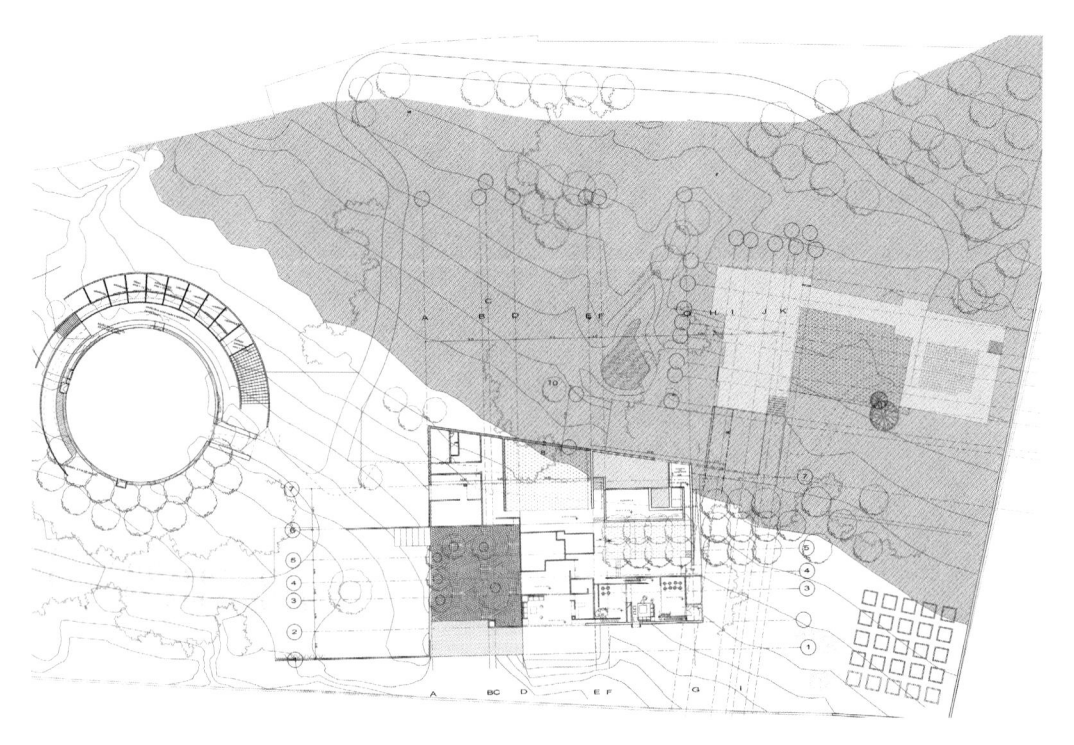

Plan

Rancho La Rosilla is a private residence and equestrian complex located in the remote southwest outskirts of the colonial city of Aguascalientes, Mexico. In Spanish, the term *rosilla* refers to the color red, like the soil around the property, though in this case it is also a reference to the owner's name. Situated on a gently sloping site that overlooks a beautiful lake, named after Mexico's former President Abelardo Rodríguez Luján (1932–34), the property also offers stunning views across a serene and arid Mexican landscape with the dramatic Cerro del Muerto (hill of the dead) of Aguascalientes as the backdrop. In plan the complex is spread out like an ancient Roman villa with the stables on the western end of the site, arranged around a circular riding arena and bull ring with high masonry walls, ramps, and stairs providing access and intrigue to the circus-like space. The slope of the site required cut and fill to even out the surface of the ring, with the stables on the higher part of the site allowing open views to the south. The rancho, with its gardens and living, dining, and entertainment spaces occupies a large horizontal area at the center of the site—parallel with the lake—and is much more open with courtyards, terraces, and water features looking out over the countryside. A rectangular cactus-walled arrival court mediates between the rancho and the stables, creating a sequence of continuous outdoor garden spaces that unite the horses, residents, and visitors alike. A tall chimney stack marks the center of the property where all the spaces come together. The private quarters with seven private bedrooms are in the eastern portion of the site offering the greatest privacy to the family members and their guests. Masonry construction clad in stucco is used throughout the project to achieve a minimalist sensibility for the walls, roofs, and terraces, with wooden doors and stone paving used to accent the largely blank surfaces in a rustic manner. Like the landscape around it, the project is painted in a taupe earth tone. However, the rancho's courtyard is colored in dramatic hot pink in the tradition of Mexico's leading modernist architect, Luis Barragán, who used clean lines and bright colors to create great emotional effect. In this sense, the Rancho La Rosilla is both a traditional Mexican farmstead, and a work of engaging modern minimalist design.

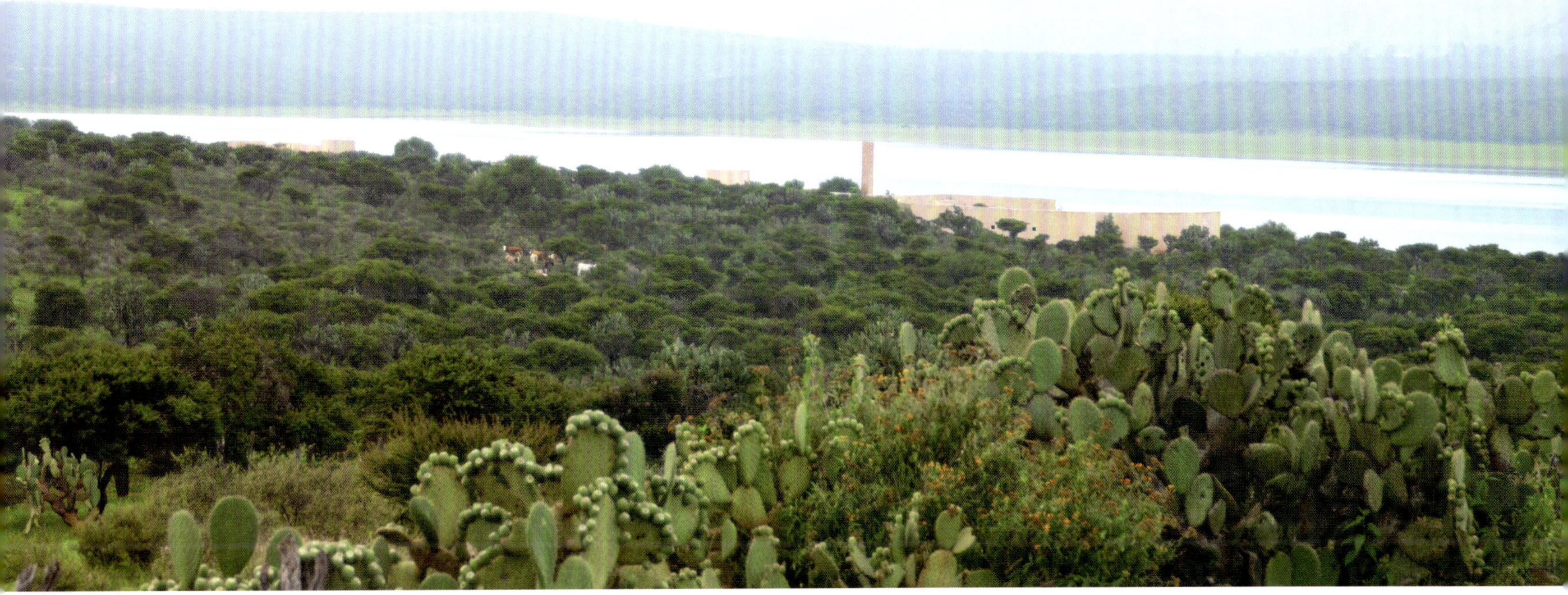

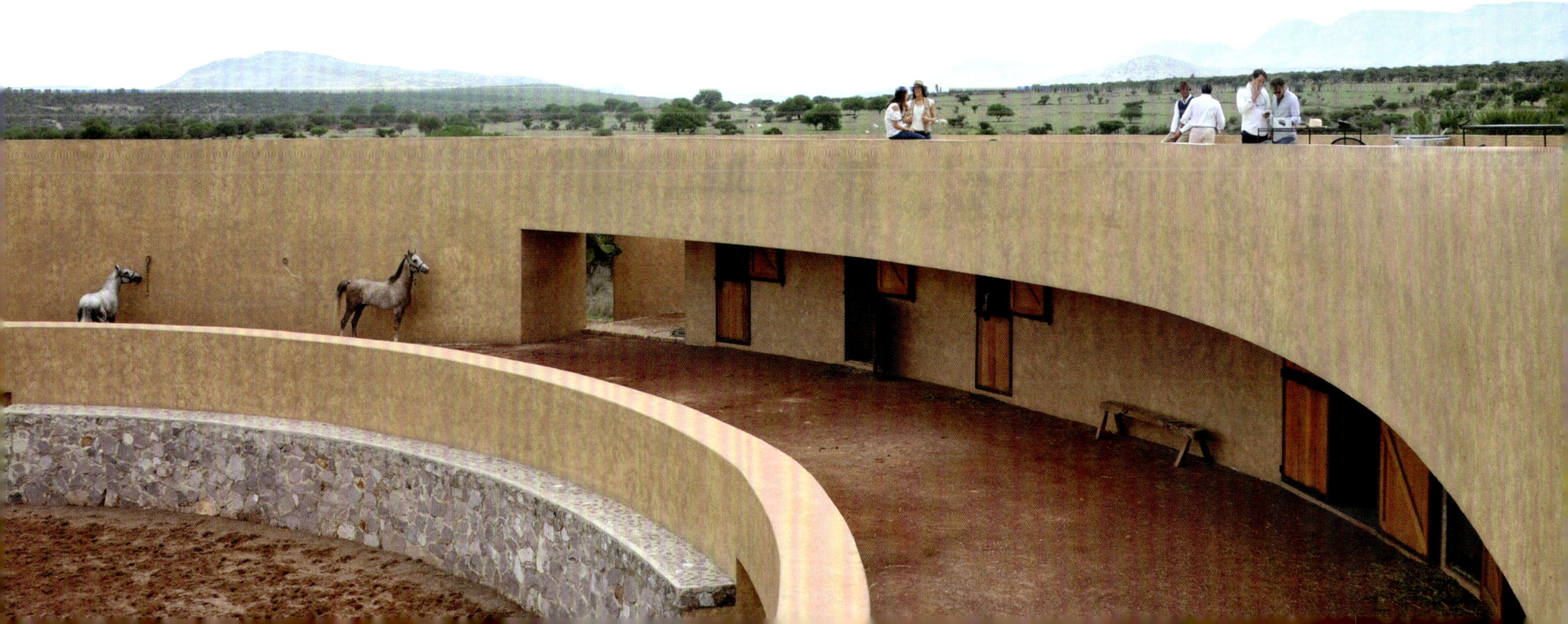

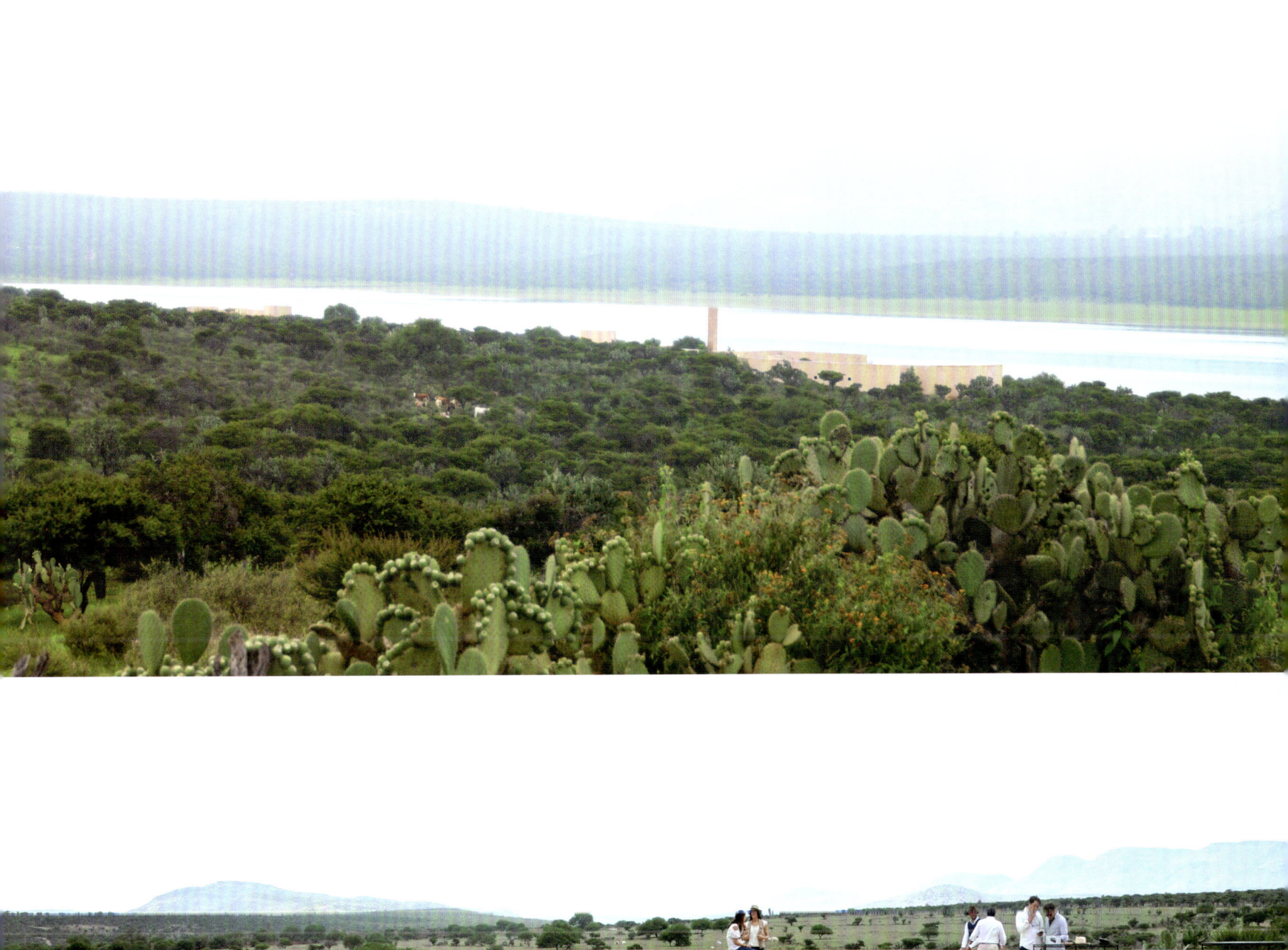

180 TALL ARQUITECTOS

LA ROSILLA 181

182   TALL ARQUITECTOS

LA ROSILLA

184 TALL ARQUITECTOS

LA ROSILLA **185**

Pabellon El Mirador

Manuel Cervantes Estudio

Valle de Bravo, México

Building Area:
459 m²

Site Area:
95 hectares

Architect in Charge:
Manuel Cervantes Céspedes,
José Luis Heredia Álvarez

Project Team:
Israel Caballero Campos, Deyanira Yarza Barrón, María Luisa Leal Rosales

Interior Designer:
Habitación 116

Landscape Designer:
Entorno, Taller de paisaje

Photographer:
Rafael Gamo

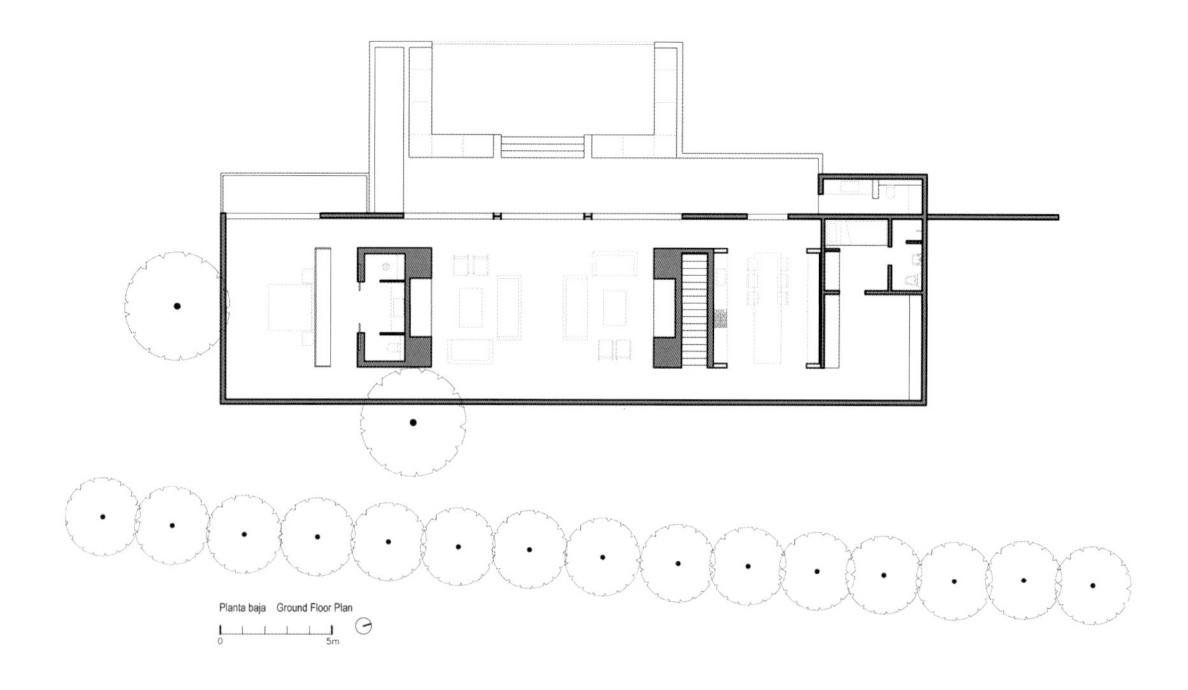

Plan

Perched near the top of a hill in Mexico's Valle de Bravo, a municipality 156 km southwest of Mexico City, El Mirador Pavilion is a striking private residence in the form of a simple rectangle with a unique horse pavilion above it. Situated in the middle of a dense forest, the project appears to emerge out of the landscape, the structure follows the contours of the terrain and generates two levels that clearly define the program for the private and equine functions. The main residence below consists of a combined living and dining entertainment space, with a well-equipped kitchen and generous master suite on either end. Imbedded halfway into the hill with rustic stone retaining walls surrounding the exposed end, the residence opens to a private outdoor terrace. The upper pavilion is a semi-open volume that sits on the stone foundation and allows the horses and riders to find shelter and rest after a long day of riding. Accessed separately from the house at the back, the pavilion has generous proportions and a distinctly rustic appearance. A drinking trough is placed within the open pavilion, visually linked to a large reflecting pool, which also harvests rainwater that is reused for services. The architects designed a series of metal frames that form the main part of the structure with recycled railway sleepers used as fill for the walls, and wooden beams supporting the roof. The structure defines two volumes separated by a low "step and repeat" wall for the horses, with the entire system exposed at the end bay overlooking the reflecting pool and distant landscape. The various stones used for the retaining walls, paving, as well as the tones and textures of the interiors, all blend into the woodland and aim to remain unaffected by the passage of time, while the earth accumulating between the joints of the materials allows for the sporadic growth of plants and moss that change the environment according to the season. The term mirador means vantage point or lookout in Spanish, but in this case, it is the horse that is on view as much as the landscape in the distance. In this sense, the Mirador Pavilion is a miniature temple to the noble quadruped.

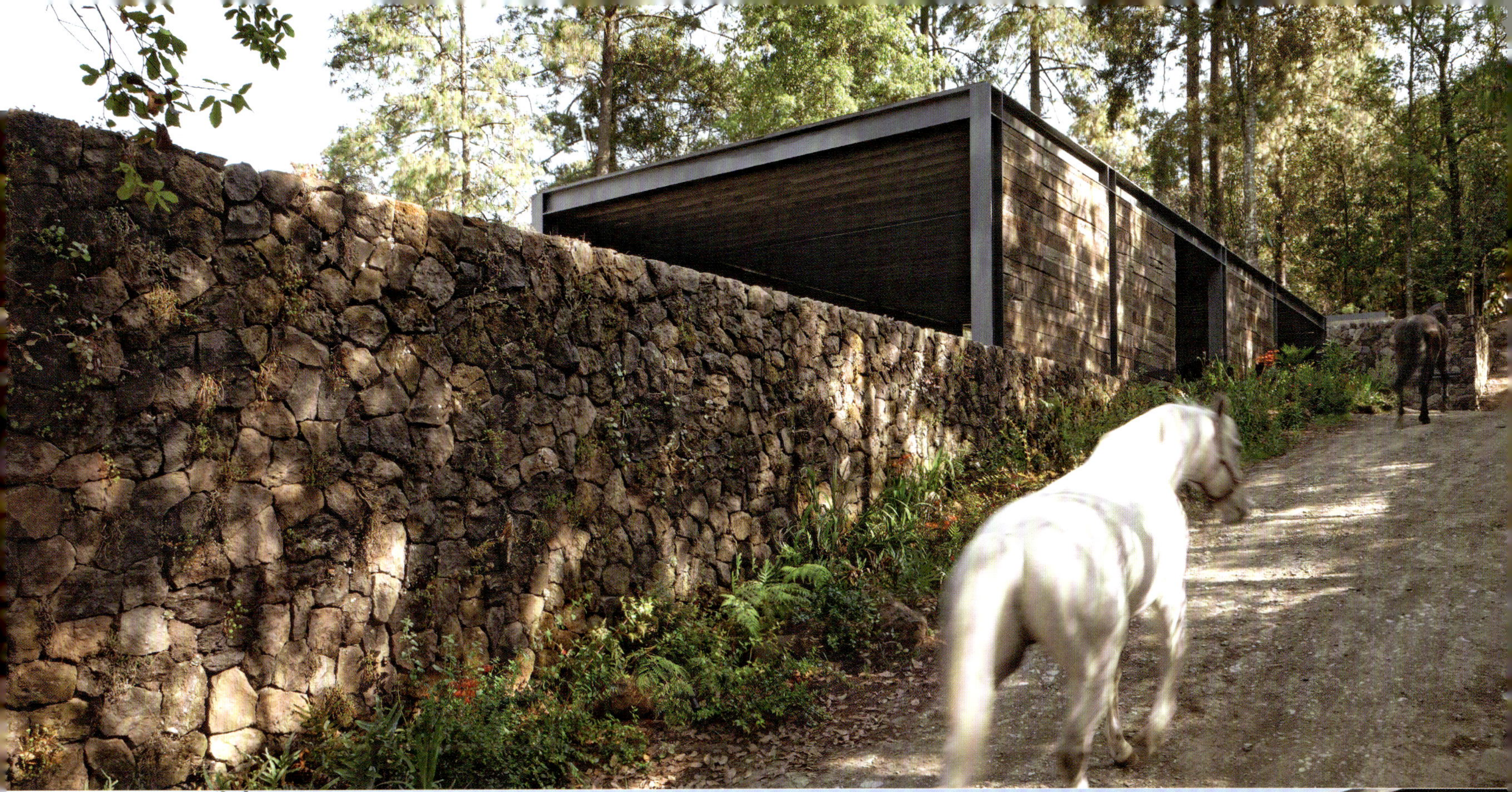

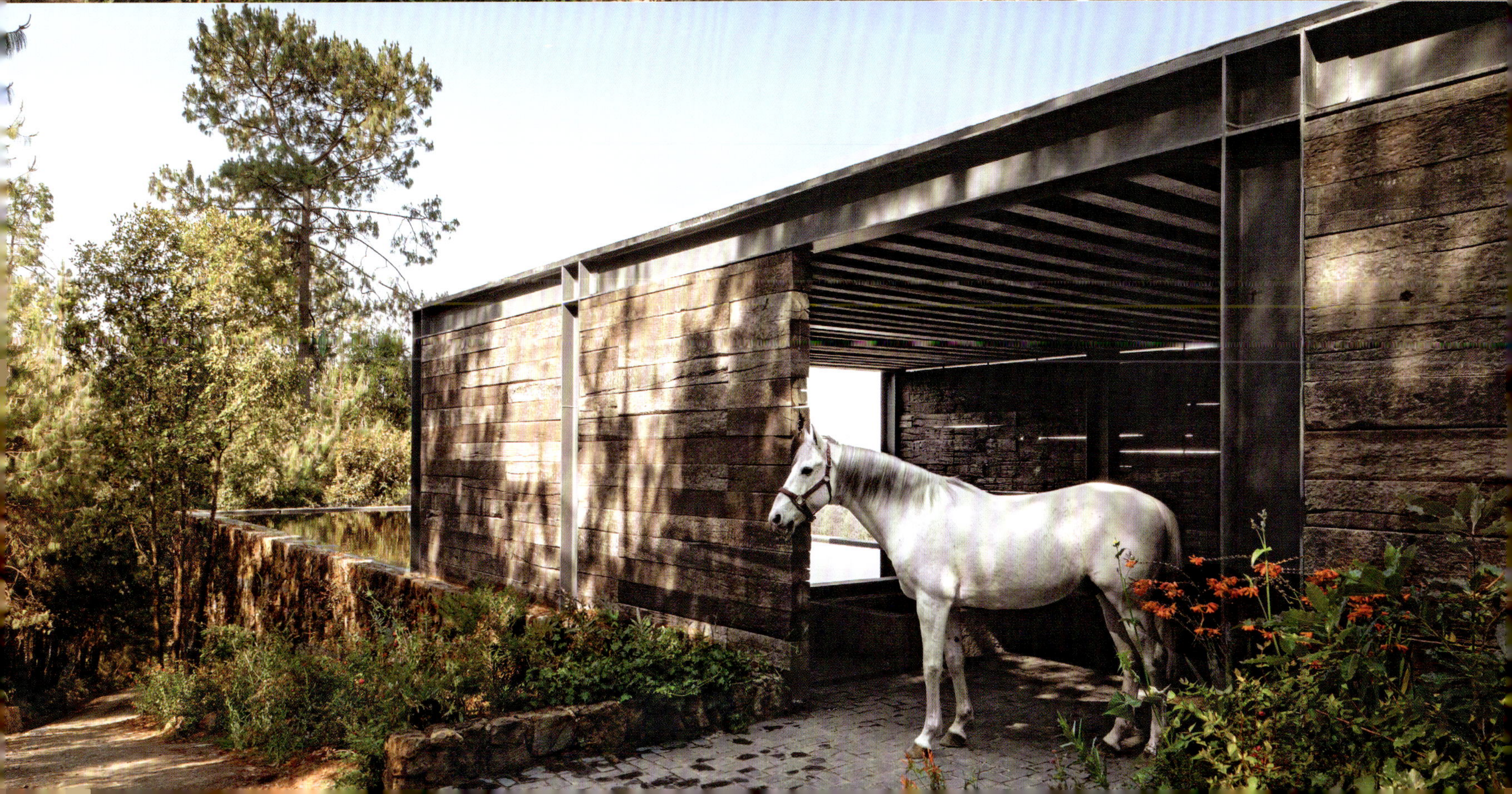

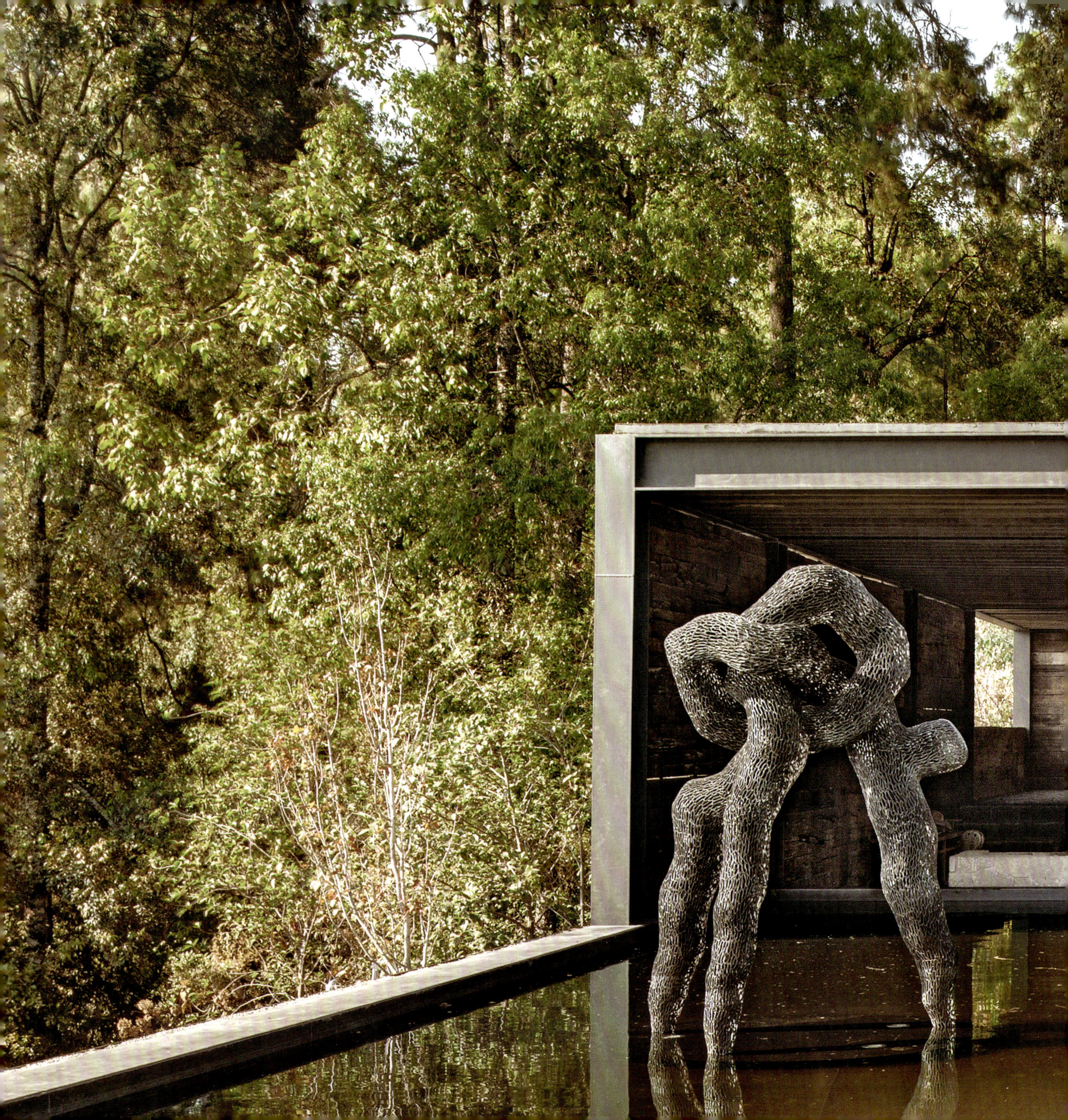

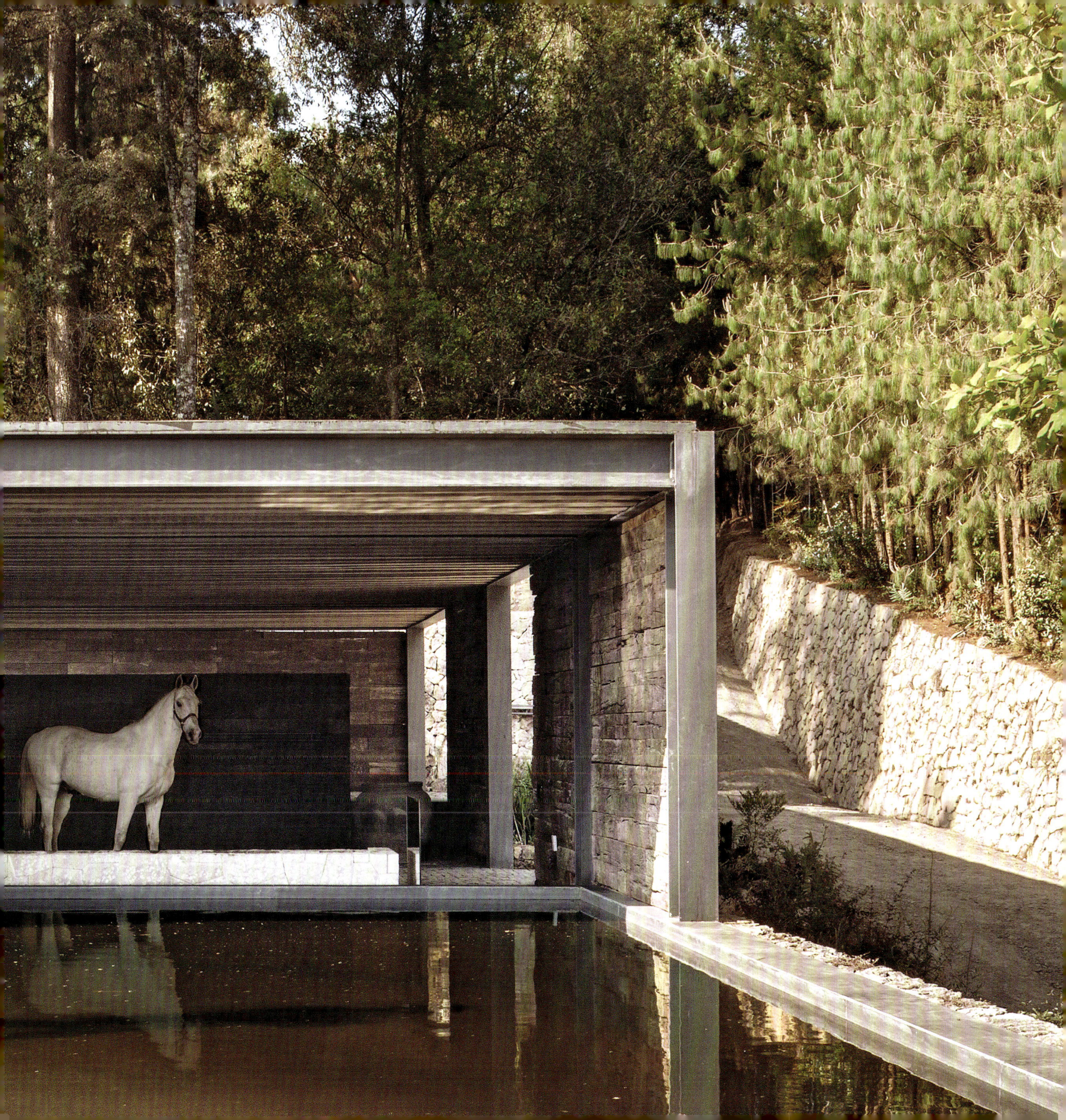

192 MANUEL CERVANTES ESTUDIO

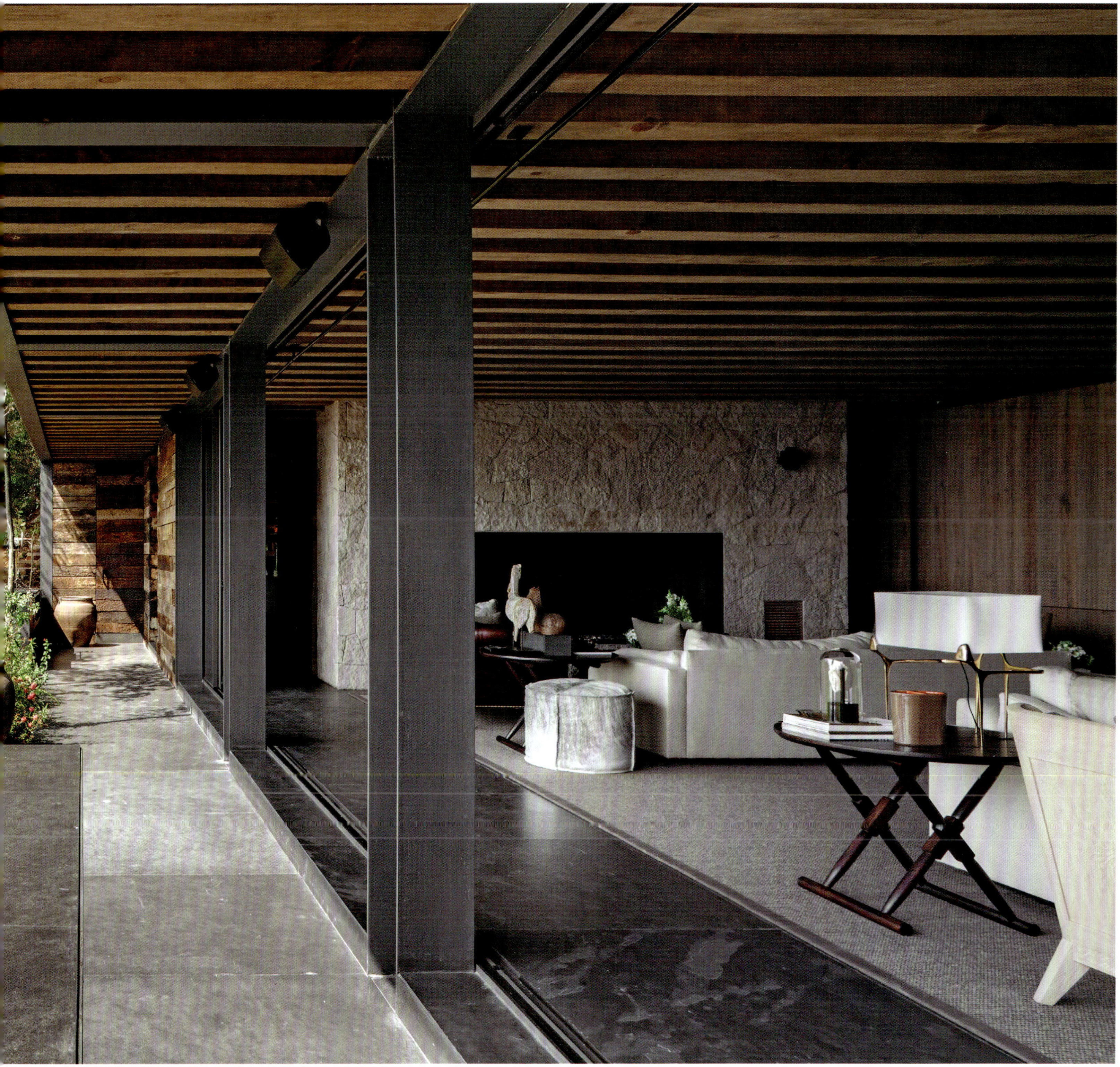

194 MANUEL CERVANTES ESTUDIO

PABELLON EL MIRADOR 195

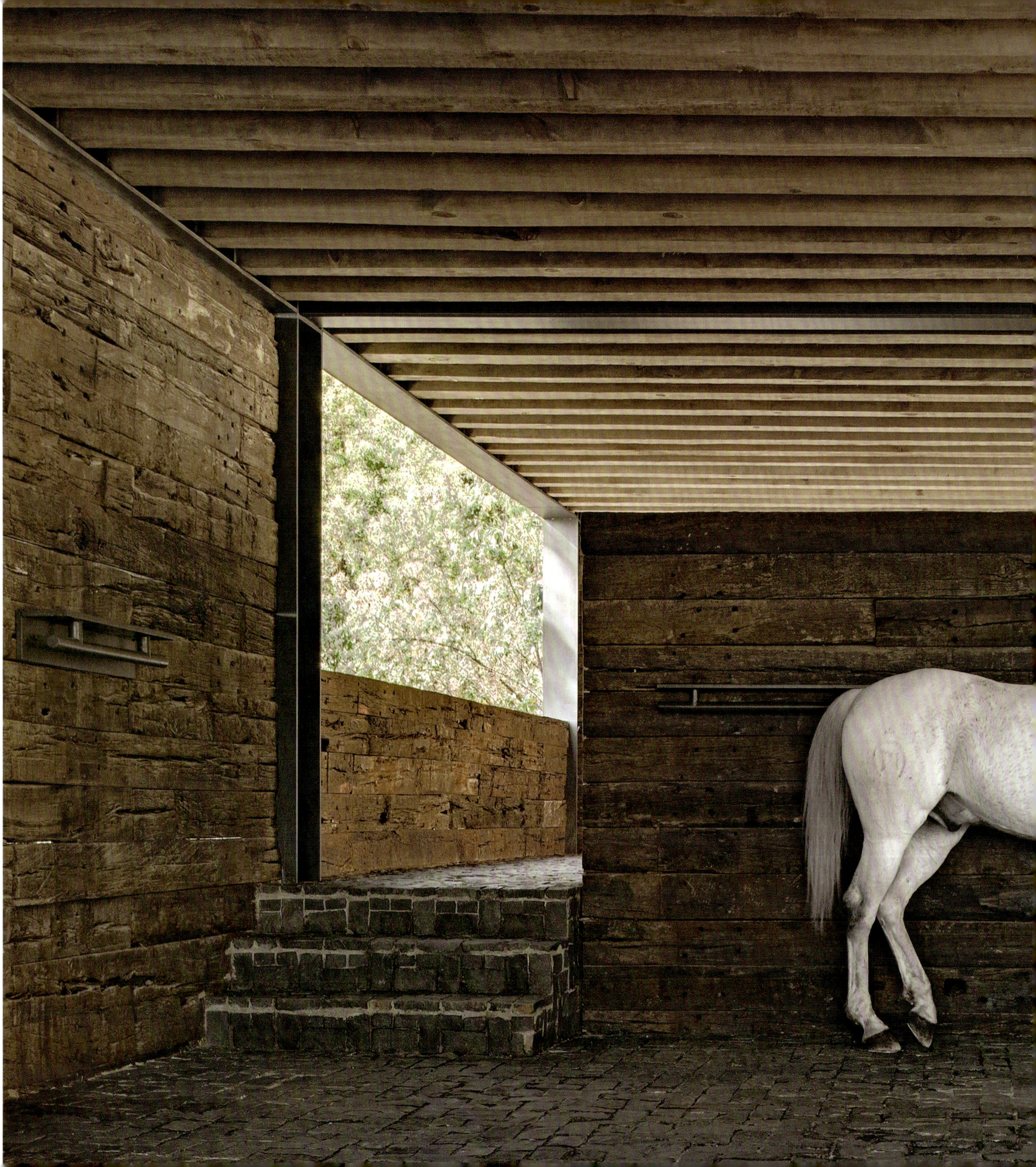

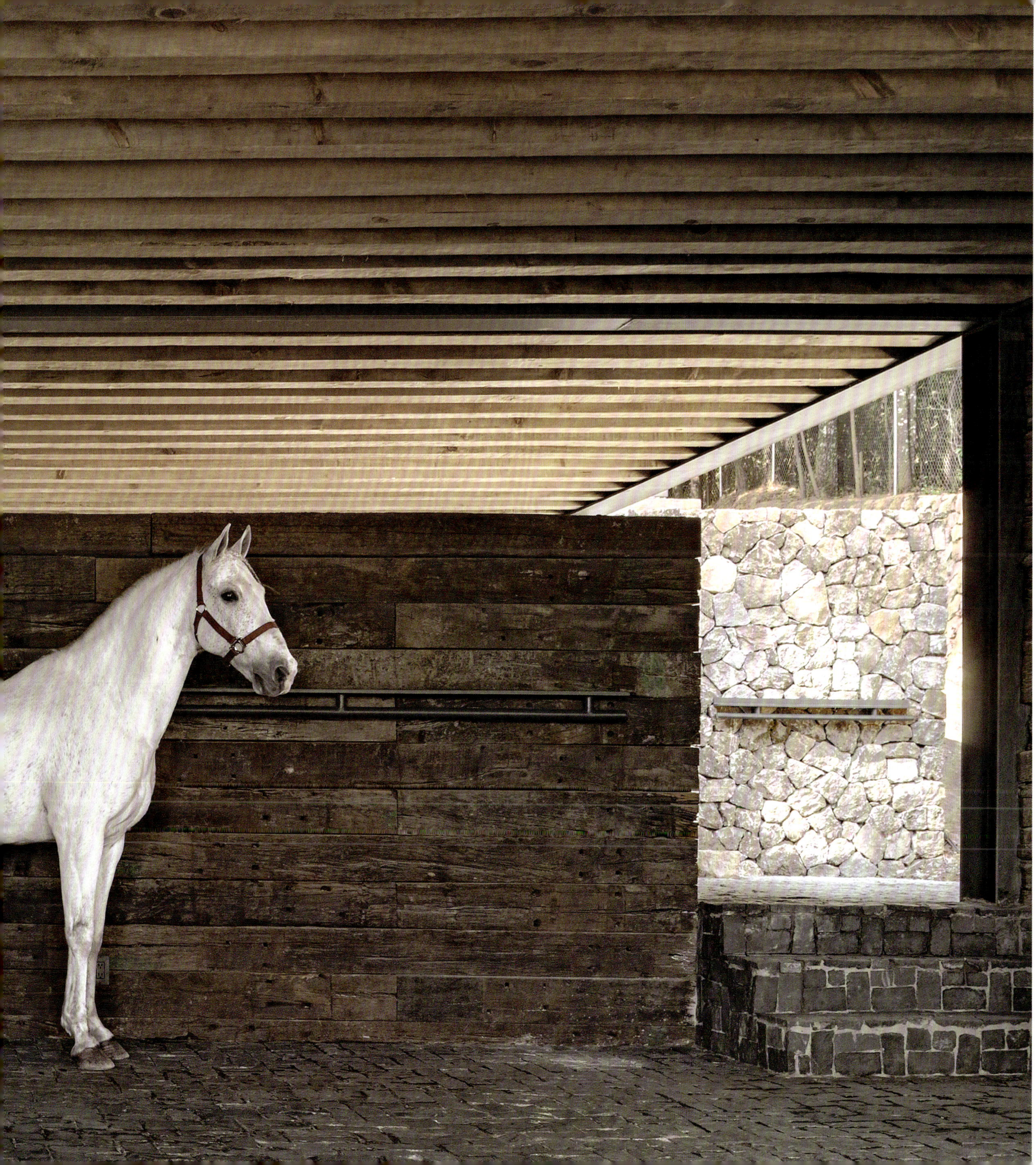

Equestrian Centre
Carlos Castanheira Architects

Leça da Palmeira, Matosinhos, Portugal

Building Area:
3,150 m²

Site Area:
38,800 m²

Architect in Charge:
Carlos Castanheira

Project Team:
Orlando Sousa, Fernanda Sá,
Joana Catarino, Cátia Carvalho,
Pedro Afonso, Adele Pinna,
Sofia Conceição, Inês Bastos,
Diana Vasconcelos, Nuno Campos

Photographer:
Fernando Guerra | FG+SG

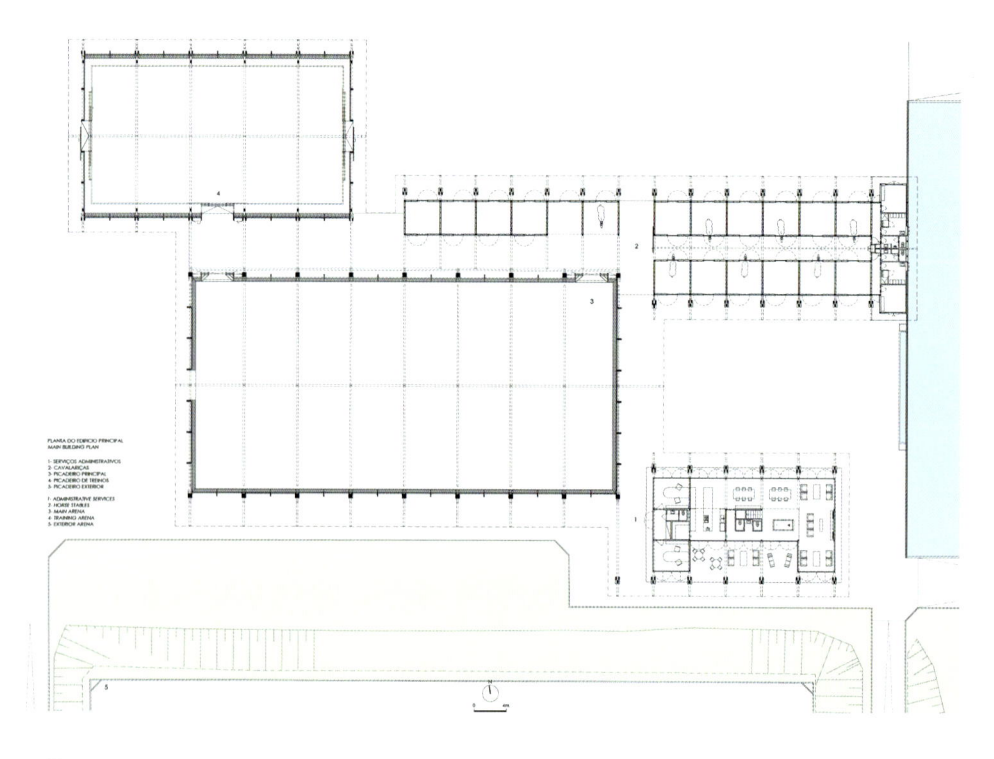

Plan

The Equestrian Centre located at Cabo do Mundo, Leça da Palmeira, Portugal, is a complex built to be inhabited by horses and the people working there who also love horses. The site, overlooking the Atlantic, was configured to create outdoor terraces where a riding arena, paddocks, jumping arenas, and riding paths were built. In plan, the project consists of four separate buildings, one large—and one small—indoor riding arena, a stables wing, and an administrative building, centered around a courtyard overlooking a large water basin. The various functions were then connected by a series of gently sloped large gable roofs. The stable building brief required the use of timber in the structure, partitions, walls, and ceilings throughout. The two covered riding arenas, differing in size, provided a structural challenge due to the considerably large spans required to cover them. Consequently, structure defines the space and use of the facility, and is both the foundation and the finished product throughout. The structure defines the building because every element is both structure and space. As noted by the architect:

"We always worry about the well-being of the people who will inhabit the spaces that we design and hope to see built. To inhabit is to occupy those spaces and to perform the vital functions of comfort, of work or pleasure. In reality, it is to do with ordering and giving form to functions. We are functionalists, if only because Architecture has to be functional and so it forces us to be so too. If not, we'll be condemned to discomfort, absurdity and eventually ridicule ... When we practice our profession, we enter deeply into the lives of the eventual inhabitants and users and get to know them well and intimately. What they like, what they don't like. This is always the way, as should be the case, irrespective of who these users or habitants are."

With giant metal roofs punctuated by large dormer windows, sloping walls, and intricate structural system, the project is centered on function and comfort. Indeed, the Equestrian Centre is a unique place where one lives with, for, and off of the horses.

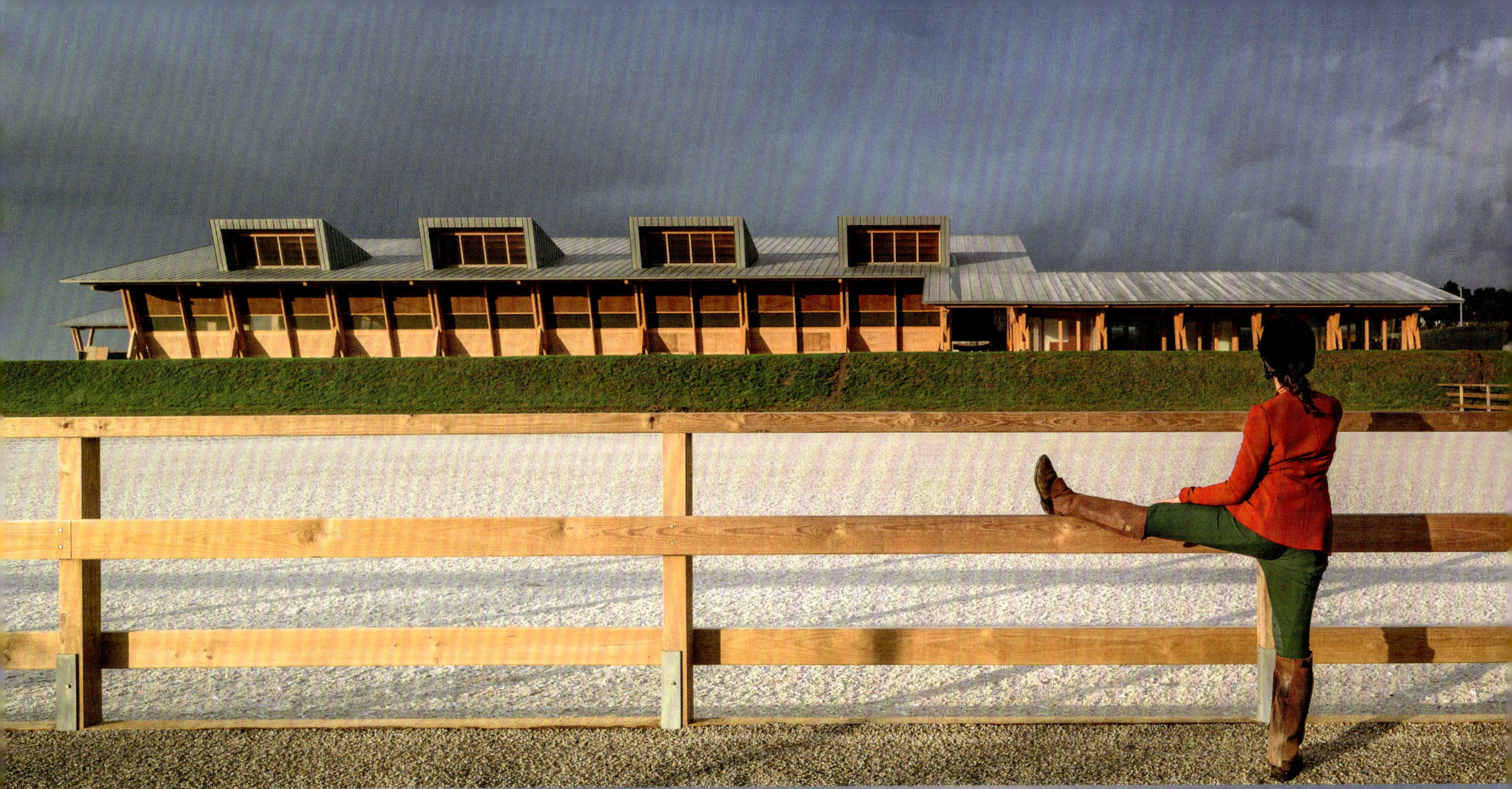

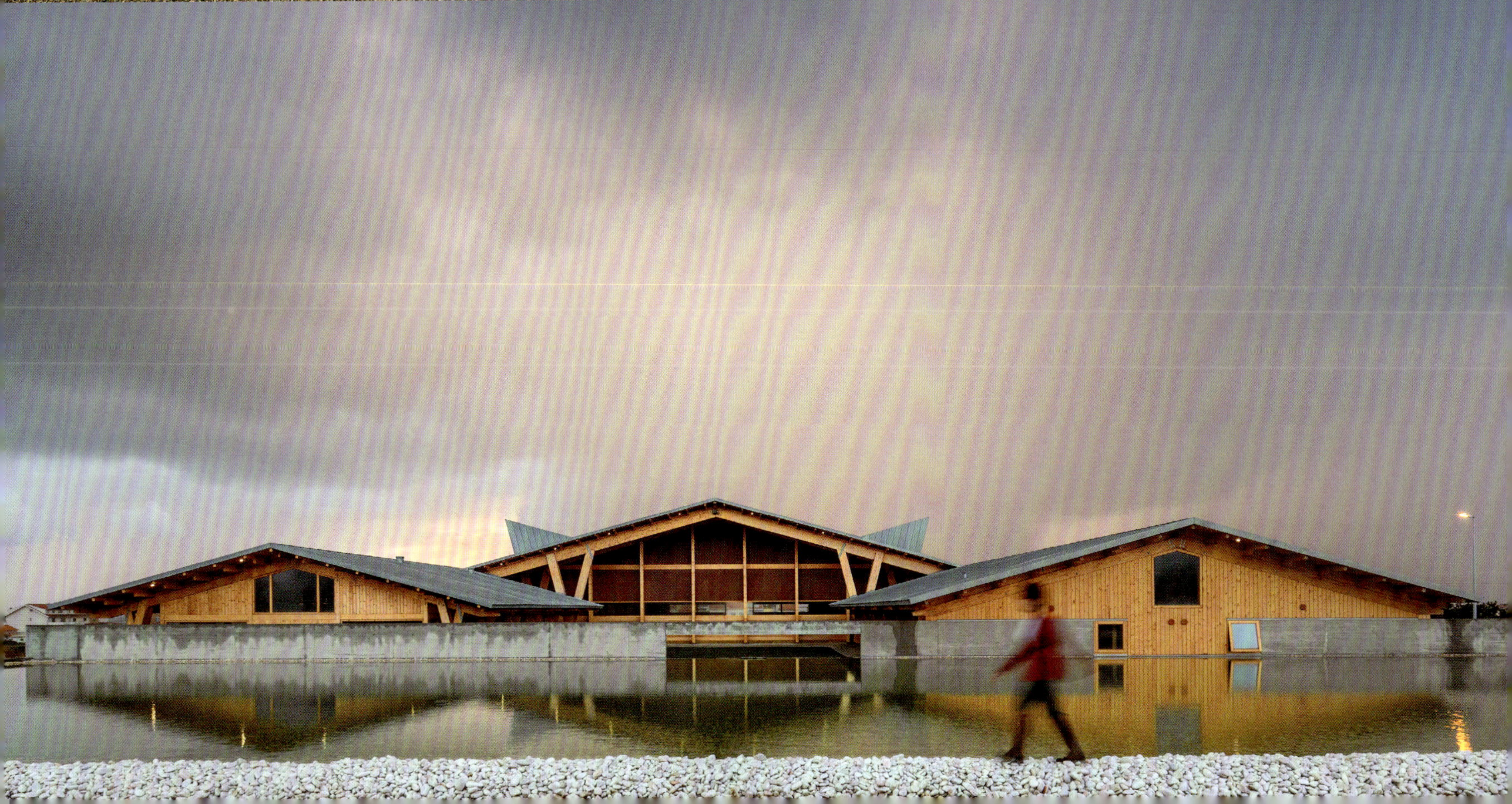

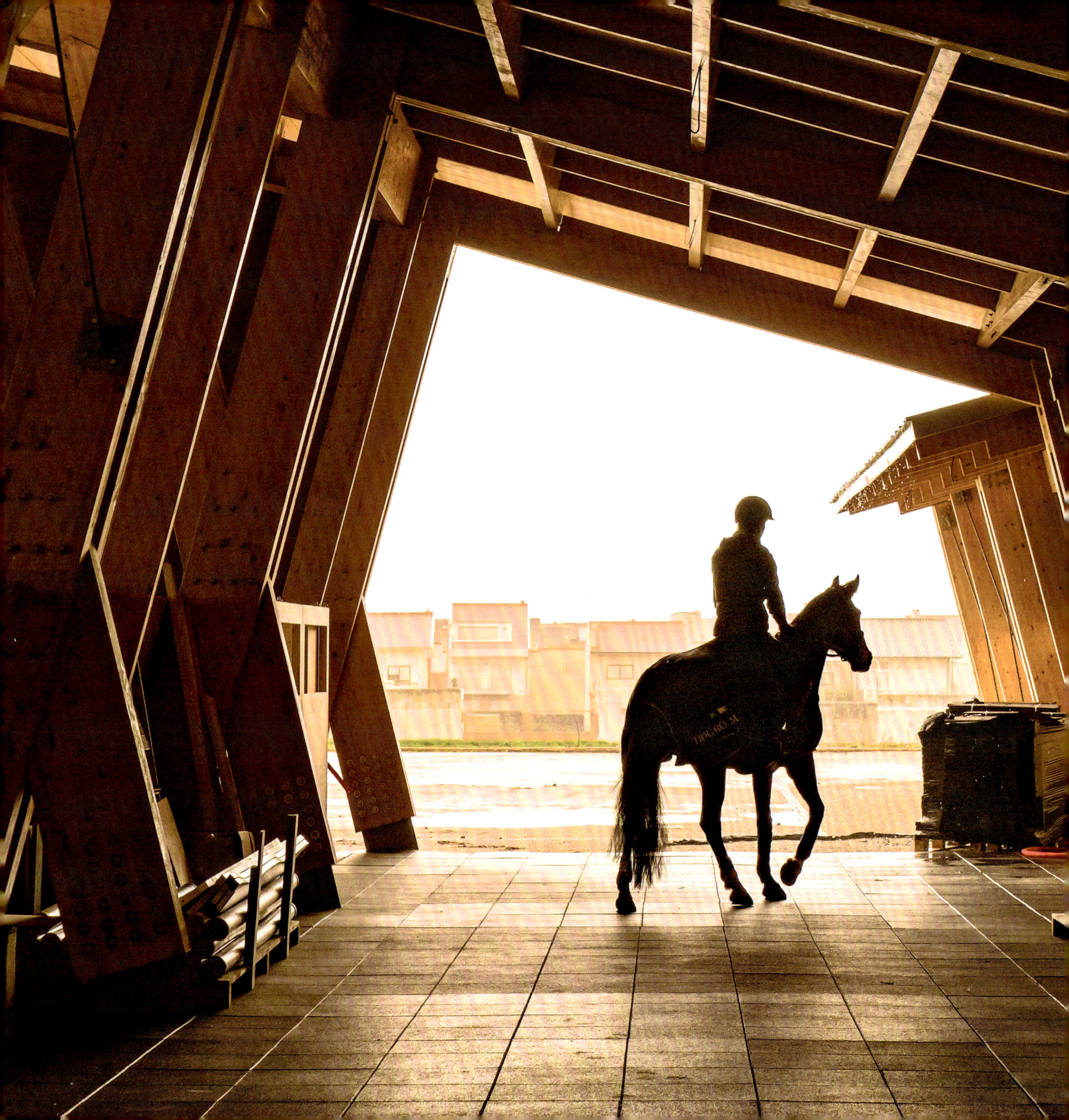

EQUESTRIAN CENTRE **203**

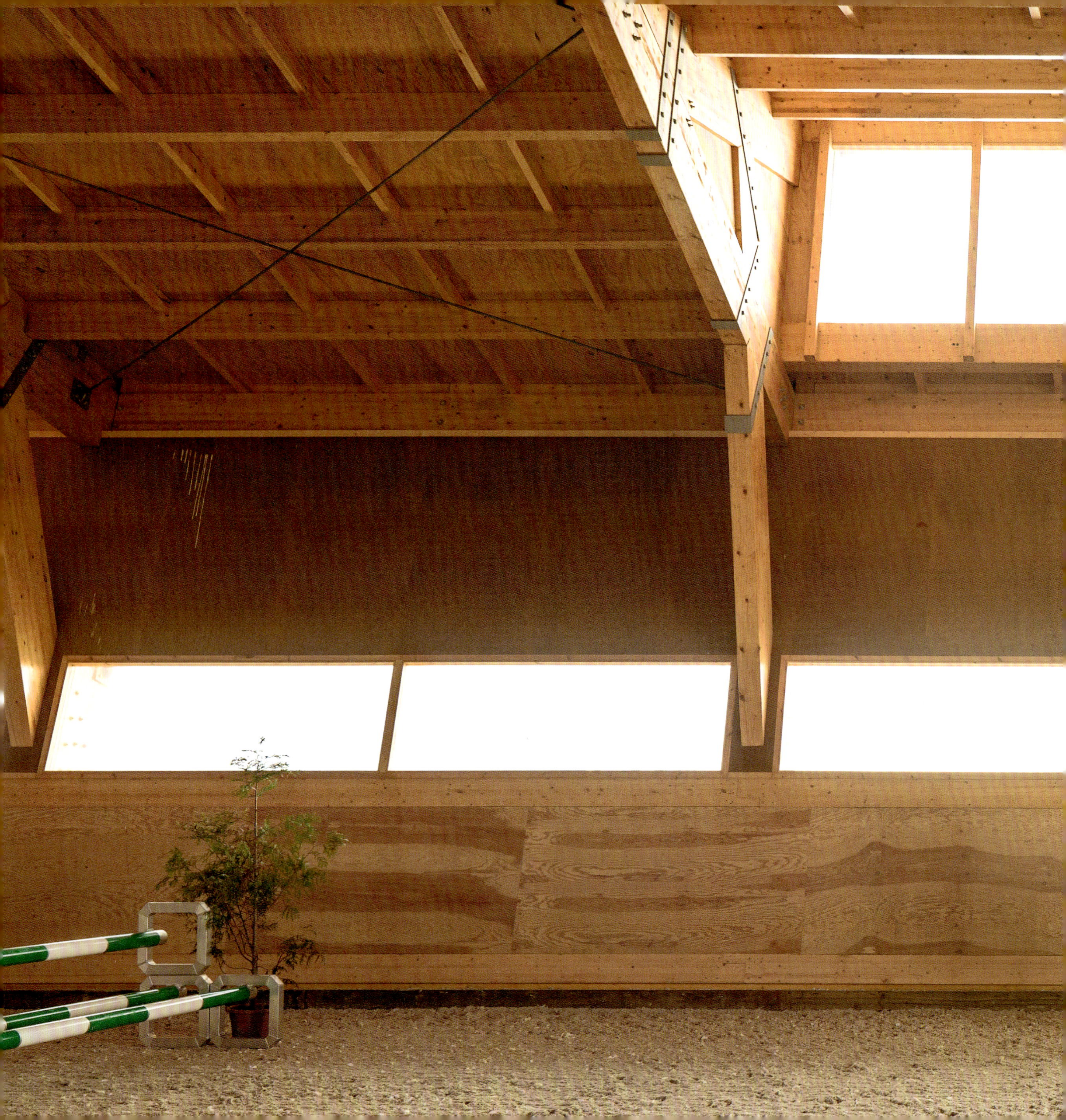

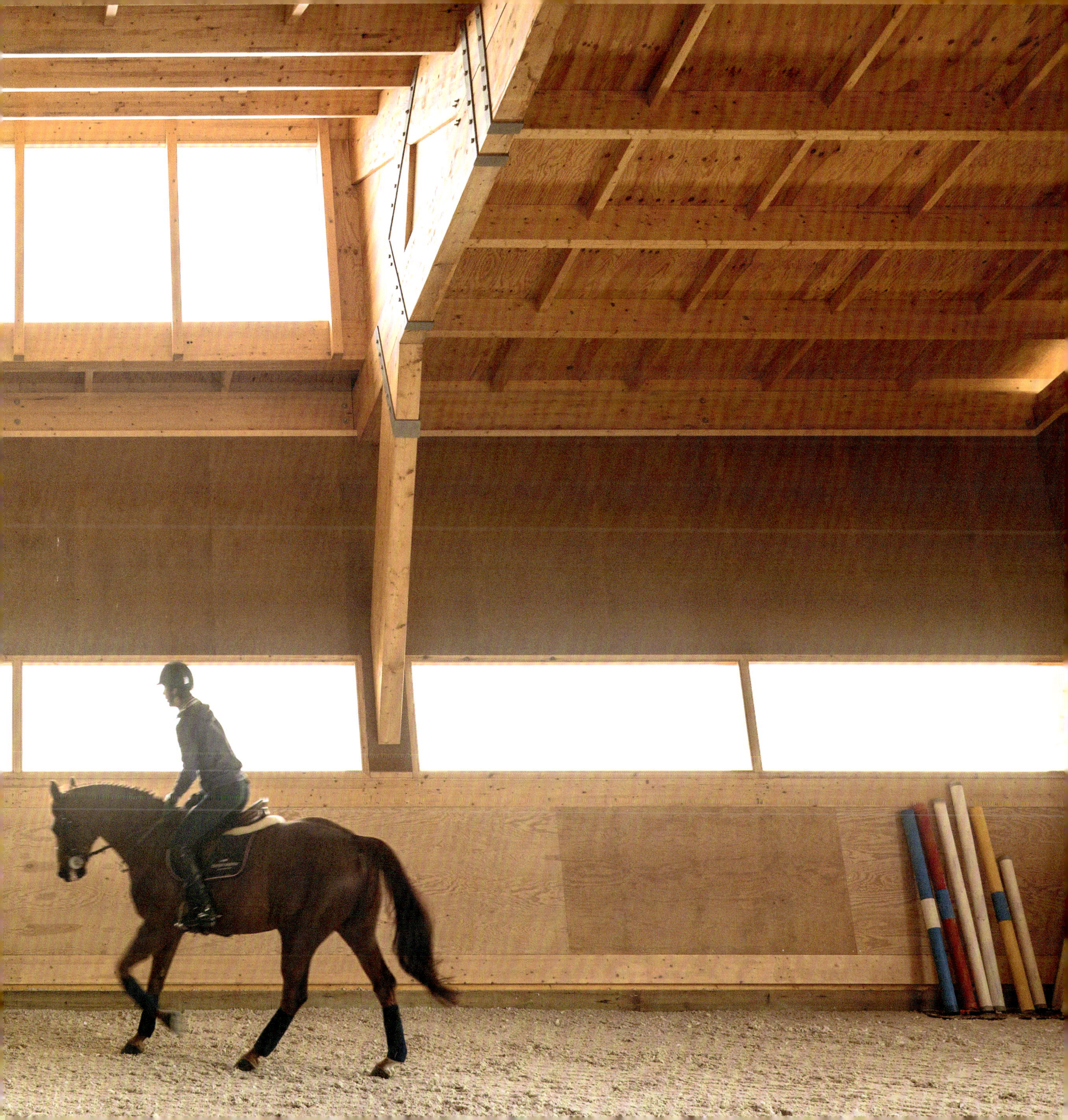

La Stella Ranch
AE Arquitectos

Tapalpa, Jalisco, Mexico

Building Area:
750 m²

Site Area:
10 hectares

Architect in Charge:
Andrés Escobar

Project Team:
Sergio Romo, Javier Rosales, Alejandra Rojas, Josué Carrillo

Interior Designer:
Mumo Interiorismo

Landscape Designer:
Juan Montaño

Photographer:
Lorena Darquea

Plan

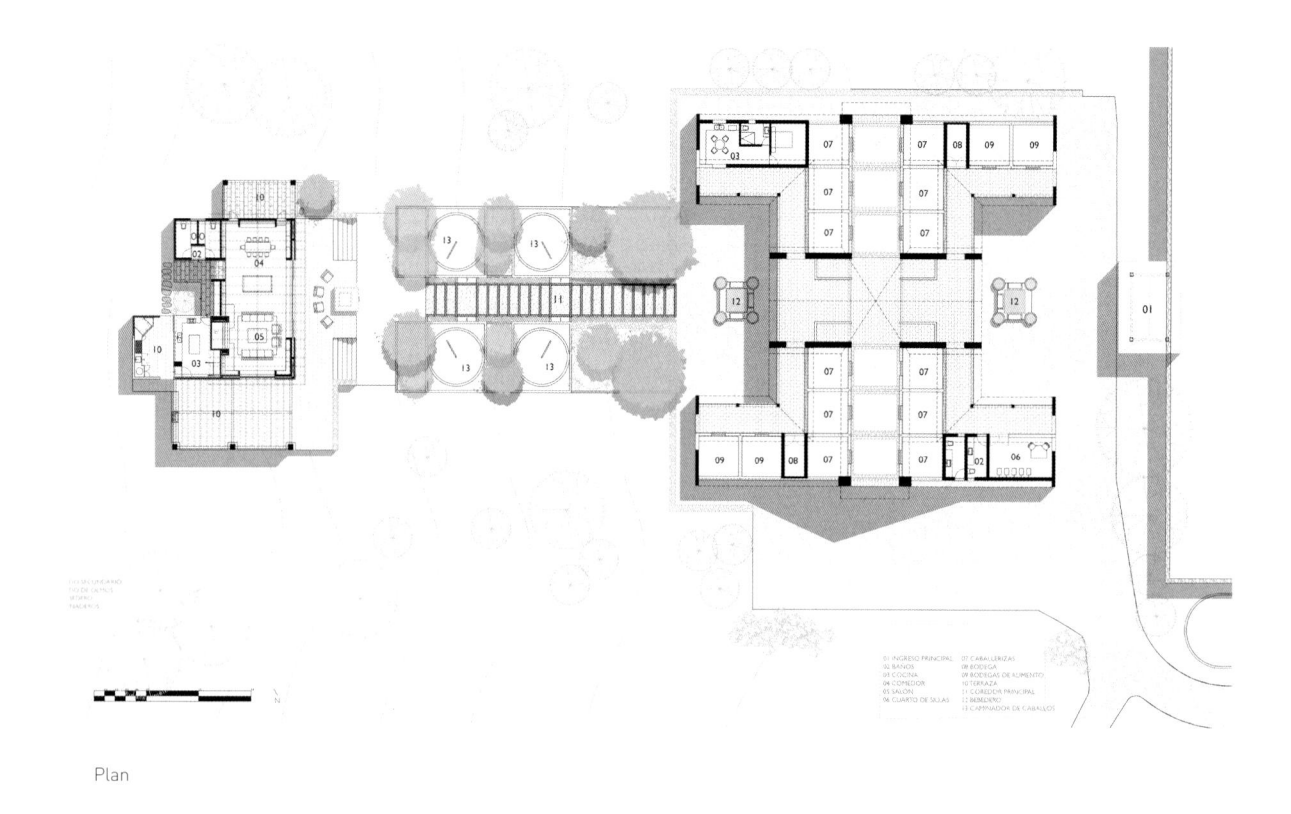

Located south of the city of Tapalpa in the western state of Jalisco, Mexico, the Rancho La Estela is a private equestrian complex situated on a verdant site overlooking a large lake and dam. Consisting of a large equestrian complex and private residence connected by a landscaped garden, the property also contains an outdoor riding arena, a circular training ring, and several open fields for riding. The project was originally designed to raise Spanish "Andalusian" horses and for this reason, the design had to follow many specific guidelines and specifications for the horses. The plan of the equestrian complex is formed by two buildings—both in the shape of a horseshoe—facing one another and joined by a large central corridor. A series of very high exposed masonry walls provide the basic structure for the facility. These are then covered by a massive timber, steel, and tile roof structure that is entirely open at the ends and in the center, creating a breezy and open atmosphere for the horses. A covered pavilion north of the stables building provides a viewing are for the large outdoor riding arena. The residential building is located south of the stables, with many social areas and terraces for entertaining. At the center of the house is a large open living and dining space that opens directly to the landscaped garden facing the stables. Covered outdoor terraces on either side of the great room allow for privileged views of the stables and the surrounding mountains, lake, and dam. All the building materials, including stone masonry, heavy timber, and steel, were selected to enhance the experience of the place by providing a breadth scale that was comparable to the large horses. Pine wood was used to supplement the structure and carpentry of the whole, and different kinds of stone and clay tiles cover the walls, roofs, and decorative planters. All of these materials give a special vernacular quality to the project that underlines the traditional domestic architecture of Central Mexico.

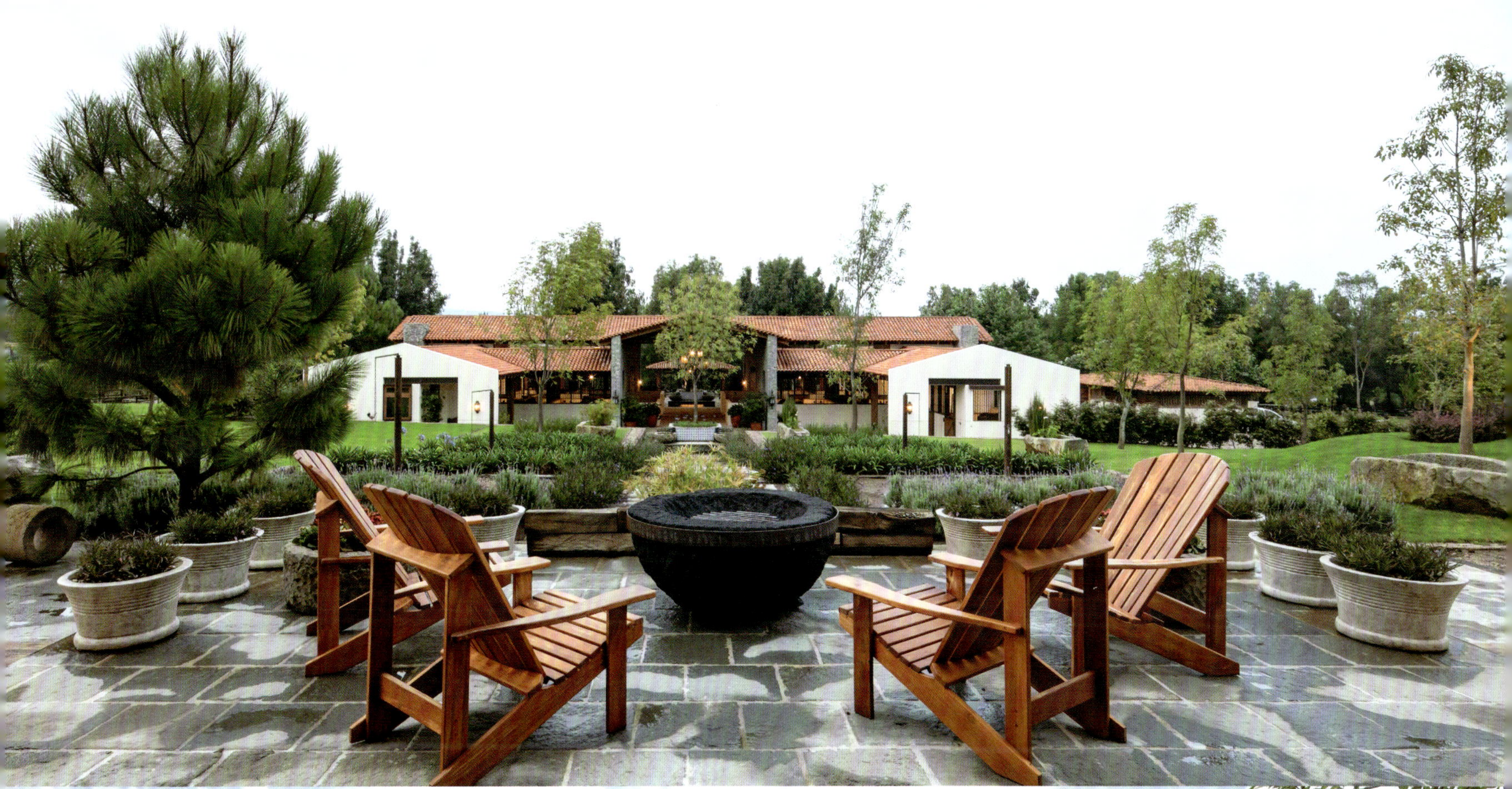

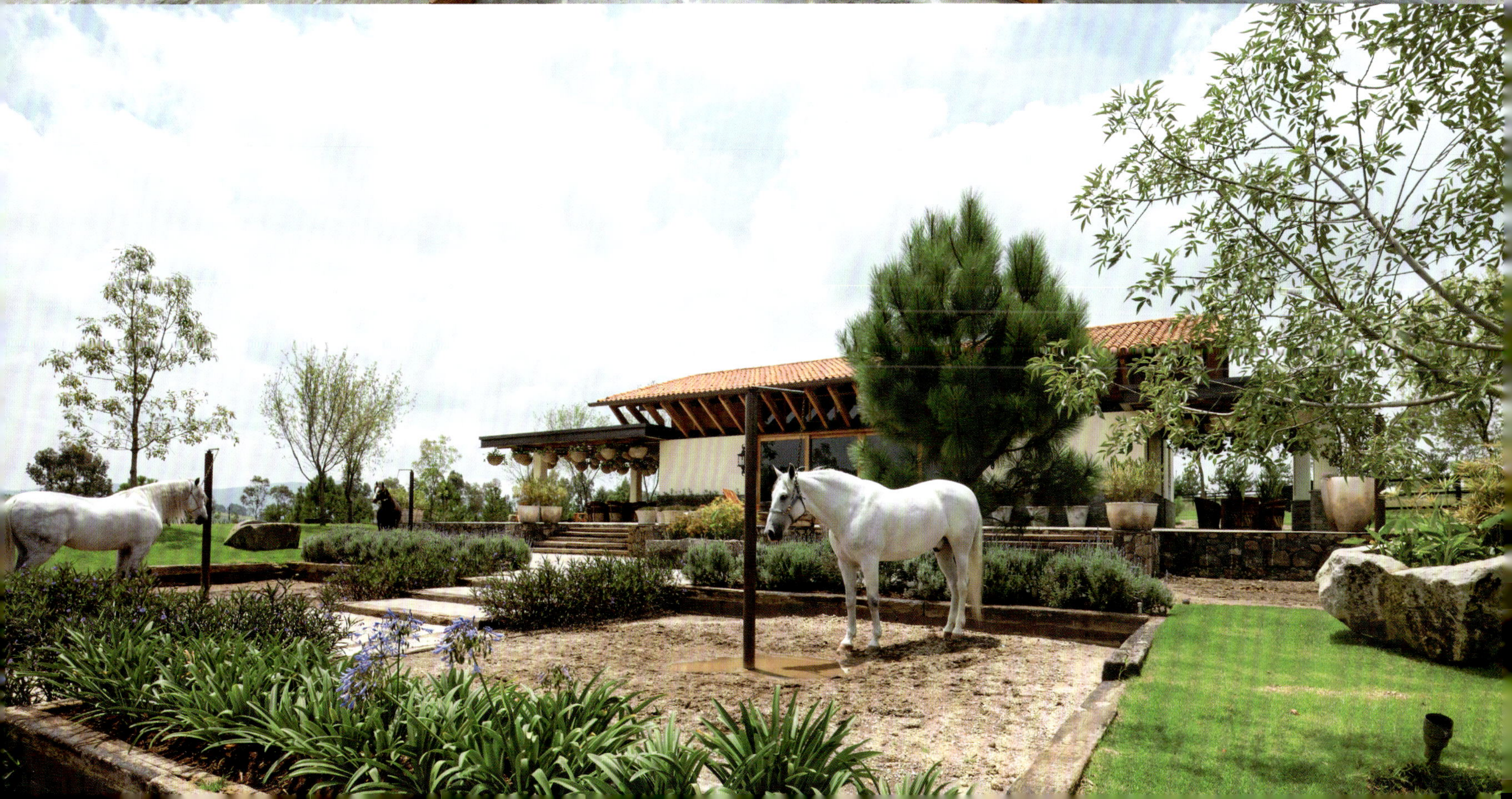

210 AE ARQUITECTOS

LA STELLA RANCH 211

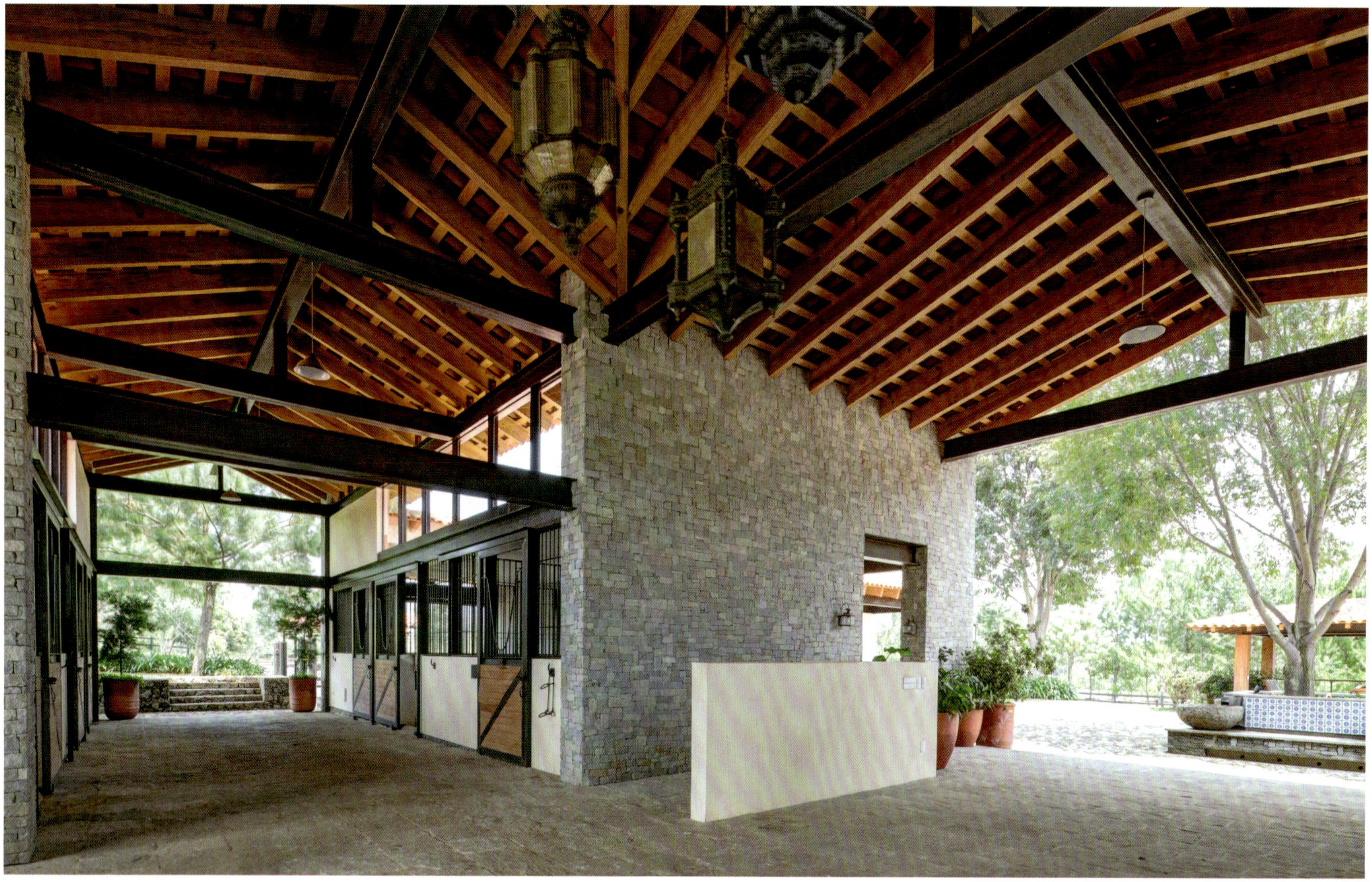

LA STELLA RANCH

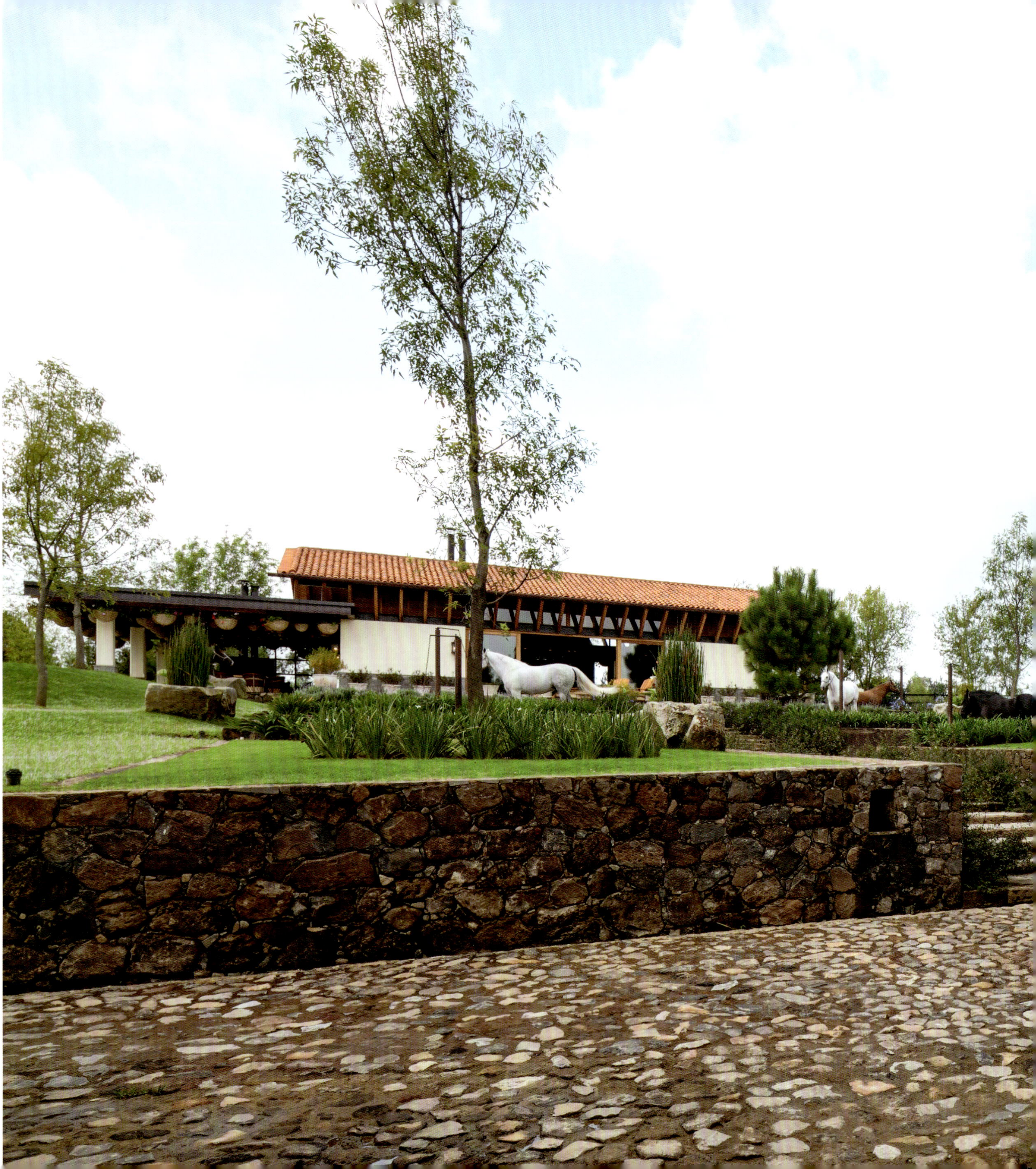

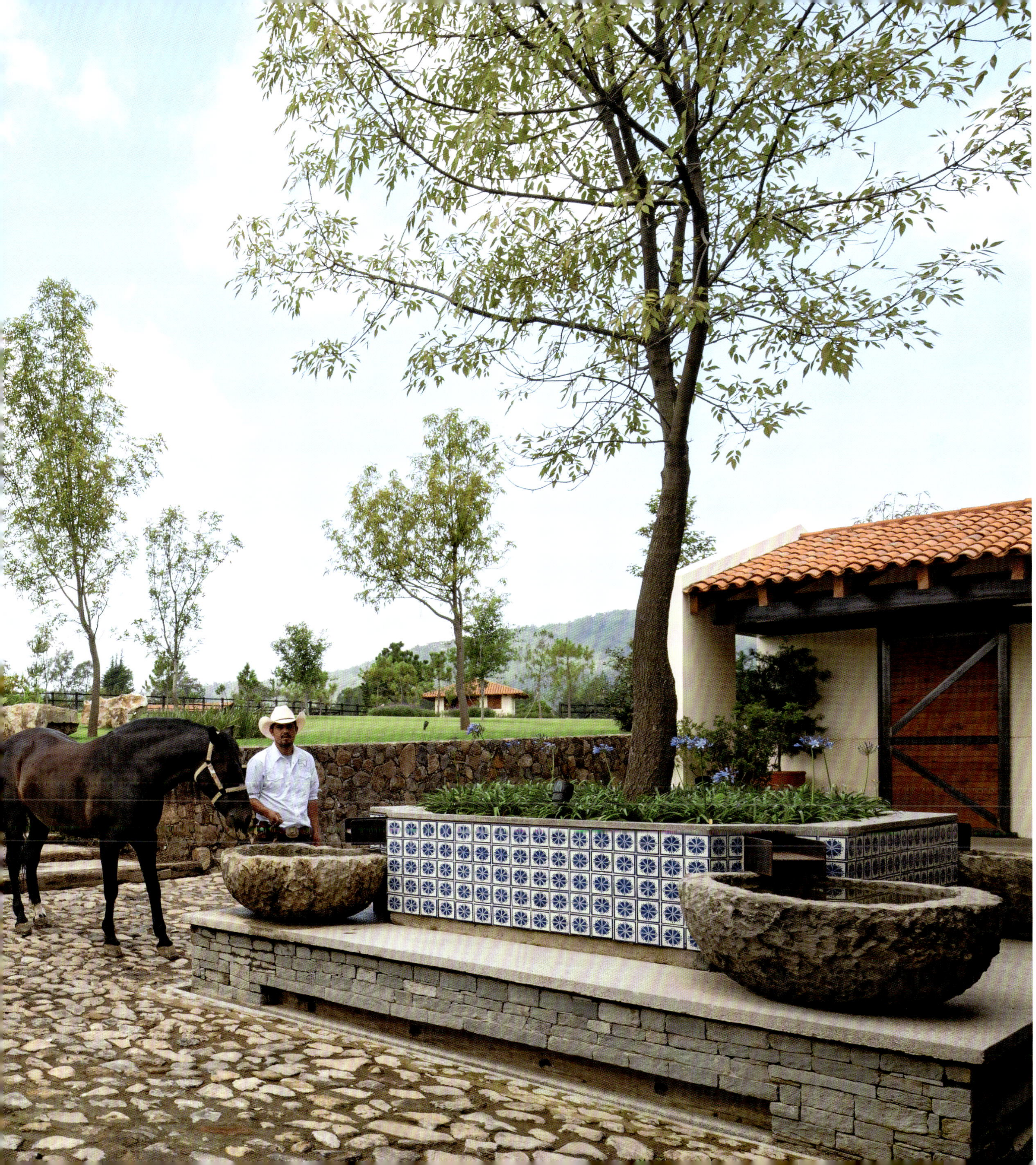

Proyecto Ecuestre
Manuel Cervantes Estudio

Valle de Bravo, Mexico

Building Area:
5.1 acres

Architect in Charge:
Manuel Cervantes Céspedes,
José Luis Heredia

Project Team:
Israel Caballero, Deyanira Yarza
Ameyalli Téllez, Adrian Izquierdo
(Structural Engineer), IESH, Samuel
Nischli (Electrical Engineer)

Photographer:
Rafael Gamo

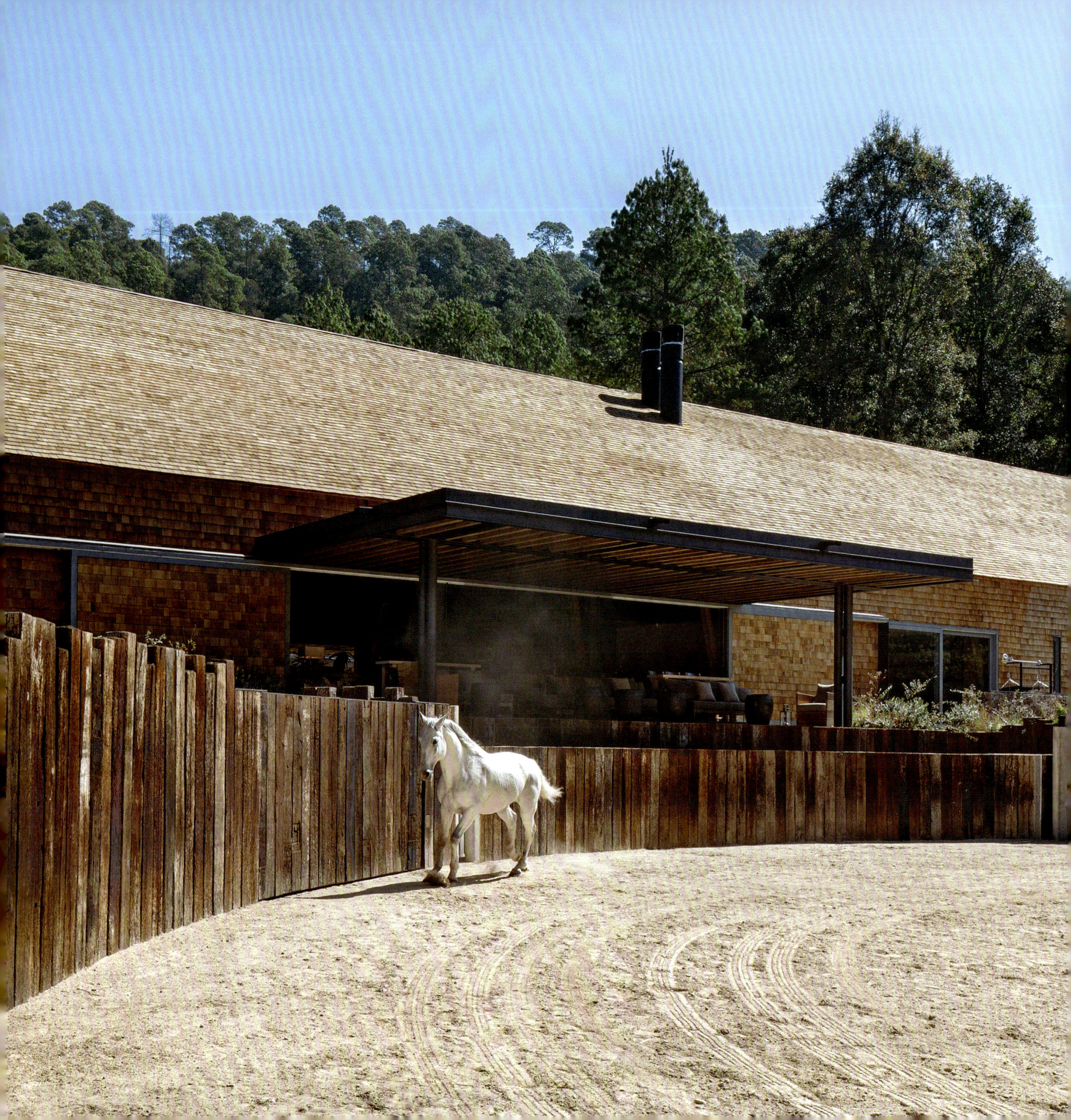

Plan

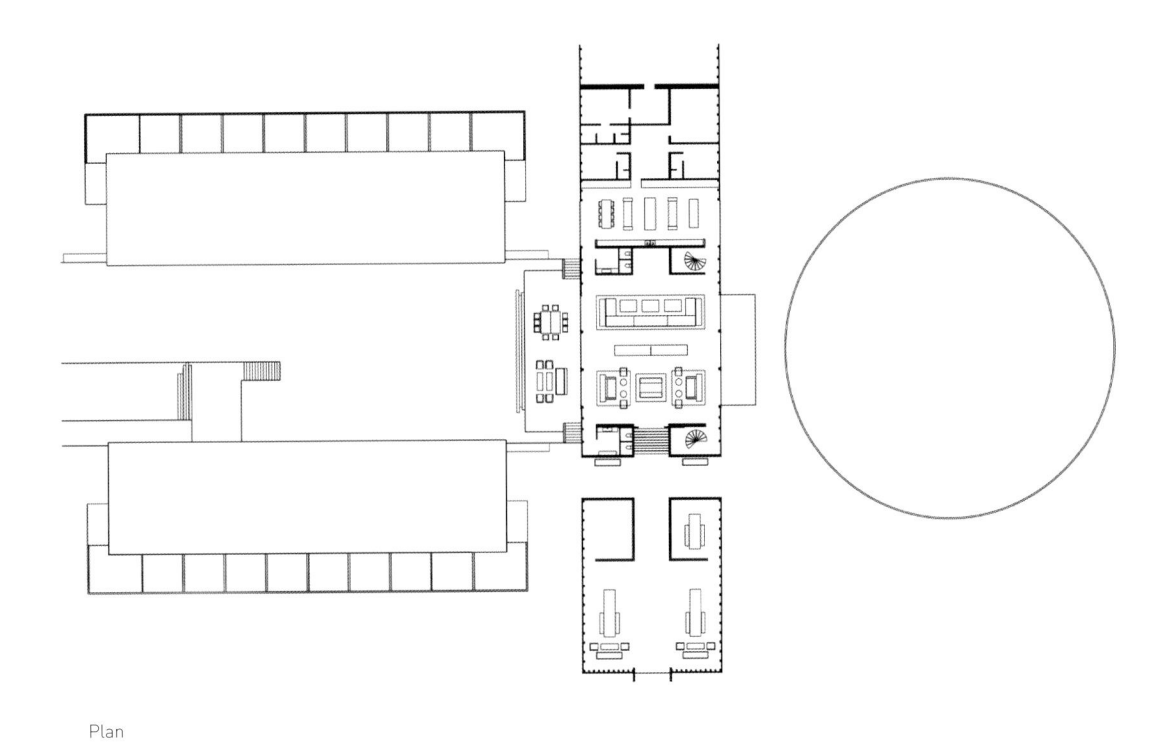

When the architect received the commission for this project in Valle de Bravo, Mexico, the client already had a well-defined idea of what he wanted: to raise horses and live close to them in the same space. The project is situated in a clearing in the middle of a dense forest, surrounded by oak, ocote, pine, and arbutus trees. The architect chose to leave the smallest possible footprint on the site—an approach that pleased the client. The topography of the site had a gentle slope, and so the architecture was integrated into its context. In plan the complex consists of a long barn-like structure that serves as residence and auxiliary functions, with two rows of stabled extending on one side and a large circular riding arena on the other. Different spaces were created through earthworks that nest the stables within the topography, not obstructing the views over the dense mountain vegetation. In doing so, the visual impact of the project's size was significantly reduced. The architects visually narrowed the heights required by horse riders on their mounts and suitable proportions were maintained for people. The spaces were joined together by paths that are shared by people and horses alike. Gently sloping ramps are used to walk around and discover the buildings. Another defining quality of the project is the intersection between interior and exterior: every space is filled with views of the surrounding woods and vegetation, and natural lighting and ventilation are employed throughout. In its structure and materials, the project keeps complexity to a minimum. The use of repeated structural frames is a straightforward approach to balancing form and function. This unfussy construction style creates a unique atmosphere in which no extra flourishes are needed. The wood and metal elements that shape the main hall create a welcoming and dark-toned atmosphere, with light openings as a compositional feature. Rustic finishes, and window and door openings create clearly defined patterns throughout. The house and stables are joined together initially through circulation routes and then by the similarity of the finishes, connecting the human to the equestrian world.

220   MANUEL CERVANTES ESTUDIO

PROYECTO ECUESTRE 221

222 MANUEL CERVANTES ESTUDIO

PROYECTO ECUESTRE **223**

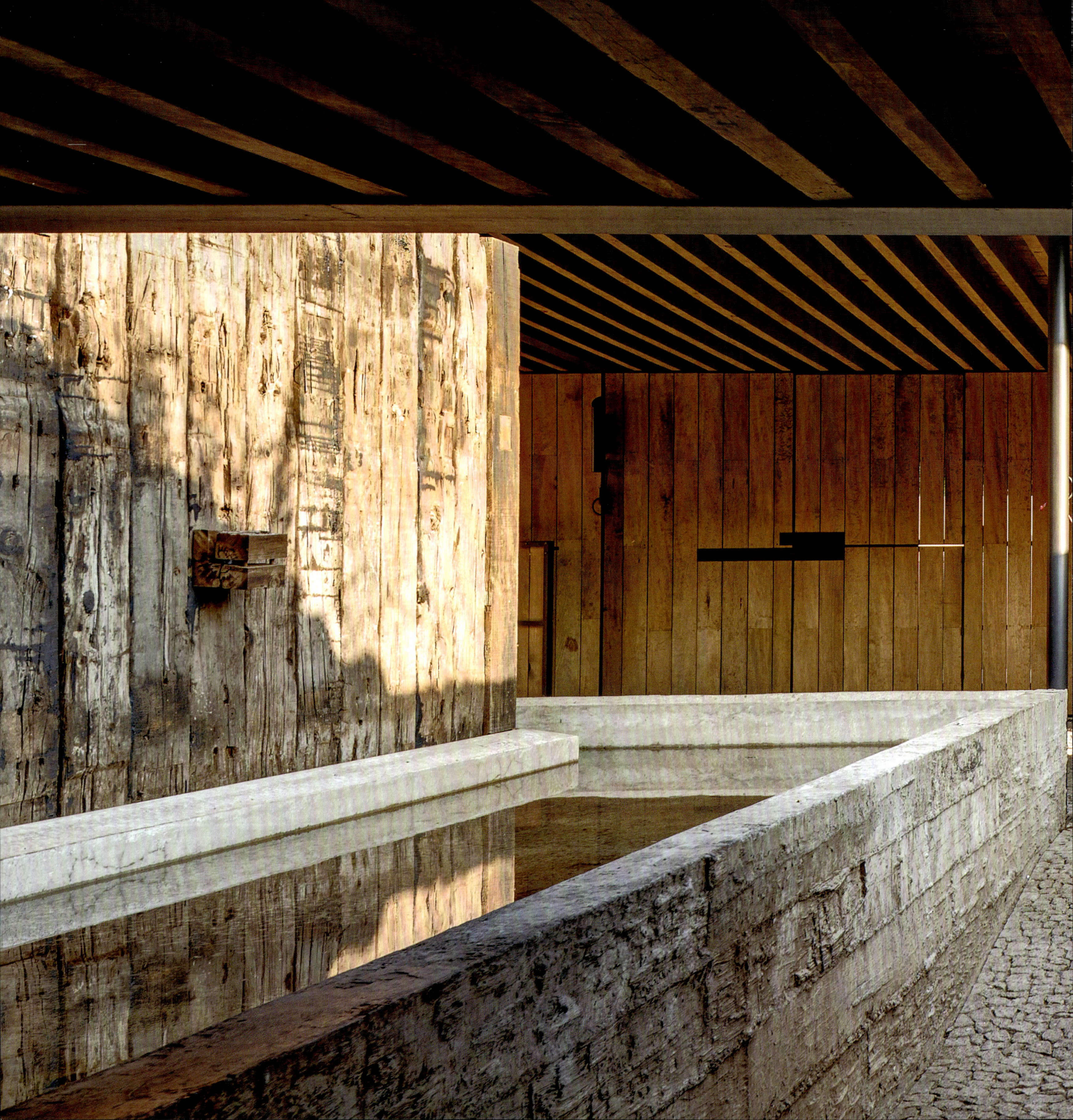

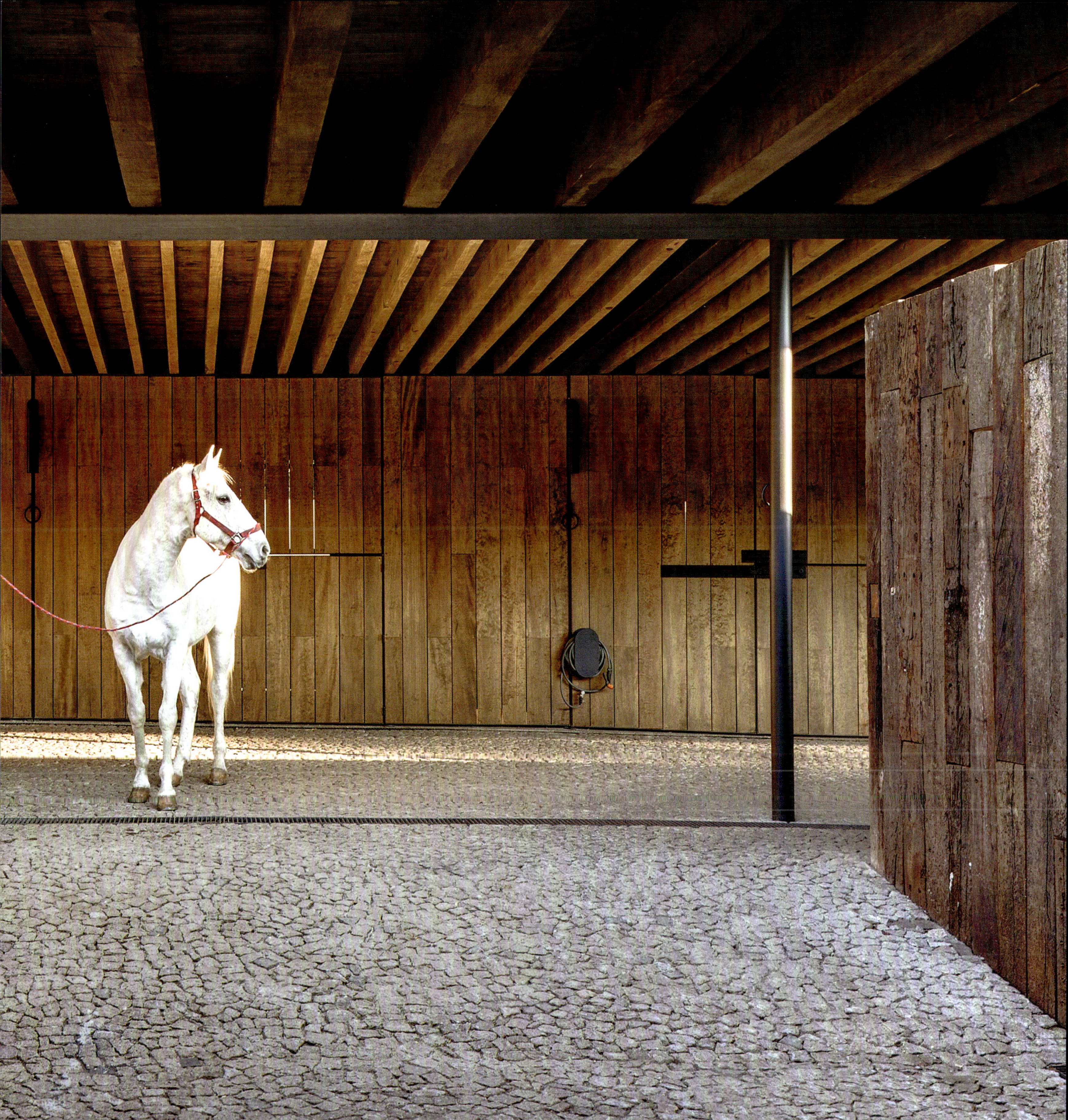

226 MANUEL CERVANTES ESTUDIO

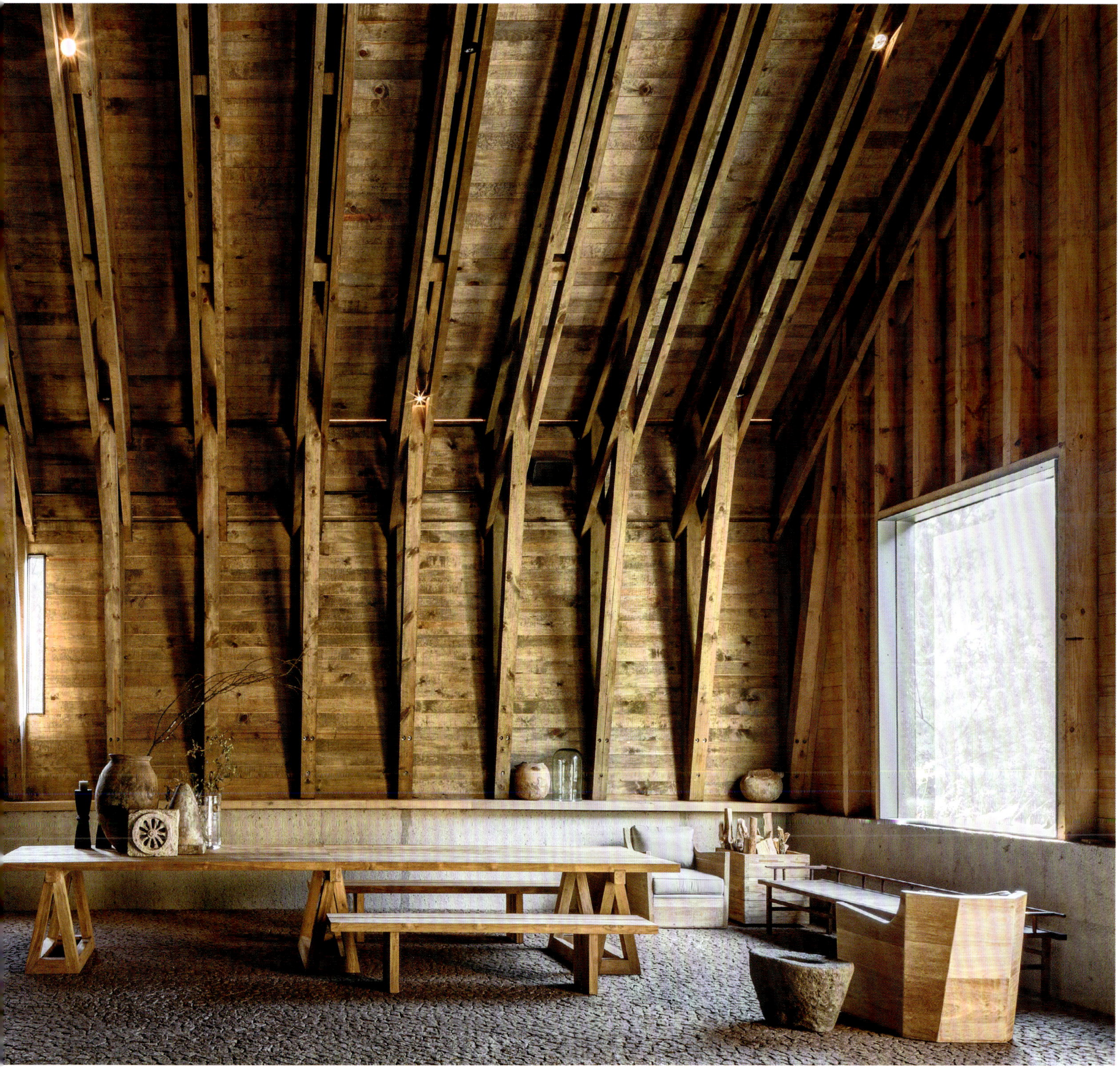

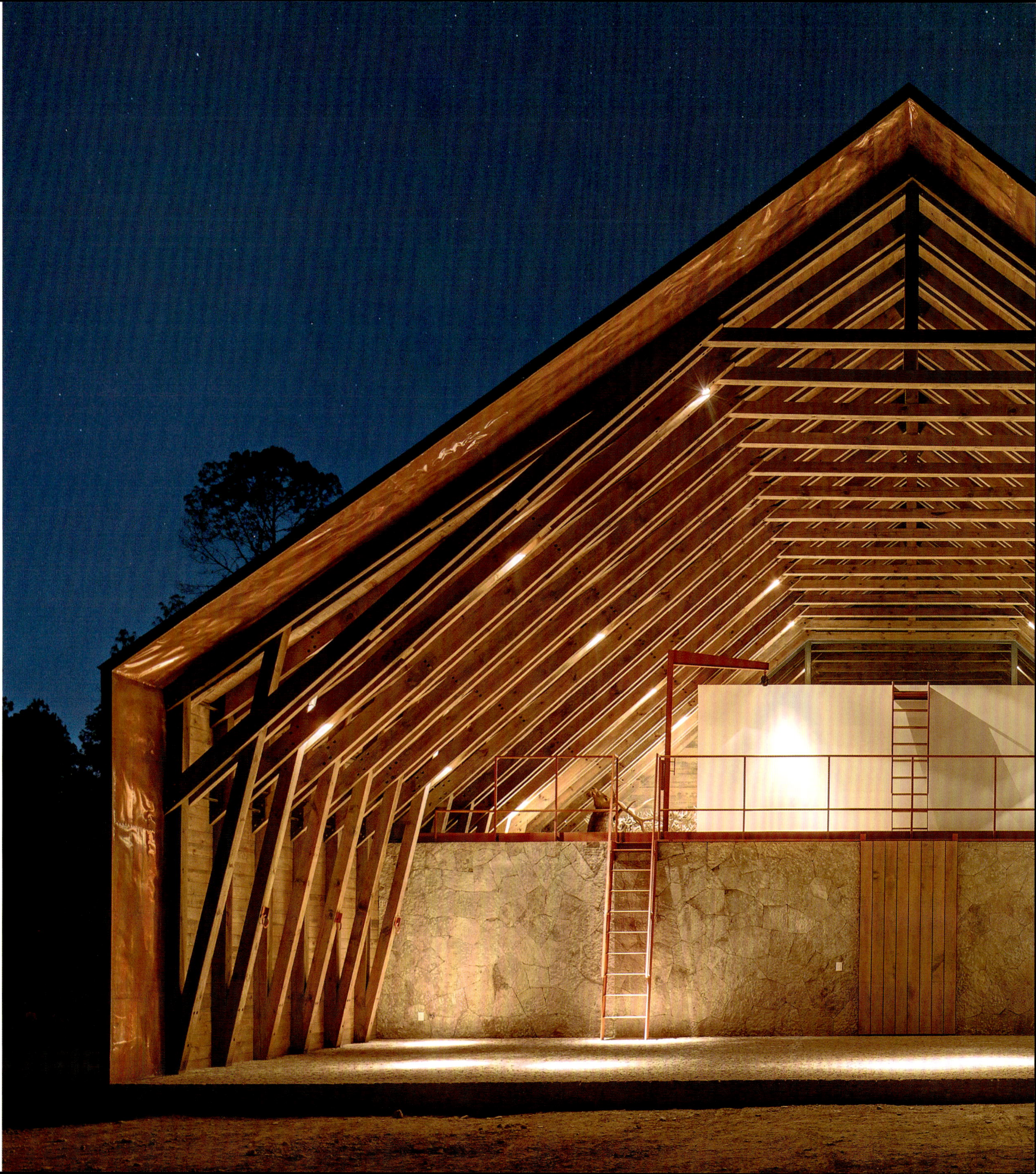

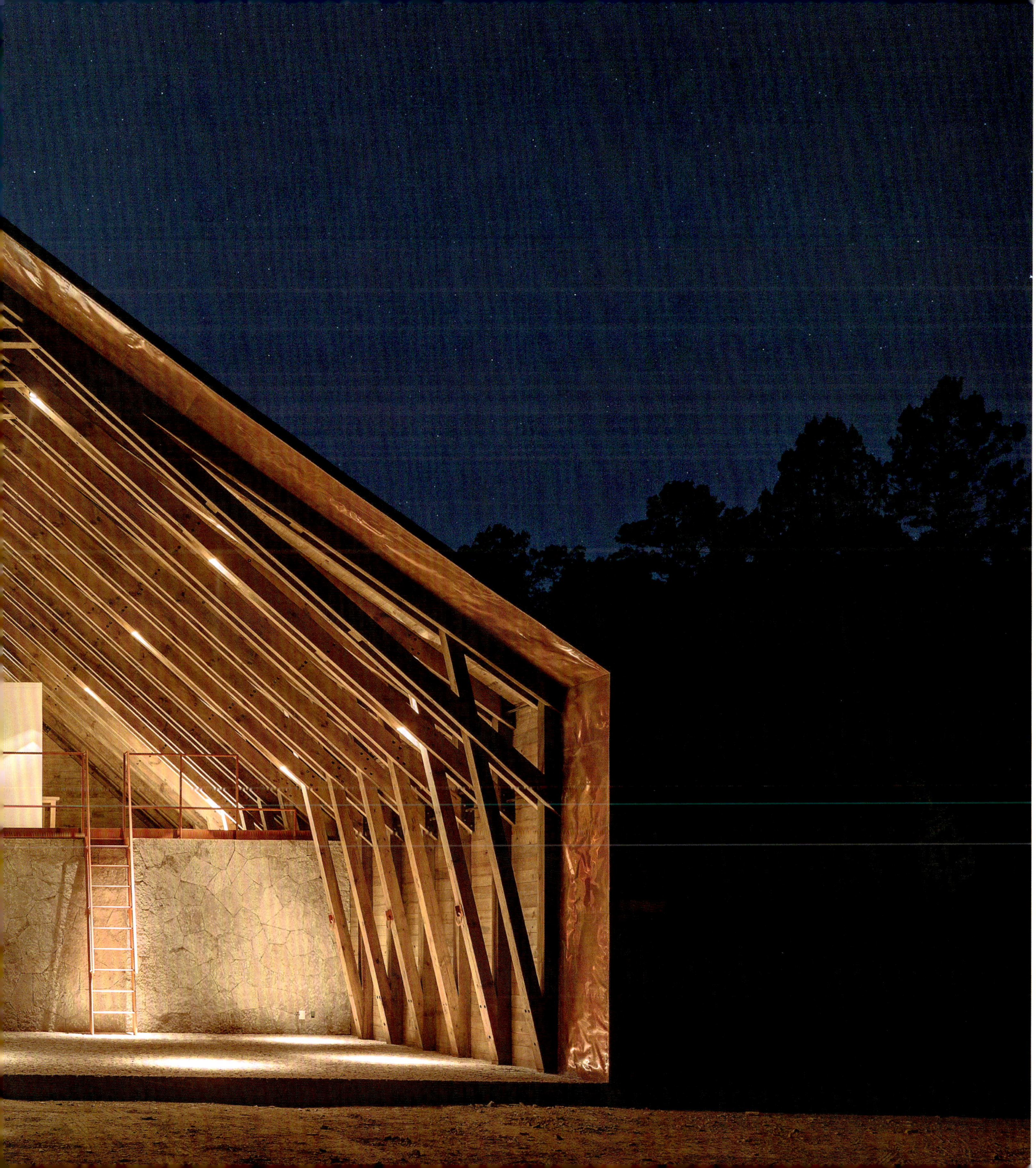

Kekkapää Stables
POOK Architects

Espoo, Finland

Building Area:
120 m²

Site Area:
8 hectares

Architect in Charge:
Pentti Raiski, Katariina Rautiala

Project Team:
ET Suunnittelu Ltd, HVAC: Hevacplan Ltd,
Electricity: JT-Sähkötekniikka Ltd

Photographer:
Kuvio Oy

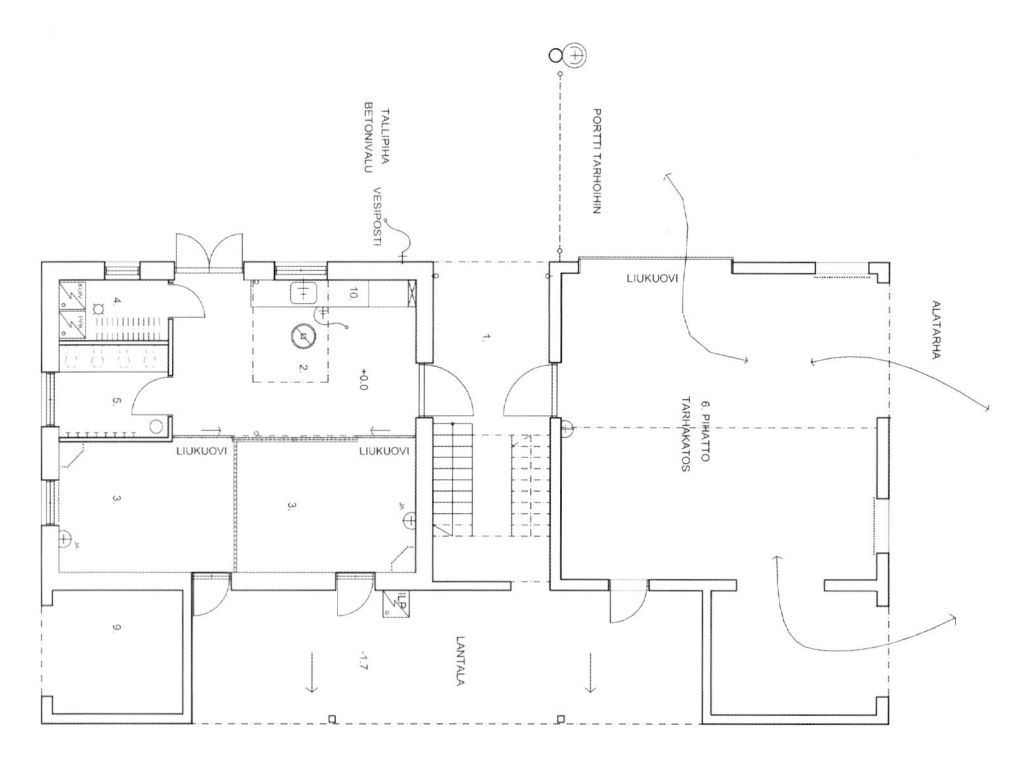

Plan

This simple and modest stable building is situated in a highly valued landscape in rural Espoo, a city on the outskirts of Helsinki, Finland. Horse management is a significant component of the region's local agriculture. The area has many small stables and well-connected riding trails throughout the countryside. Horse keeping, for its part, allows for the preservation of the landscape for cultivation and grazing. Wood is also a natural building material for the area. The Kekkapää Stables is a small private stable that also includes a track area for cross country training. The aim of the project was to nestle the simple rectangular building in the picturesque landscape; its long facade following the direction of the forest edge, bringing the building's sloped gable into the woods. In additional to the landscape, the siting created wind shelters in the outdoor spaces to protect against the prevailing southwestern winds. The massing is based on the steep, a-centric gabled roof, under which all the central functions are located. The plan of the building paid special attention to the ease of everyday activities and durability of building parts. In horse keeping everyday chores are repetitive; smooth organization for feeding, cleaning and horse care are essential. The free-range area and stables are linked directly to the forest pasture, care locations are multifunctional and close by, the manure storage area opens out directly from the stalls and the free-range area, and the riding arena and connections to riding trails are in the courtyard. The aim was to avoid unnecessary walking distances. All horizontal structures and cladding were built with conifer wood. Sturdy floor planks were directly attached to a laminated timber floor structure. This achieved a simple structure, gave the room height, and provided a natural stratification of warmth. The wooden-lattice structure ceiling is insulated with cellulose wool and ventilated from the gable. Sturdy tongue-and-groove spruce boards were used for the facade and interior cladding. The stalls and free-range areas that are exposed to direct wear from use by horses are primarily of steel or concrete. Unimpregnated wood was also used liberally in interior cladding because of the material's hygroscopic characteristics. The management of fluctuations in humidity and maintaining functional ventilation in the stable area are important to the horse's well-being. Ventilation is primarily pressure force ventilation, with an option to increase efficiency using mechanical venting. Heat generated from the horses is used in the stable spaces to supplement heating generated by hot air pumps, which are also used to decrease humidity as necessary.

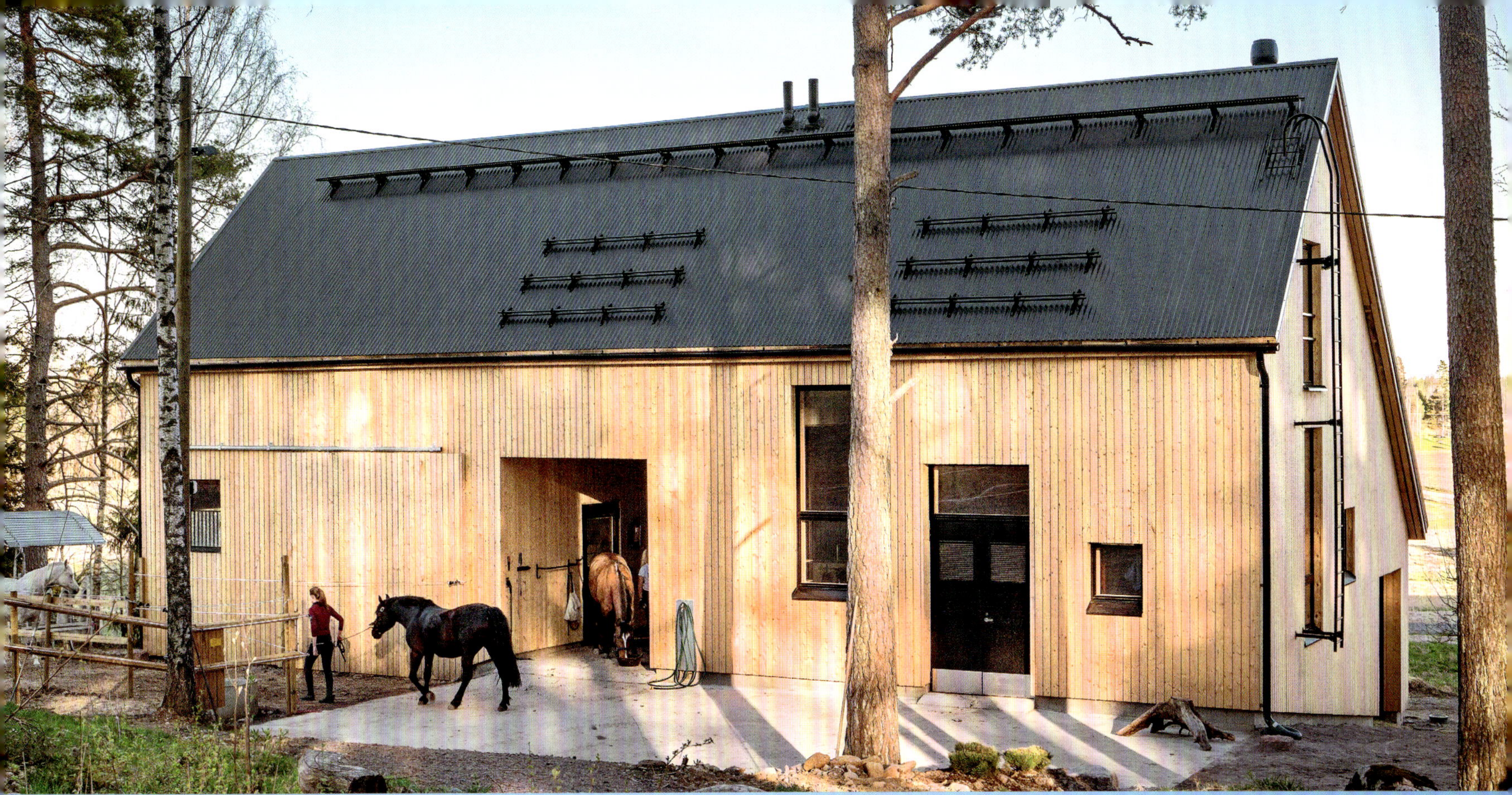

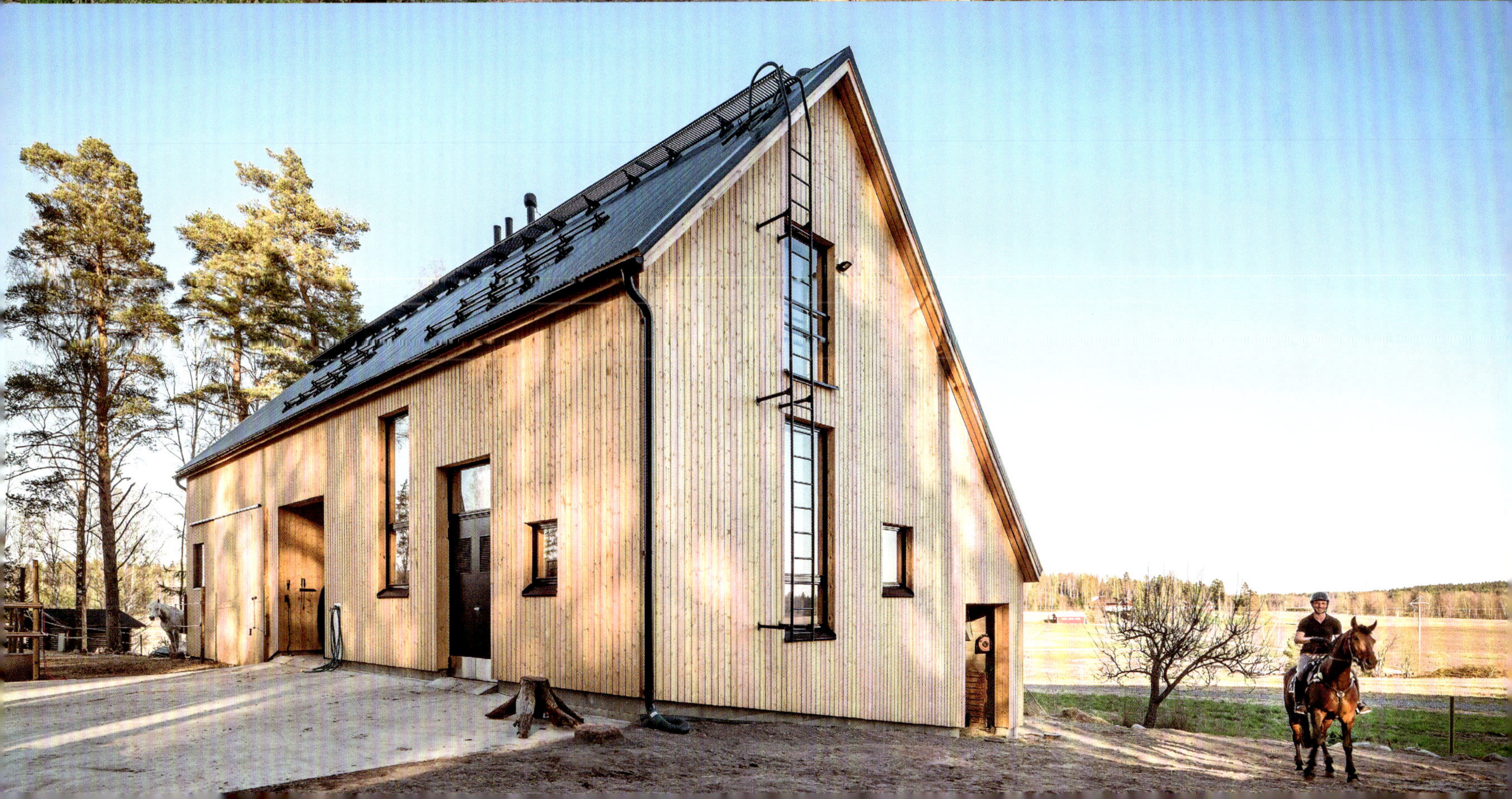

POOK ARCHITECTS

KEKKAPÄÄ STABLES 235

Caballerizas Sanint

Simón Vélez, Felipe Sanint, Marcelo Villegas

Pereira, Colombia

Building Area:
648 m²

Site Area:
52 hectares

Architect in Charge:
Simón Vélez, Felipe Sanint, Marcelo Villegas

Project Team:
Stefana Simic

Photographer:
Nicolas Cabrera Visual

1. ESPEJO DE AGUA.
2. PICAPASTO.
3. BODEGA ALIMENTO.
4. SILLERO
5. CABALLERIZAS.
6. HABITACIÓN.
7. BAÑO.

Plan

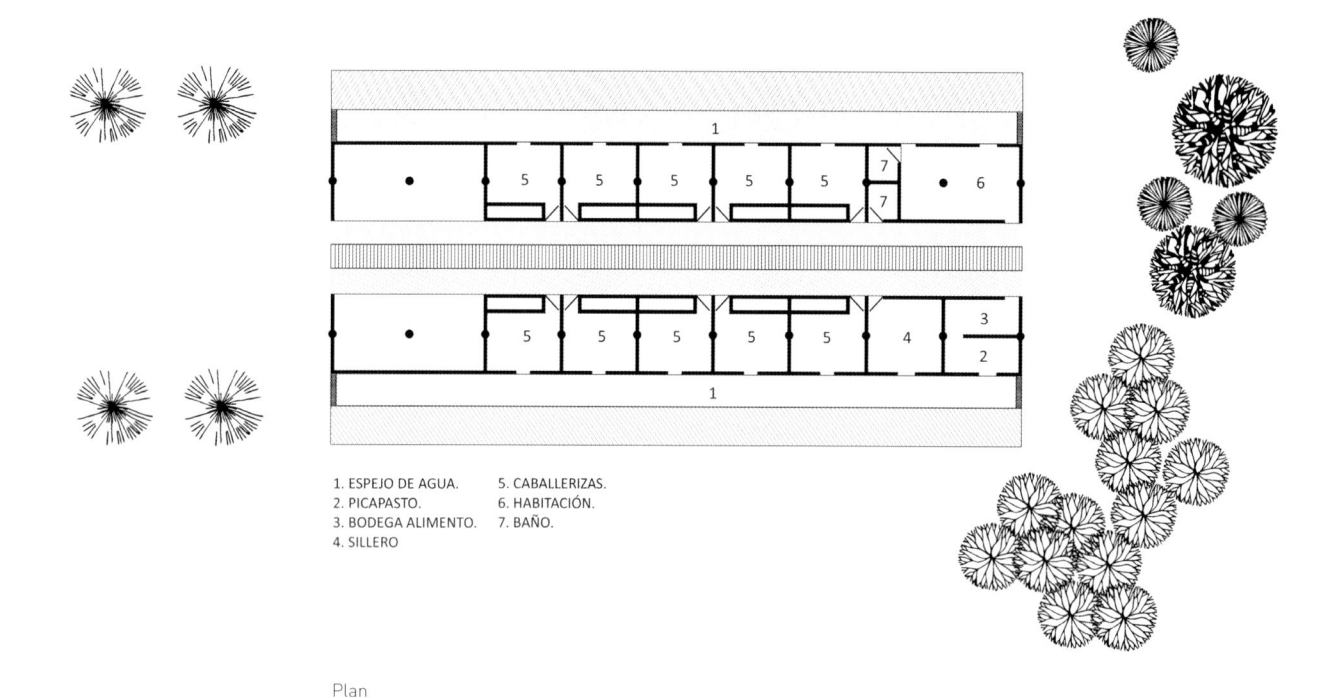

The Caballerizas is an open stables pavilion located in a lush agricultural region on the outskirts of the city of Pereira, Colombia, an area famous for its coffee-growing and production. Situated in the foothill of the Andes, the landscape is both mountainous and tropical, with bucolic rolling hills, rows of palm trees swaying on the horizon, and patches of dense vegetation that contrast with the open fields for farming. The simple yet beautiful rectangular structure sits on an open knoll and consists of approximately 10 stables with a central aisle and open service area at one end, all beneath a massive wood and tile gable roof supported by dendriform (tree-like) bamboo columns that spring from rows of circular concrete pillars. The branching columns support a series of curvilinear beams, cross-beams, and rafters with deep projecting eaves that extend well beyond the interior stalls below and give the impression that the roof is actually undulating like a pagoda. The low walls of the building are all made of concrete as well and have delicately curved corners to protect the horses from any unnecessary injury. Narrow vertically slit windows in the stalls allow the horses to peer out from the structure as if their heads were mounted on a wall for honorific display. Continuous water channels on each long side provide a cooling effect to the stables and reflect the building's clever structure, if not the striking horses themselves. Inside, horizontal wooden slats divide the stalls from the central aisle and allow the feed and water troughs below to be filled as necessary. The central aisle and perimeter terraces are made of poured concrete slabs with incised herringbone patterns that provide appropriate friction for the horses. The rustic yet cleverly conceived and detailed Caballerizas Sanint reminds us that architecture is the art of building and that human artifice and invention can flourish in the simplest of programs and siting, and in the careful selection and fitting together of materials. The ancient Roman writer Vitruvius argued that the art of architecture emerged from the primitive hut, and I sincerely believe that this is what he had in mind.

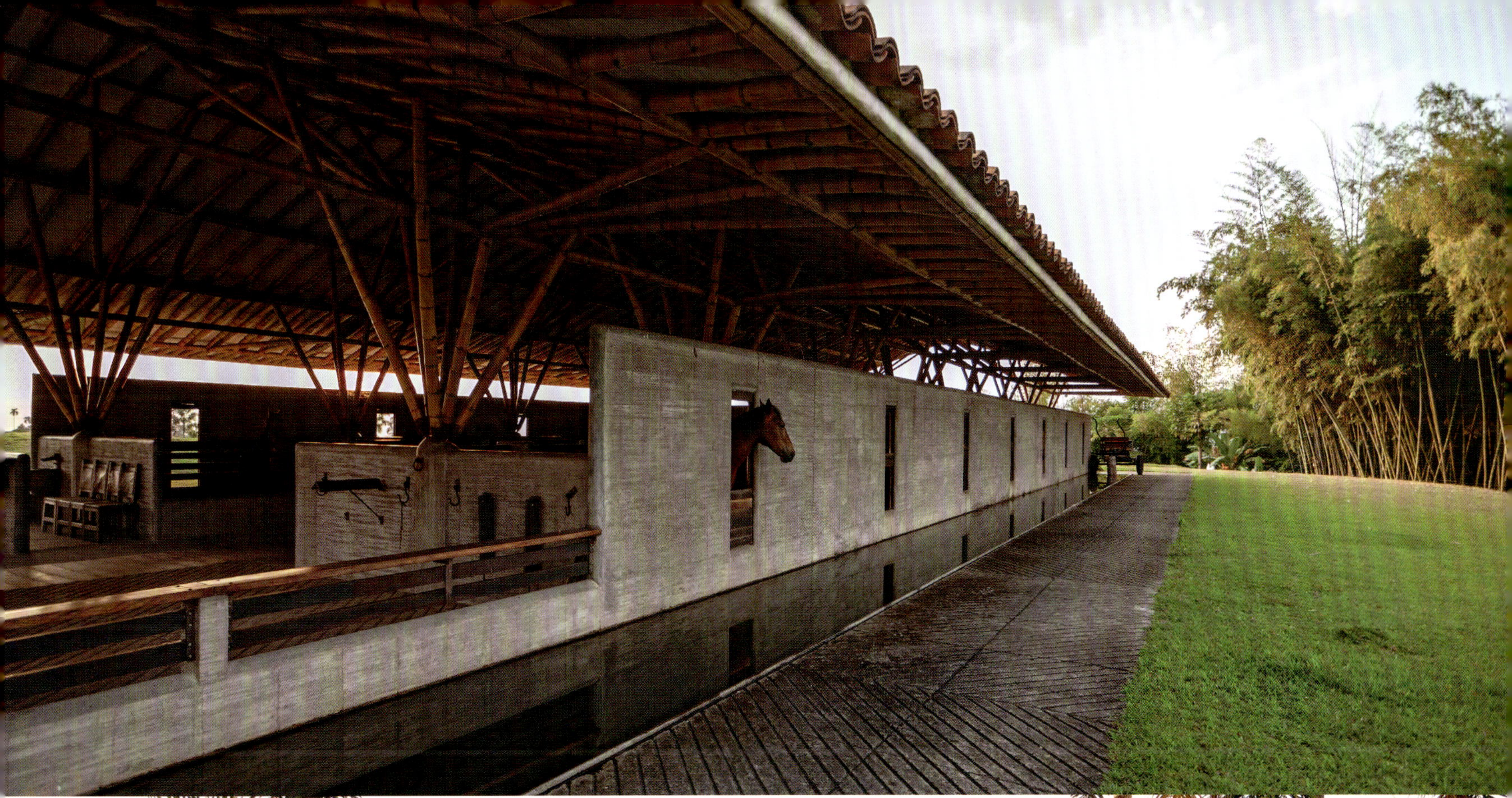
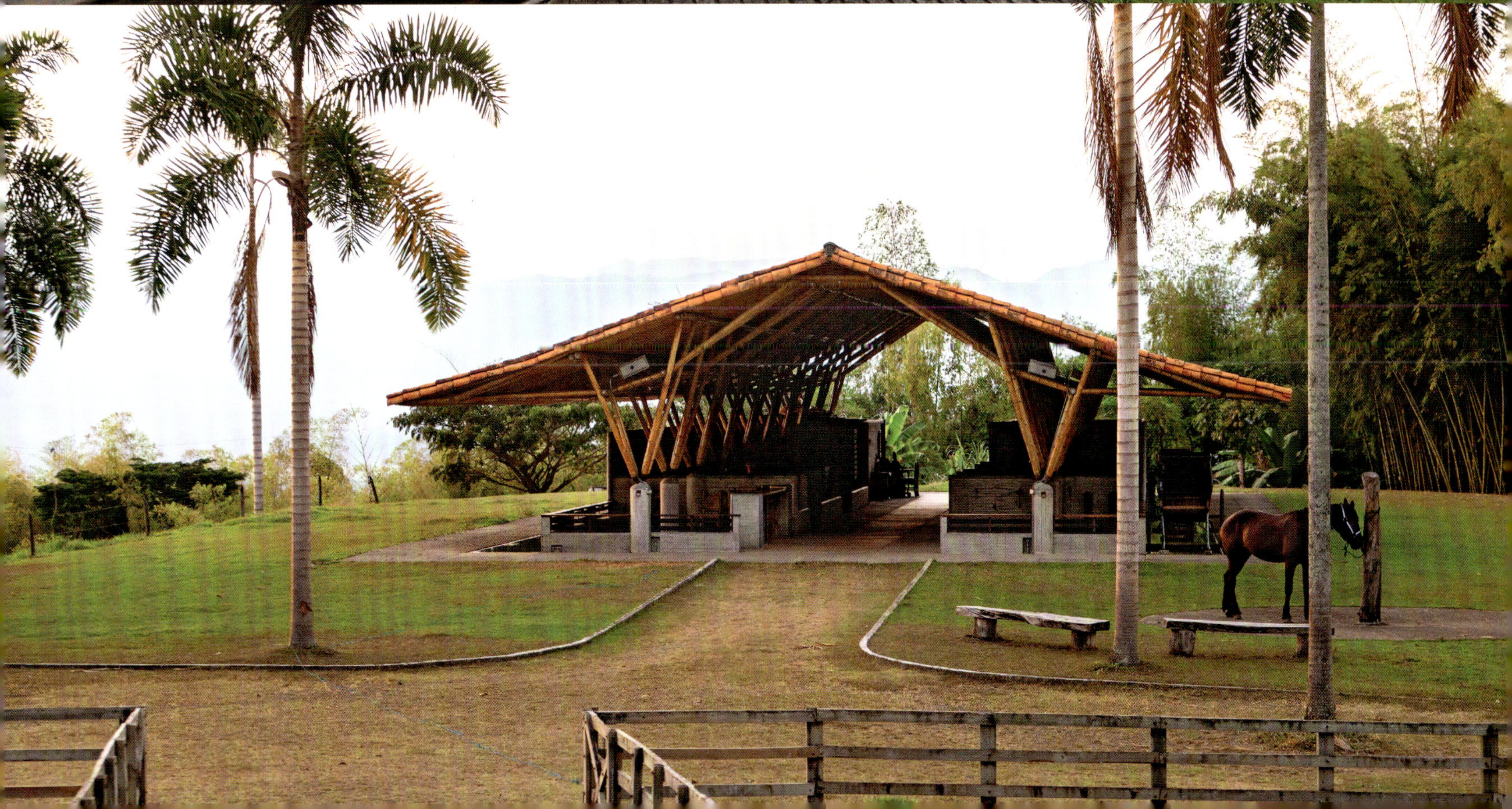

240 SIMÓN VÉLEZ, FELIPE SANINT, MARCELO VILLEGAS

CABALLERIZAS SANINT 241

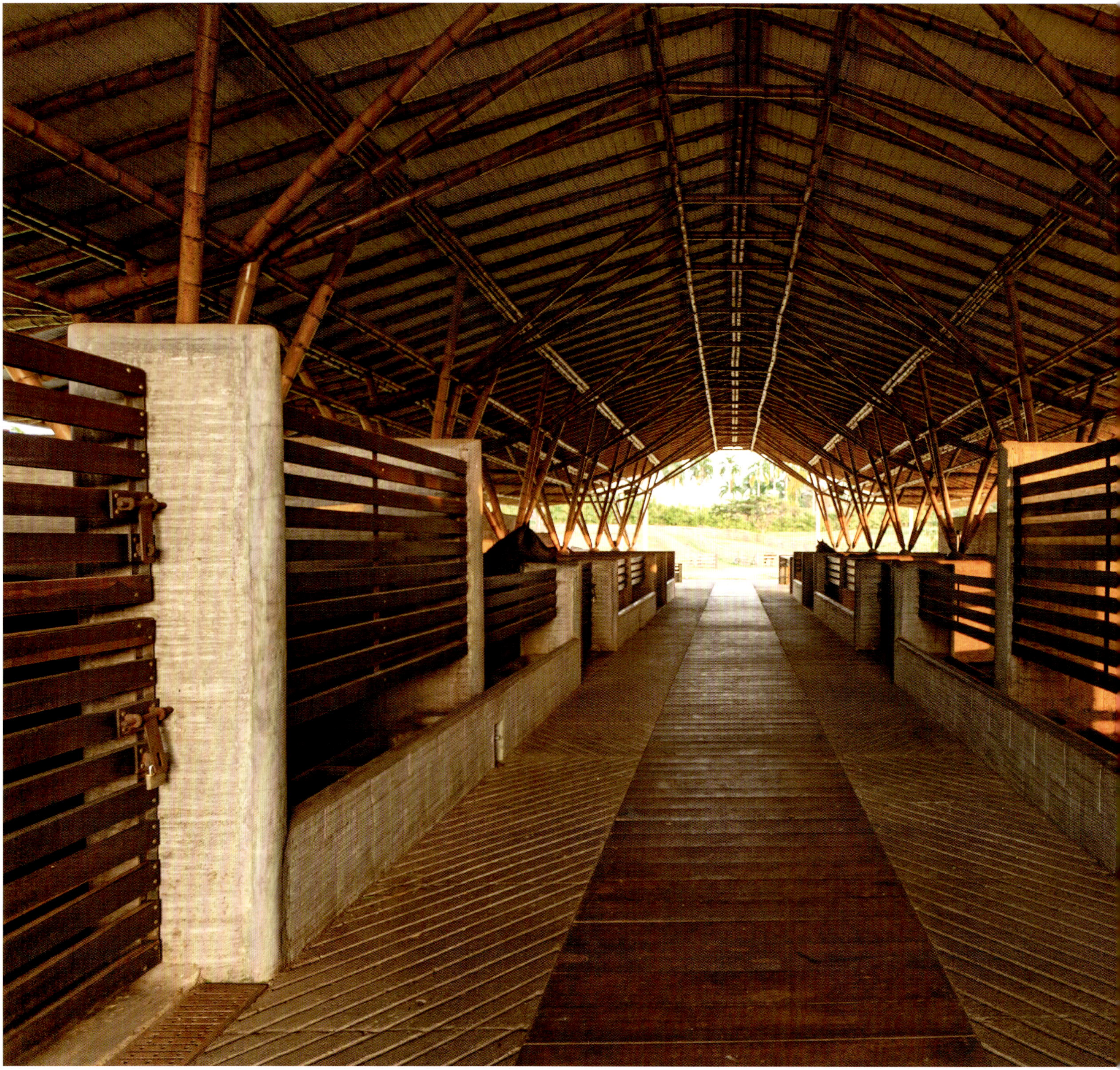

CABALLERIZAS SANINT **243**

244 SIMÓN VÉLEZ, FELIPE SANINT, MARCELO VILLEGAS

CABALLERIZAS SANINT

Hípica La Llena
Vicente Sarrablo + Jaume Colom

La Llacuna, Barcelona, Spain

Building Area:
1,245.06 m²

Site Area:
5 hectares

Architect in Charge:
Vicente Sarrablo, Jaume Colom

Project Team:
Pere Riba, Jordi Riba

Interior Designer:
Vicente Sarrablo, Jaume Colom

Landscape Designer:
Vicente Sarrablo, Jaume Colom

Photographer:
José Hevia

Plan

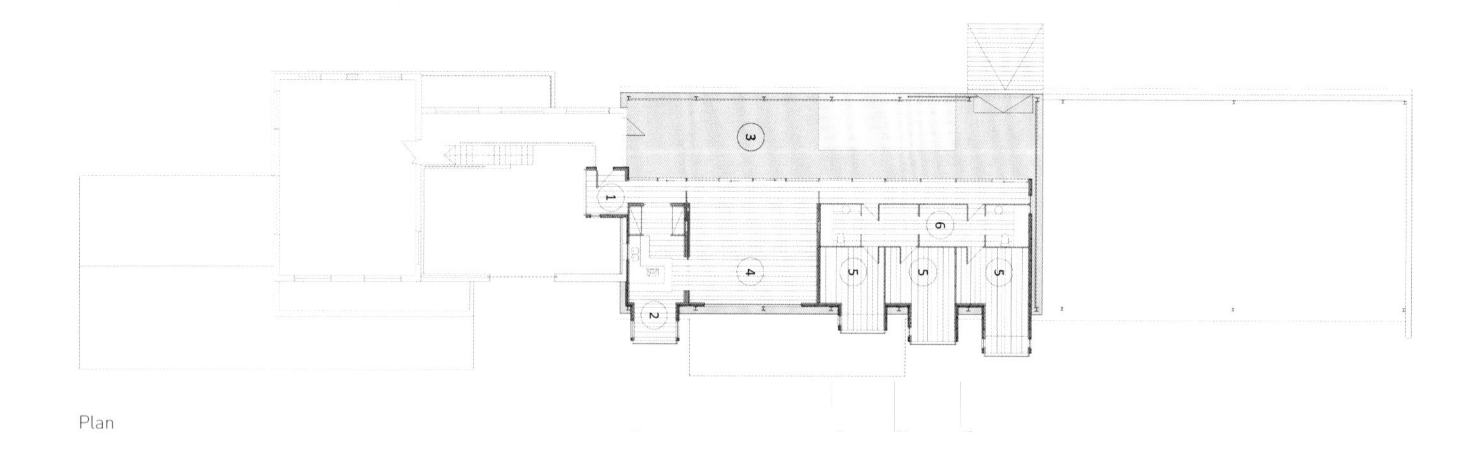

Hípica La Llena is an equestrian center located on the outskirts of the rural village of La Llacuna, in the province of Barcelona, Spain, that came about from the transformation of an existing rustic stable building into a new combined modern residence and horse stable. By adding a new large pitched metal roof, the architects were able to insert a new house in the upper part of the stable building in the space previously occupied by the hayloft. A vast covered terrace faces south, thus moving the house to the north façade, turning it into an overhanging modernist dwelling that looks out over the circular training rink and large outdoor riding arena. The house has a ventilated cool roof that takes advantage of the space between the existing upper surface of the pitched roof and a new plywood roof underneath that adapts to the shape of the metal trusses. This new roof offers a double curve that is concave in the living and dining room, and convex in the three bedrooms and kitchen. The final part of the structure is a floor-length window with spectacular views of the equestrian center below. CNC cut laminated wood panels were used for the partition and support walls as well as the curved ceiling. The outer finish of the walls employs the same autoclave treated wood that surrounds the original barn. Inside, the wood is left as it is, with a distressed paint finish on the vertical partitions and a transparent varnish on the ceiling. The stables are located beneath the house in the original barn structure, with adjacent paddocks, and a vast open hay storage that is kept underneath the shed extension provided by the new roof. Throughout this book we have considered several contemporary architectural projects that have focused on the unique theme of living with horses—or even living beneath them—but this project, more than anything, explores the rare possibility of living above them, like very distinct barn cats.

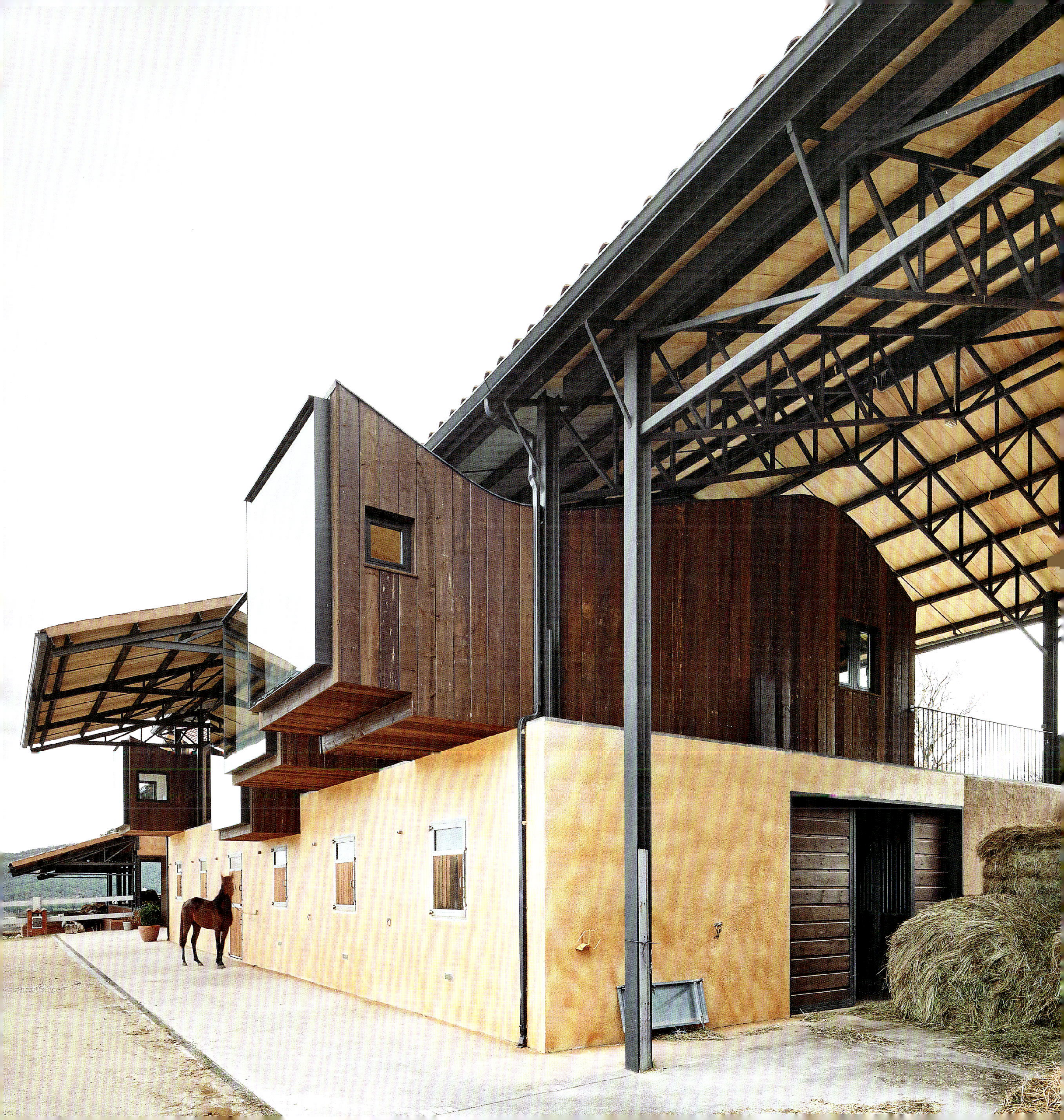

VICENTE SARRABLO + JAUME COLOM

HÍPICA LA LLENA 251

Cutting Horse Ranch
Lake|Flato in association with gh2 Gralla Architects

Weatherford, Texas, United States

Building Area:
7,432 m^2

Site Area:
175 acres

Architect in Charge:
David Lake, Ted Flato

Project Team:
Ted Flato, Bill Aylor, Ryan Jones, Cameron Smith, Raina Tilden, Lewis McNeel

Landscape Designer:
MESA Design Group

Photographer:
Frank Ooms

Key
1. Arena
2. Walker
3. Hydrotherapy
4. Training Barn
5. Mare Barn

Plan

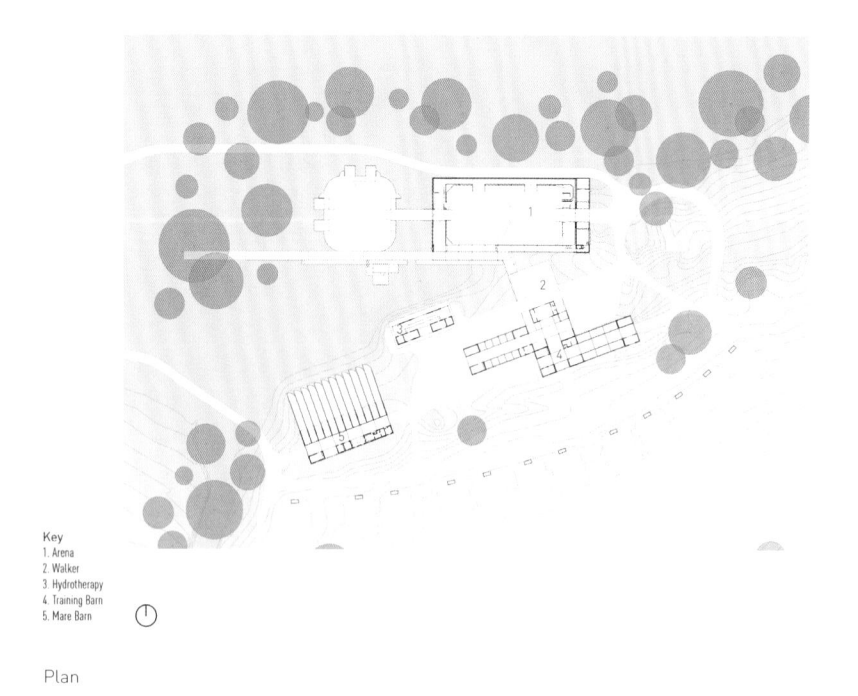

The Cutting Horse Ranch is a large equestrian complex for the care, training, and breeding of cutting horses (trained for working with cattle), situated in the Cross Timbers plains of Texas, on the outskirts of the town of Weatherford just west of Fort Worth. The vast property contains 75 acres of pastures, roads, and trails for riding, both indoor and outdoor arenas, horse barns, cattle pens, paddocks, and additional structures for hydrotherapy, horse walking, and other related services such as tack room, vet space, wash areas, storage, and offices. The complex is situated adjacent to a tree-lined creek that provides protection from the north wind, with the barns, pens, arenas, and paddocks taking advantage of the views and breezes from the south. The large indoor and outdoor riding arenas are cut into the sloping section of the site minimizing their height and impact on the landscape. The horse barns, walker, and hydrotherapy shed are located on an angle to the arenas parallel with the downward slope of the site, with paddocks radiating in a gentle curve along the slope. The arena and barns are connected by a continuous ramp—covered by a gable—that also contains a long water trough adjacent to the outdoor arena and gathering pavilion, while the hydrotherapy barn is a free-standing structure between the two. The horse barn contains 22 stalls on either side of a central aisle, and the mare barn consists of 12 stalls with walkout pens. The buildings all adopt the classic barn shape, though instead of being timber, they are all made of exposed steel clad in perforated corrugated metal which provides both natural light and ventilation as well as eliminating the need for operable windows. The office and other air-conditioned spaces are clad in wood and galvanized metal. Several loafing sheds are spread around the fields, and wooden fences provide an appropriate familiarity to the rolling pastures. Seen from a distance, one would hardly know that underneath the classic gable shapes lies a very subtle and nuanced modernist sensibility.

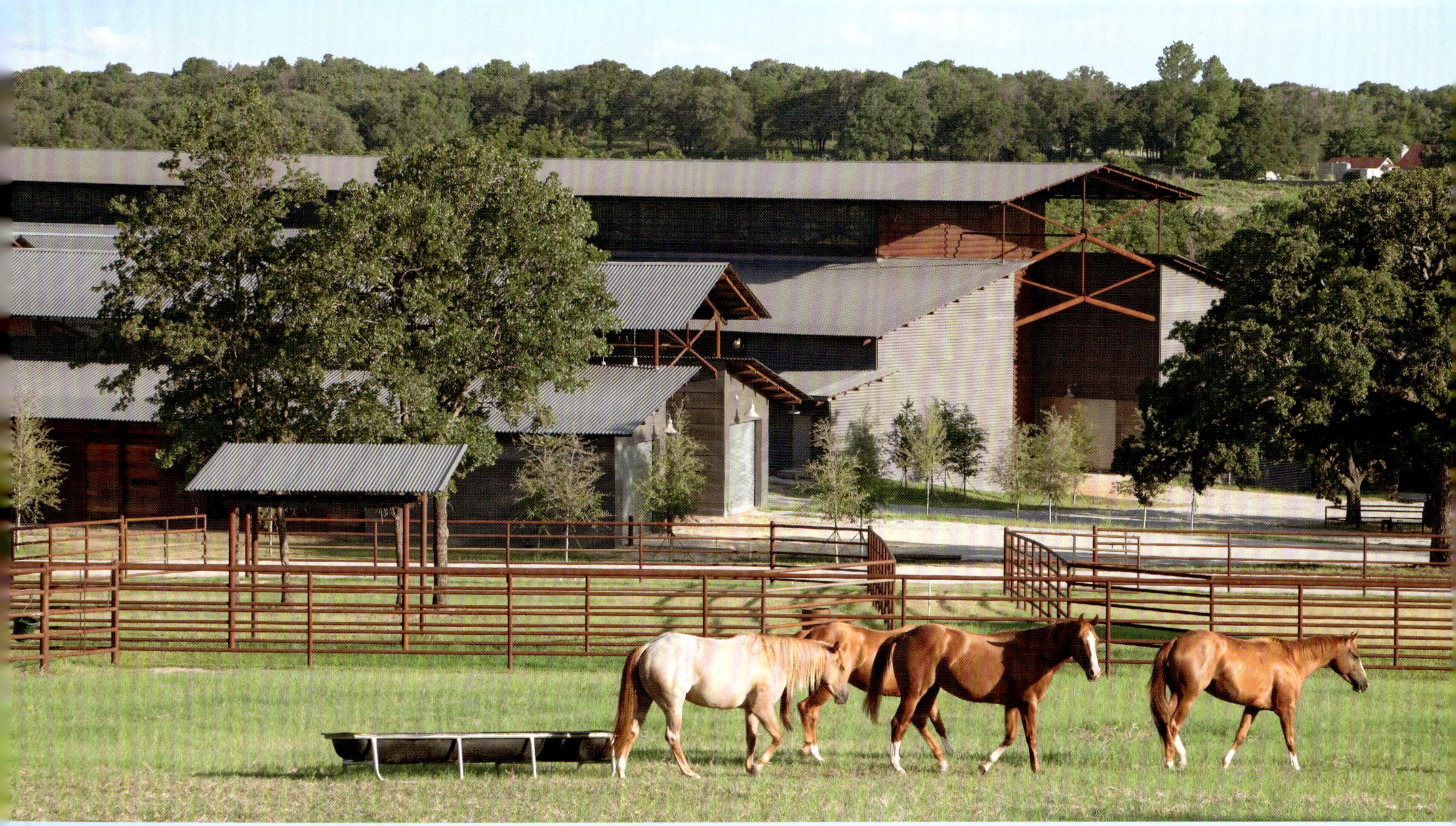
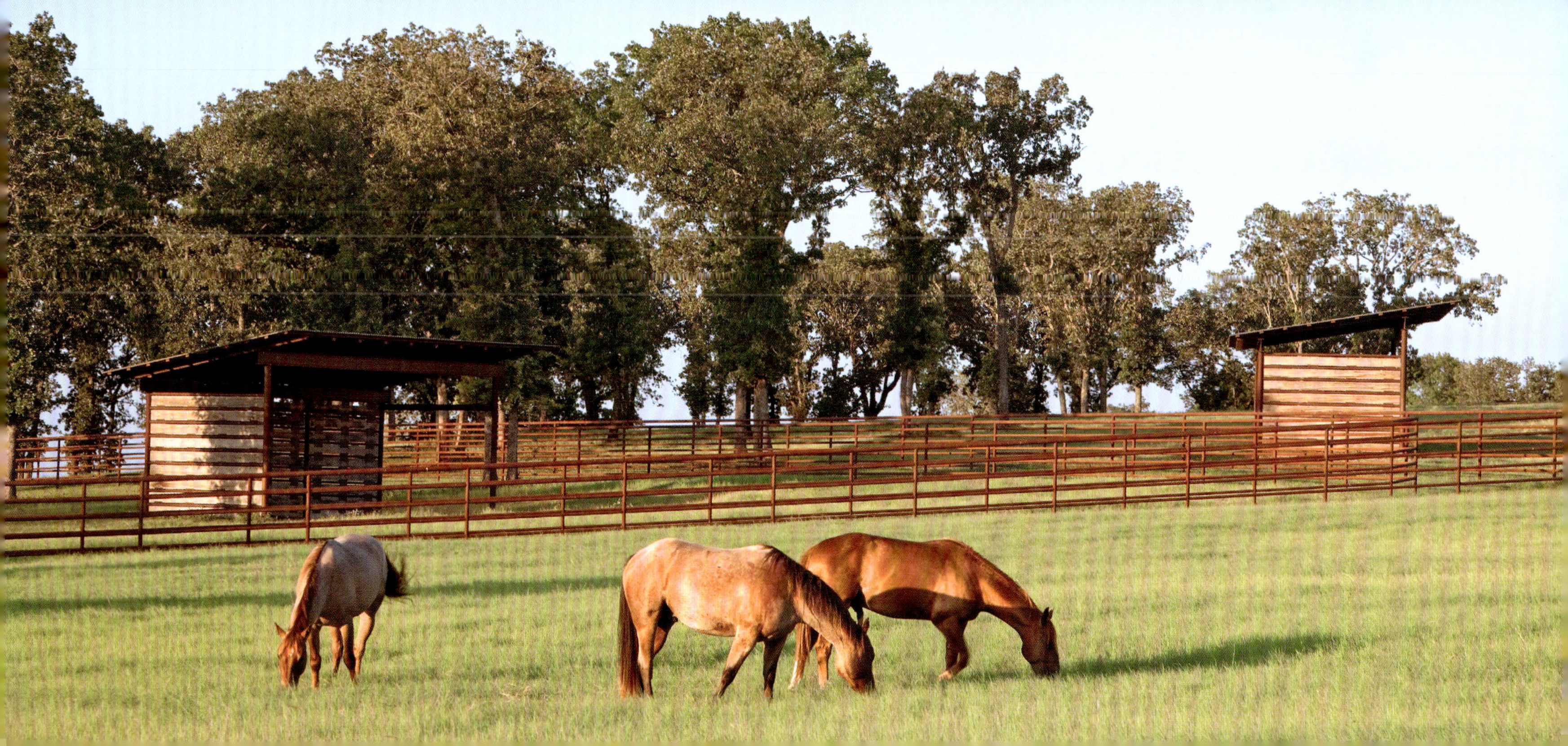

256 LAKE|FLATO IN ASSOCIATION WITH GH2 GRALLA ARCHITECTS

CUTTING HORSE RANCH 257

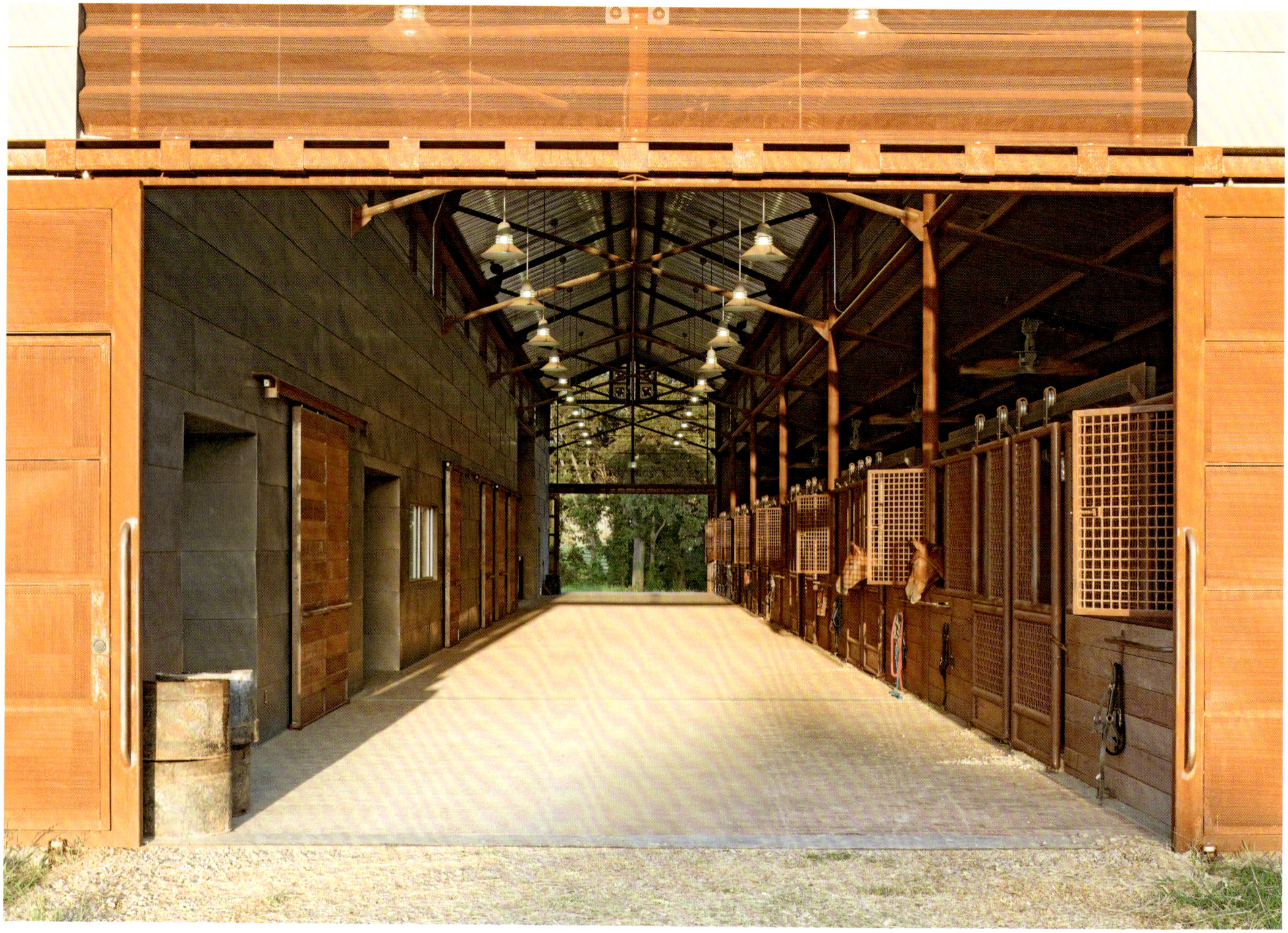

CUTTING HORSE RANCH **259**

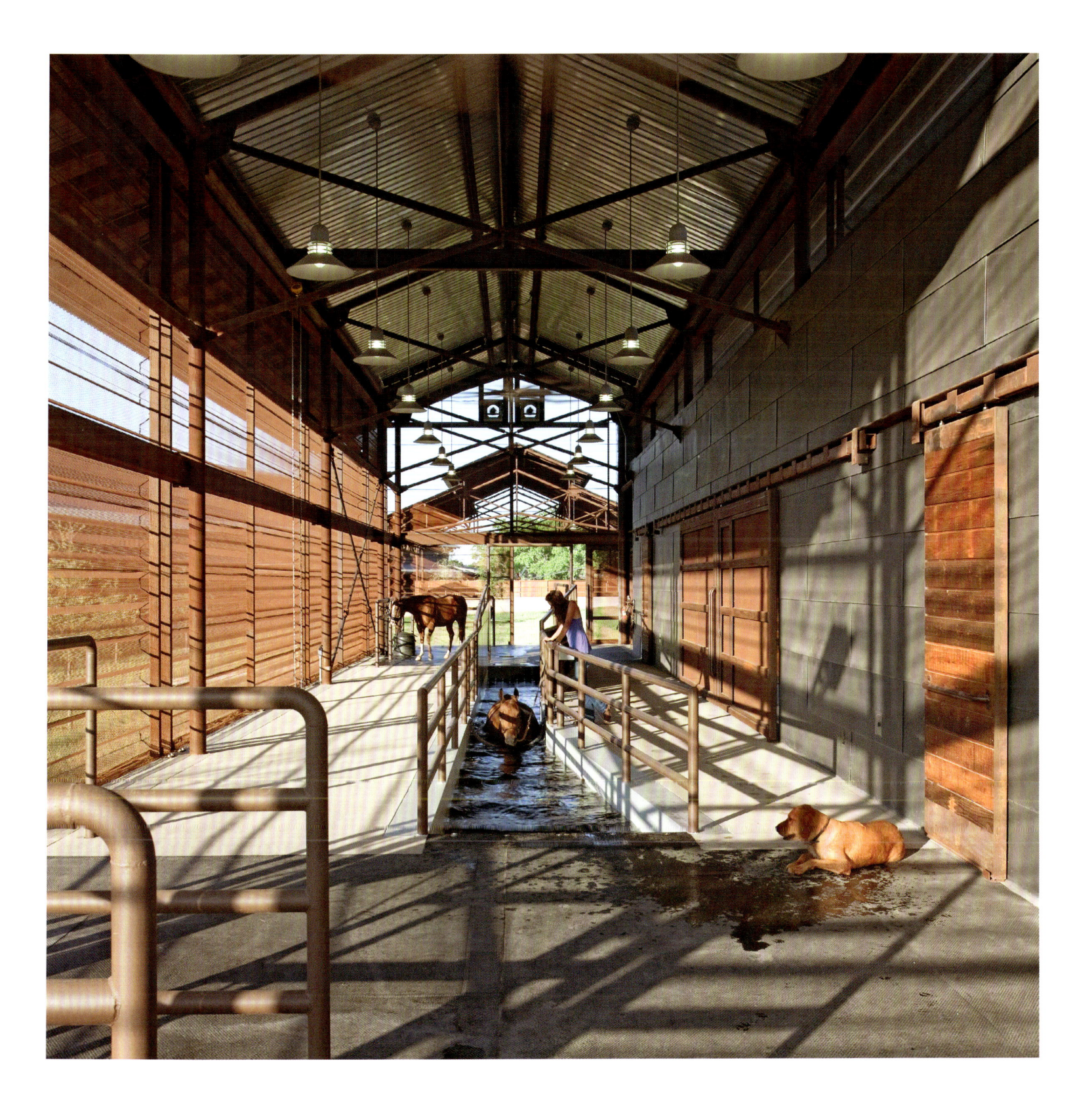

260 LAKE|FLATO IN ASSOCIATION WITH GH2 GRALLA ARCHITECTS

CUTTING HORSE RANCH **261**

APPENDIX

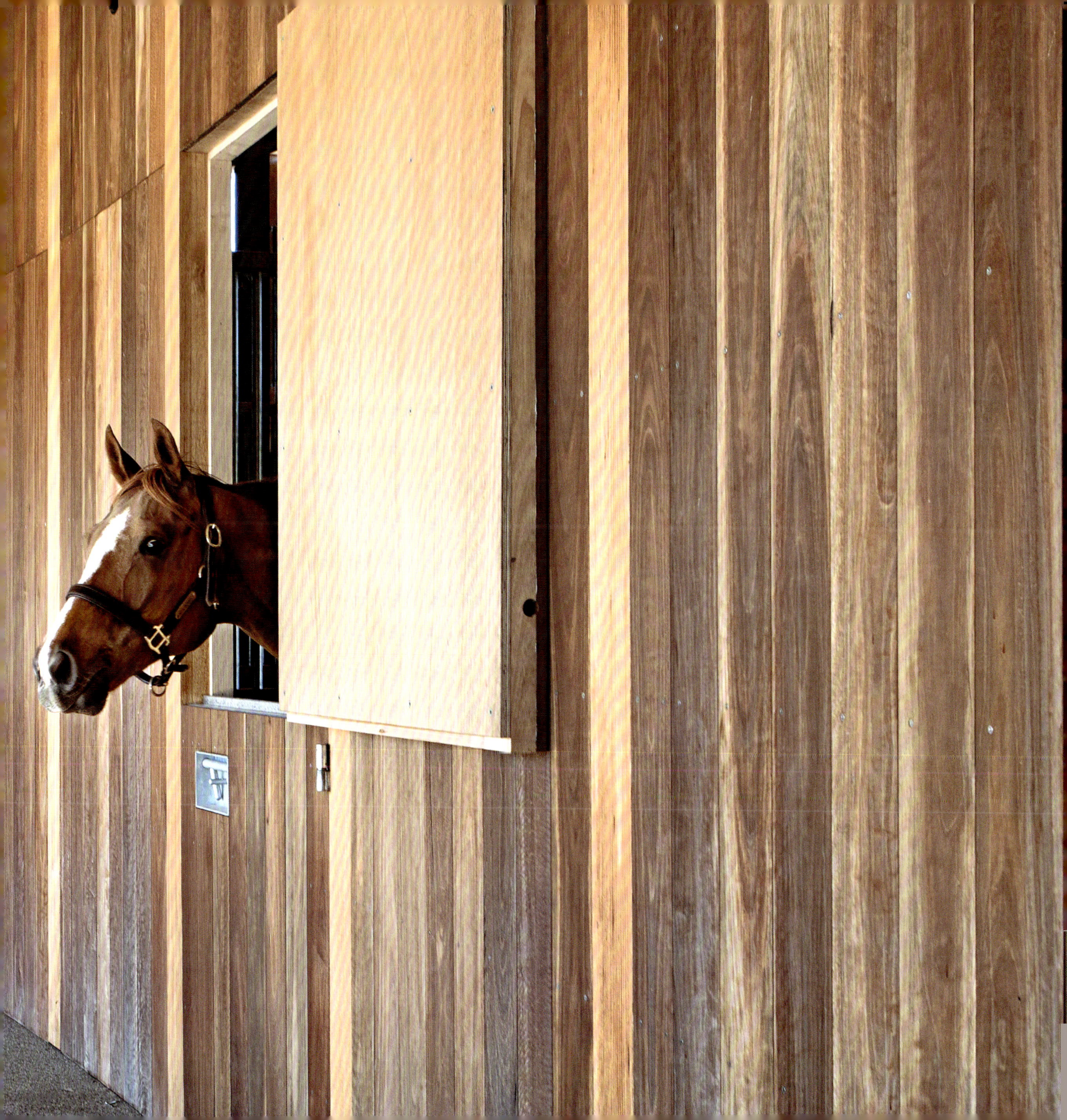

ARCHITECTS' PROFILES

BLACKBURN, JOHN is the President and Senior Principal of the firm Blackburn Architects, which he founded in 1995 in Washington, DC. John has over 40 years of experience, having received his Master of Architecture and Urban Design degree from Washington University in St. Louis in 1972. John's experience includes the management of a full range of project types and services, including programming, existing facility evaluation and master planning, new construction, adaptive reuse, and historic preservation. A renowned worldwide leader in the design of healthy and sustainable equestrian facilities, John's projects range from polo barns and thoroughbred-training facilities to therapeutic riding centers and private ranches.

BUCHANAN, RICHARD D., AIA, co-founded Archer & Buchanan Architecture in 1996 with a focus on custom residential design and country property planning. Born into a family of horsemen and veterinarians, Richard enjoys equestrian facility design, drawing on his extensive personal experience and knowledge for an on-point approach. Always keeping practicality and animal well-being at the forefront, Richard marries functionality with regional character in design that becomes more beautiful with age.

CARTER, JAMES F. is known for his unique approach to beautiful, confident, and visionary architecture, epitomizing the grace and generosity that comes, in part, from living in the American South. After graduating from Auburn University, James established his own firm in 1994, which since then has become nationally recognized for doing things the "old-fashioned way." The firm is respected by his peers as "clever in a subtle way," and beloved by his clients throughout the Southern, mid-Atlantic and Northeast regions. Originally from Monroeville, Alabama, James excels in sophisticated ease and his designs exude decorum and comfort.

CASTANHEIRA, CARLOS graduated in architecture from the School of Fine Arts of Porto, and the Academy of Architecture in Amsterdam. In 1993 he founded the practice Carlos Castanheira & Clara Bastai, Arquitectos in Porto with Maria Clara Bastai. Working mainly in the private sector, he has also participated in several competitions, presented in conferences, has been involved in setting up architectural courses and workshops, curated and organized exhibitions, and has edited and published several books and catalogues. Since the time he was a student, he has been collaborating with the Portuguese architect Álvaro Siza in various projects in Portugal and abroad.

CERVANTES CESPEDES, MANUEL graduated in architecture from the Anahuac University in Mexico, and in 2004 founded MANUEL CERVANTES CESPEDES/ CC ARQUITECTOS. In 2006 his firm began to focus on urban projects and mass transport, leading to research around multimodal transfer centers and transit oriented developments. He has designed projects for institutes such as the Mexican federal institute for worker's housing, and other government agencies, as well as urban and architectural projects throughout the Americas. He has given workshops and conferences in several universities in Mexico, the United States, Spain and Portugal, and has also been honored with national and international awards.

COLOM, JAUME AND SARRABLO MORENO, VICENTE have been working jointly since 2003. Their work has been published in several specialized journals and blogs including Archdaily, Tectonica, ConArquitectura, Detail, and Costruire in Laterizio. They have also obtained several awards such as selection to the 2016 Spanish Biennial of Architecture and Urbanism for the "Barcelona Ceramics Exhibition" in which they received the prize for "Flexbrick, ceramic textile," the Prize Technal for "La Llena, Equestrian Center" (2015), the Prize Catalonia Construction for "Mingo house" (2010), an ASCER Award for "Versatile Slats" in Casa Barcelona (2005), and selection to the 2004 FAD Awards for the "DCPAL Stand" at Construmat.

ESCOBAR, ANDRES founder of AE Arquitectos, was born in Guadalajara, Mexico, in 1975. He studied architecture at the Western Institute of Technology and Higher Education (ITESO) in Guadalajara, and at the Polytechnic University of Madrid (UPM). The firm was established in 1999 and since then, it has developed work in residential and commercial projects, and in urban planning, both at the regional and national scale. The three areas of the studio's work are carried out in parallel, with clearly differentiated teams to develop each project.

FLATO, TED AND LAKE, DAVID Since co-founding Lake|Flato in 1984, Ted Flato has received acclaim both nationally and internationally for his artful and practical regional designs that leverage each unique site, incorporate indigenous building forms and materials, and respond to the context of their landscape. By employing sustainable strategies in a wide variety of building types and scales, Ted seeks to conserve energy and natural resources while creating healthy built environments. His recent focus has been on residential, higher education and eco-conservation projects, including the ASU Polytechnic Academic Campus in Mesa, AZ; the new Midtown Arts & Theater Center in Houston, TX; and the Naples Botanical Garden Visitor Center in Florida.

GLEYSTEEN, MARCUS received a Bachelor of Fine Arts in sculpture from Cooper Union and a Master of Architecture from Columbia University in 1983. His early career was in the offices of S.I.T.E., Payette Associates, the Architects Collaborative, and Moshe Safdie Architects. He was a founding member of Elkus Manfredi Architects, before establishing his own firm in Boston in 1996 with his wife, Judy Glysteen. As the Principal-in-Charge of MGa, Marcus brings over 30 years of professional experience, spanning a broad range of project types, from residential, institutional and corporate architecture, to interior design, master-planning and urban development. Marcus's dedication to clients, along with his passion for art and architecture, is shared by the entire firm.

HEREDIA ÁLVAREZ, JOSÉ LUIS (Mexico City 1970) graduated as an architect from the Universidad Autónoma Metropolitana in Mexico City in 1994. He worked for several Mexican firms, including ABAX and KMD, before joining Manuel Cervantes Estudio in 2010. As architectural designer in the firm, he has participated in several projects working in such areas as hospitality, equestrian, commercial, and transit oriented development (TOD). His work has been awarded in several national architecture biennials and international architectural competitions as part of the firm's design team.

LEGORRETA, RICARDO (1931 - 2011) graduated from the Escuela Nacional de Arquitectura of the Universidad Autónoma de Mexico in 1954 and started working as a draftsman in the office of José Villagrán García, the leader of Mexican functionalism. In 1965 he established his firm Legorreta Arquitectos, focusing on interpreting the architectural style of indigenous Mexican buildings. In 1991, his son, Victor, joined the firm. His buildings have been recognized throughout the world and since its foundation (now LEGORRETA®) has received several awards and has won national and international competitions. Ricardo Legorreta is well known internationally as one of the most influential Mexican architects.

LEGORRETA, VICTOR (Mexico City, 1966) studied architecture at the Universidad Iberoamericana in Mexico City. After practicing with Leason Pomeroy & Associates (Los Angeles), Martorell, Bohigas & Mackay (Barcelona), and Fumihiko Maki (Tokyo), he joined Legorreta Arquitectos in 1991. Víctor is now a partner, CEO and Design Director at LEGORRETA®. He has lectured in numerous universities and conferences in the U.S.A. and Latin America. In 2007 Victor was made an Honorary Member of the American Institute of Architects (AIA), and in 2018, LEGORRETA received the RIBA Award for International Excellence for their BBVA Bancomer Tower.

MILLÁN VILLAMUELAS, JOAQUÍN graduated from the Polytechnic University of Madrid, ETSAM. After working for Norman Foster (London) and Rem Koolhaas (Rotterdam), he founded OOIIO in Madrid in 2010 as a laboratory of architecture and the city. Joaquín leads OOIIO´s architecture process by looking for emotion, imagination, and aesthetics in each work, always relying on the pillars of reason, technique, and efficiency. He has taught as an assistant professor of architecture at the Polytechnic University of Madrid, as well as in several universities in Europe and Latin America. His work has been exhibited, awarded, and published in multiple journals, books, and blogs around the world.

MOLEN, MATS was born and raised on the beautiful plains of southern Sweden and from the beginning of his architectural education his interests focused on agricultural structures and the relationship between building and landscape. Upon graduation, he worked for several years at the Swedish University of Agricultural Sciences with various research and development projects related to agricultural buildings. In addition to designing many equestrian facilities, he also designs other types of buildings, all of them with the approach of exploring the relationship between the building and the landscape and the architectural expression of functions, sustainable materials, and new building technologies.

PENTTI, RAISKI (1971) AND RAUTIALA, KATARIINA (1972) both graduated in architecture from the Escuela Técnica Superior de Arquitectura in San Sebastián, Spain, in 1996, and the Helsinki Technical University in 2000. Together they founded POOK Architects Ltd. In 1997, a company focused on the design of housing, leisure and sport buildings. They have a special interest in the sustainable use of wood.

RAMOS, JUAN IGNACIO was born in Buenos Aires, Argentina, in 1955. He graduated from the University of Architecture and Urbanism of Buenos Aires in 1978. During his years of study, he worked as a draftsman in his father's studio: Ramos, Alvarez Forn, Ostman, Arquitectos. Between 1979 and 1989 he worked in association with the architects Francisco Billoch and Ignacio Dahl Rocha. In 1990 he founded Estudio Ramos which since then has developed more than 400 projects in Argentina, Uruguay and the United States.

RAMOS, IGNACIO was born in Buenos Aires in 1983. He carried out his studies at Florida Atlantic University in the United States and at the Anhalt+Bauhaus Foundation in Dessau, Germany. He graduated from his architectural studies in 2007, and in 2011 he completed his master's degree in architecture at Columbia University in New York. During his years of study, he worked as a draftsman in Estudio Ramos and as a collaborator with the artist Michael Singer. In 2007 he became a Partner in the firm.

REBOLLO URIBE, LILIAN is a graduate of the University of the Americas, Puebla, the National Autonomous University of Mexico, and the Autonomous University of the State of Morelos (UAEM) where she received a master's degree in Territorial Studies, Heritage and Landscape. In 2010, she founded the architecture studio APT architecture for all. She complements the work of the architecture studio by teaching in the Faculty of Architecture at UAEM. She is currently working on a project that associates architecture and participatory urban planning in order to generate proposals for the recovery and appropriation of public spaces.

SANINT FELIPE received his architecture degree from the Universidad Javeriana in Bogota Colombia and complemented his studies in London and Oxford. Sanint has developed projects in different areas, including architecture, ephemeral architecture and interior design. He has designed projects for government agencies, international fairs representing Colombia, urban city christmas decorations, stands, events and all range of TV sets and broadcast.

SEQUOIA CONTRACTING COMPANY LTD Alan Megerdichian is the owner of Sequoia Contracting Company Ltd, based in North Salem, NY. He has been in practice for over 30 years, building high-end custom residential homes and designing and developing equestrian facilities. Alan has been involved with horses for most of his life, so transitioning into constructing horse farms was a natural progression for him.

STEIN, SETH Born in New York City in 1959, Seth Stein was raised in London and began his architectural career in the offices of Richard Rogers and Norman Foster. Since establishing his own office in 1990 the small practice has completed projects in the UK and internationally ranging from coastal houses (in Finland, South Africa, Cornwall and the Caribbean) to urban projects that include art galleries, restaurants and offices.

TALL ARQUITECTOS Lázaro Gutiérrez Cortina Sainz, Leonardo Montero Tello, and Sebastián Gutiérrez Cortina Sainz make up the young firm of TALL ARQUITECTOS in Mexico City. The firm seeks to respond to the needs of their customers and users, the city, environment, programs and budgets, in a creative, clear and effective way with the goal of achieving impact. Aware of their responsibility as professionals with historical roots, TALL ARQUITECTOS aims to achieve a spiritual and emotional balance in each project by proposing the most appropriate integral approach, always supporting the aesthetic aspects with technical and functional solutions.

VELEZ, SIMON (1949) is a Columbian architect famous for the innovative use of his country's natural resources, especially its lush vegetation and Guadua bamboo, a material found in the Andes Mountain range. In a career spanning more than 20 years, largely in collaboration with the engineer-constructor Marcello Villegas, Vélez has experimented with the structural capacity of bamboo in more than 200 projects throughout the world, including luxury residences, churches, resorts, museums, and other entertainment structures. He has also persuaded numerous public administrations, town councils, and businesses concerned with the environmental impact of construction to adopt and promote Guadua bamboo as a more sustainable and responsive building material.

VILLEGAS, MARCELO has played an integral part in the development of Construction with Guadua Bamboo. A skilled craftsman, artist and builder his foundry work engineering skills are responsible for the hardware finish work and metal fixtures that make a large Guadua Bamboo structures possible. Marcelo is perhaps the most knowledgeable person on the qualities and strengths of this material. He is solely responsible for the growing popularity of Guadua bamboo through his magnificent books "Tropical Bamboo" and "New Bamboo". He has restored several ancient farm houses in his native Colombia and is well known for his Residential and Commercial building.

WATSON, ROBERT is a 55-year old architect and industrial designer based in Melbourne, Australia. Prior to starting his own practice, he gained valuable experience in London working on some world-renowned projects for the offices of both Nicholas Grimshaw and Norman Foster. He established his own practice in 1998 and has been recognized both nationally and internationally, winning awards for architecture, urban design, and industrial design projects.

WEINFELD, ISAY Born in São Paulo, Brazil, Isay Weinfeld graduated from the School of Architecture at Mackenzie University. Over the course of his near 40-year career, Weinfeld has developed projects in the most diverse areas, including architecture, furniture, and cinema. This diversity, the result of clear purpose rather than luck or chance, is based on the certainty that multidisciplinary action is essential to foster a keen creative spirit, and that professional practice grows with rigorous design, bold experimentation, and relentless research. He has been published widely and has also served as a professor of Kinetic Expression at the School of Communications of the Fundação Armando Álvares Penteado in São Paulo.

ZEGERS, MATIAS received his architecture degree from the Universidad Católica de Chile and is the founder of Matías Zegers Arquitectos (MZA). Previously, from 2005-2008, he worked with Rick Joy Architects in Tucson, Arizona, as a project architect collaborating on many of the projects within the office. In 2009 he returned to Santiago, and re-launched Matías Zegers Arquitectos. In 2011, MZA won a competition for the design of the New National Congress Library which was started in 2014. Matías Zegers has been a visiting professor at the University of Arizona, Universidad Católica de Chile, and he is currently teaching at the Universidad de Talca.

AUTHORS' PROFILES

RIERA OJEDA, OSCAR is an editor and designer based in the US, China, and Argentina. Born in 1966, in Buenos Aires, he moved to the United States in 1990. Since then he has published over two hundred books, assembling a remarkable body of work notable for its thoroughness of content, timeless character, and sophisticated and innovative craftsmanship. Oscar Riera Ojeda's books have been published by many prestigious publishing houses across the world, including Birkhäuser, Byggförlaget, The Monacelli Press, Gustavo Gili, Thames & Hudson, Rizzoli, Damiani, Page One, ORO editions, Whitney Library of Design, and Taschen. Oscar Riera Ojeda is also the creator of numerous architectural book series, including Ten Houses, Contemporary World Architects, The New American House and The New American Apartment, Architecture in Detail, and Single Building. His work has received many international awards, in-depth reviews, and citations. He is a regular contributor and consultant for several publications in the field.

DEUPI, VICTOR teaches architectural history and theory, design, and representation at the University of Miami School of Architecture. His research focuses on the art and architecture of the Early Modern Ibero-American world, and mid-twentieth-century Cuba. His books include *Architectural Temperance: Spain and Rome 1700-1759*, *Transformations in Classical Architecture: New Directions in Research and Practice*, *Cuban Modernism: Mid-Century Architecture 1940-1970*, with Jean-Francois Lejeune, and *Emilio Sanchez in New York and Latin America*. Dr. Deupi was also the President of the CINTAS Foundation dedicated to promoting Cuban art and culture from 2016-2018.

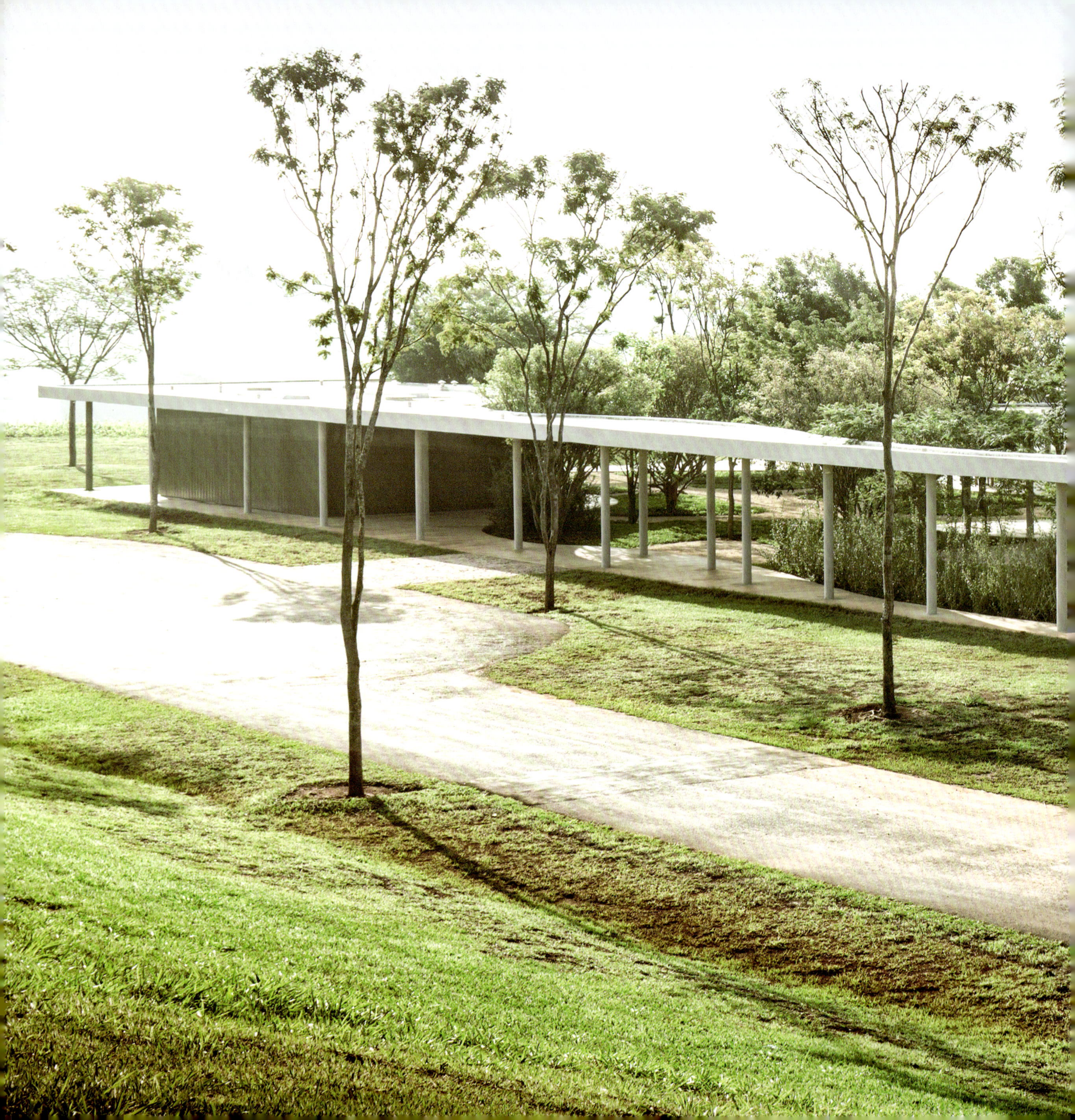

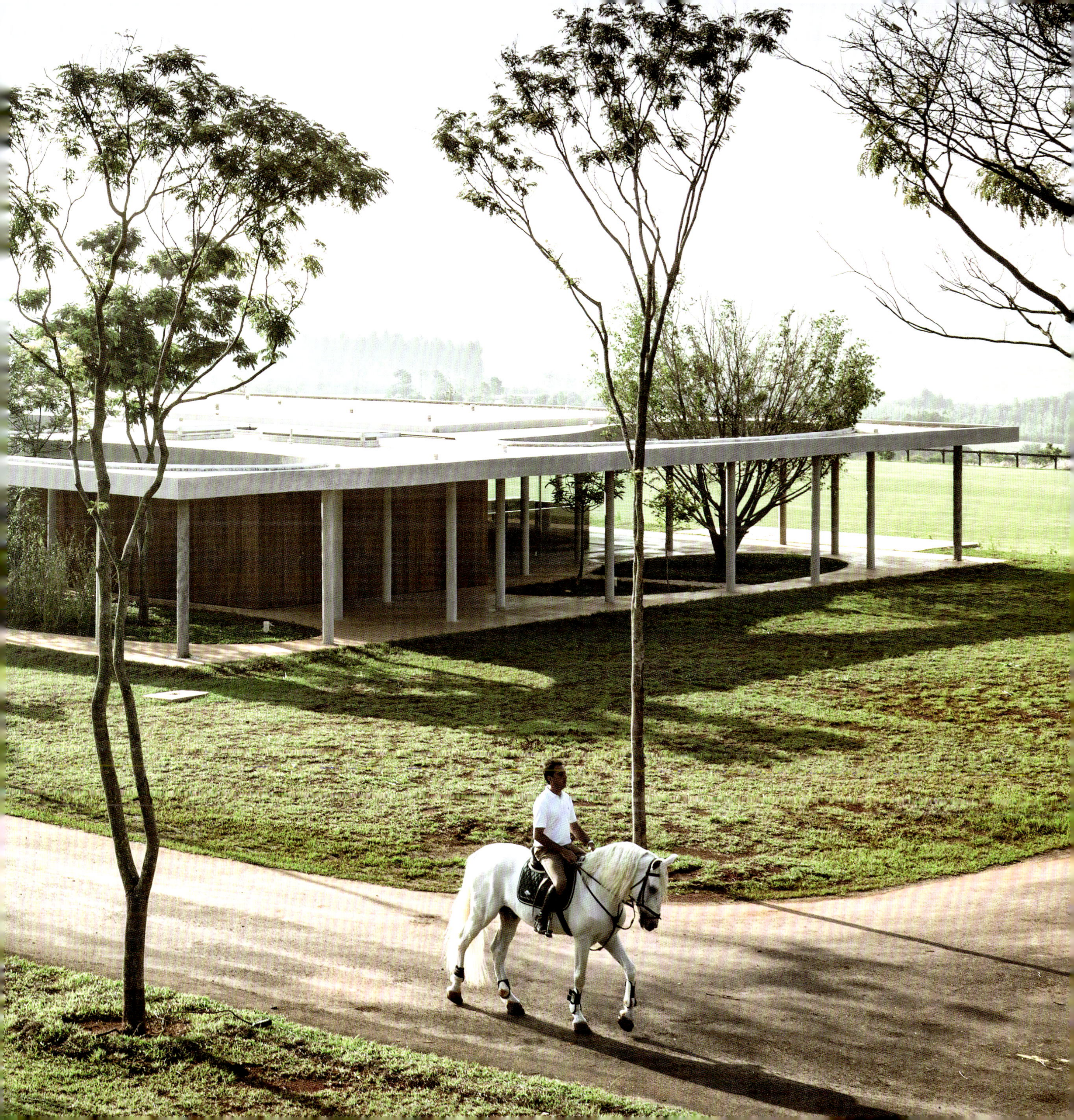

BOOK CREDITS

Edited by Oscar Riera Ojeda & Victor Deupi
Introduction by Victor Deupi
Art direction by Oscar Riera Ojeda
Graphic Design by Lucía B. Bauzá and Julia Miceli Pitta

First published in the United States of America in 2021 by
RIZZOLI INTERNATIONAL PUBLICATIONS, INC.
300 Park Avenue South, New York, NY 10010
www.rizzoliusa.com

© 2021 Oscar Riera Ojeda and Victor Deupi
© 2021 Rizzoli International Publications, Inc.

Photography credits appear throughout book by project; all photography in this book is used with permission.

Publisher: Charles Miers
Editor (for Rizzoli): Douglas Curran
Production Manager: Barbara Sadick
Managing Editor: Lynn Scrabis

Front cover: MSporthorses, Matias Zegers Arquitectos, photograph © Cristóbal Palma
Back cover photos: Please see book interior for project and photo credits.

All rights reserved. No part of this publication may be reproduced, stored in a retrieval system, or transmitted in any form or by any means, electronic, mechanical, photocopying, recording, or otherwise, without prior consent of the publisher.

Printed and bound in China

2024 2025 2026 / 10 9 8 7 6 5

ISBN-13: 978-0-8478-6856-8
Library of Congress Control Number: 2020931560

Visit us online:
Facebook.com/RizzoliNewYork
Twitter: @Rizzoli_Books
Instagram.com/RizzoliBooks
Pinterest.com/RizzoliBooks
Youtube.com/user/RizzoliNY
Issuu.com/Rizzoli

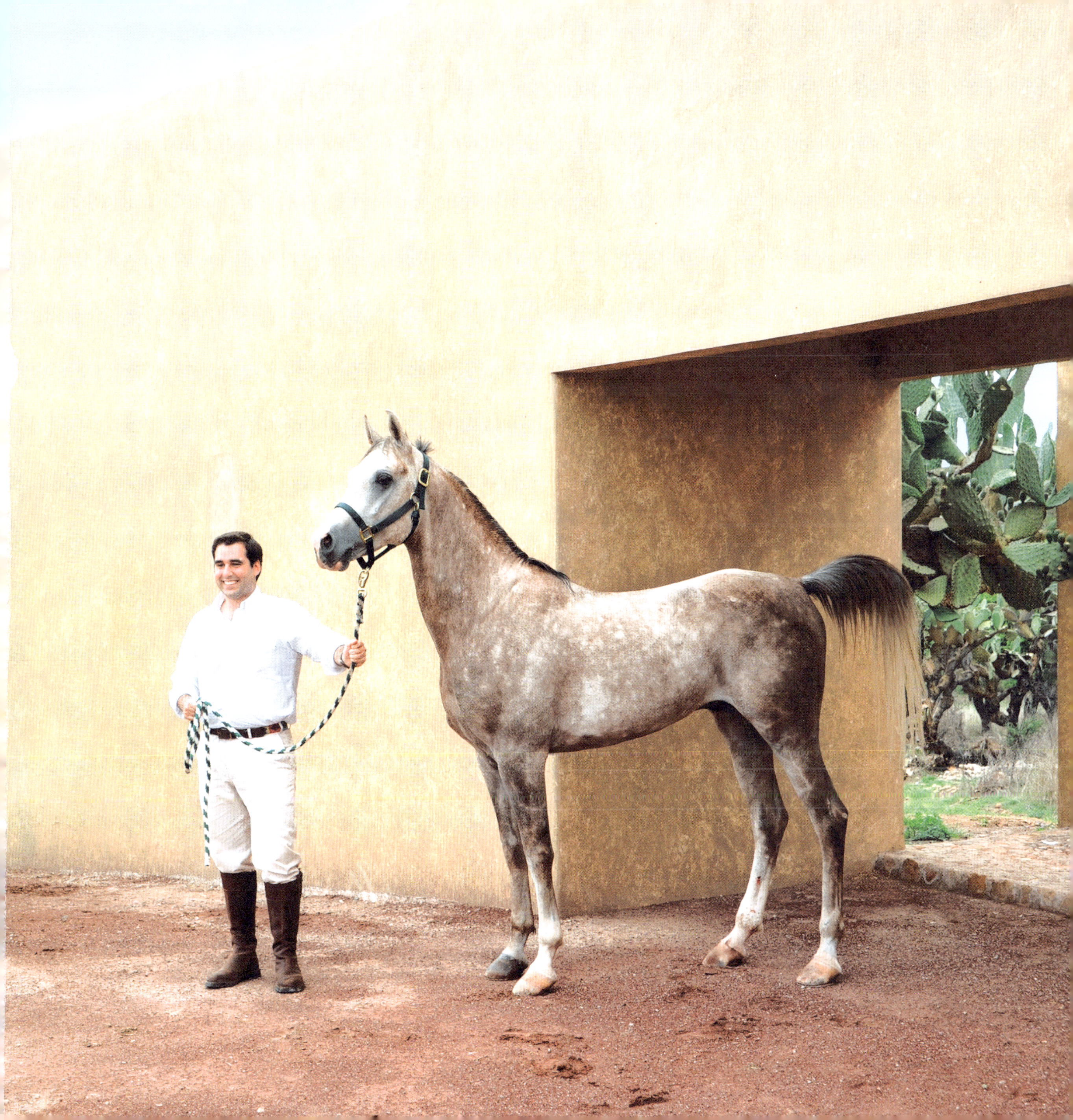

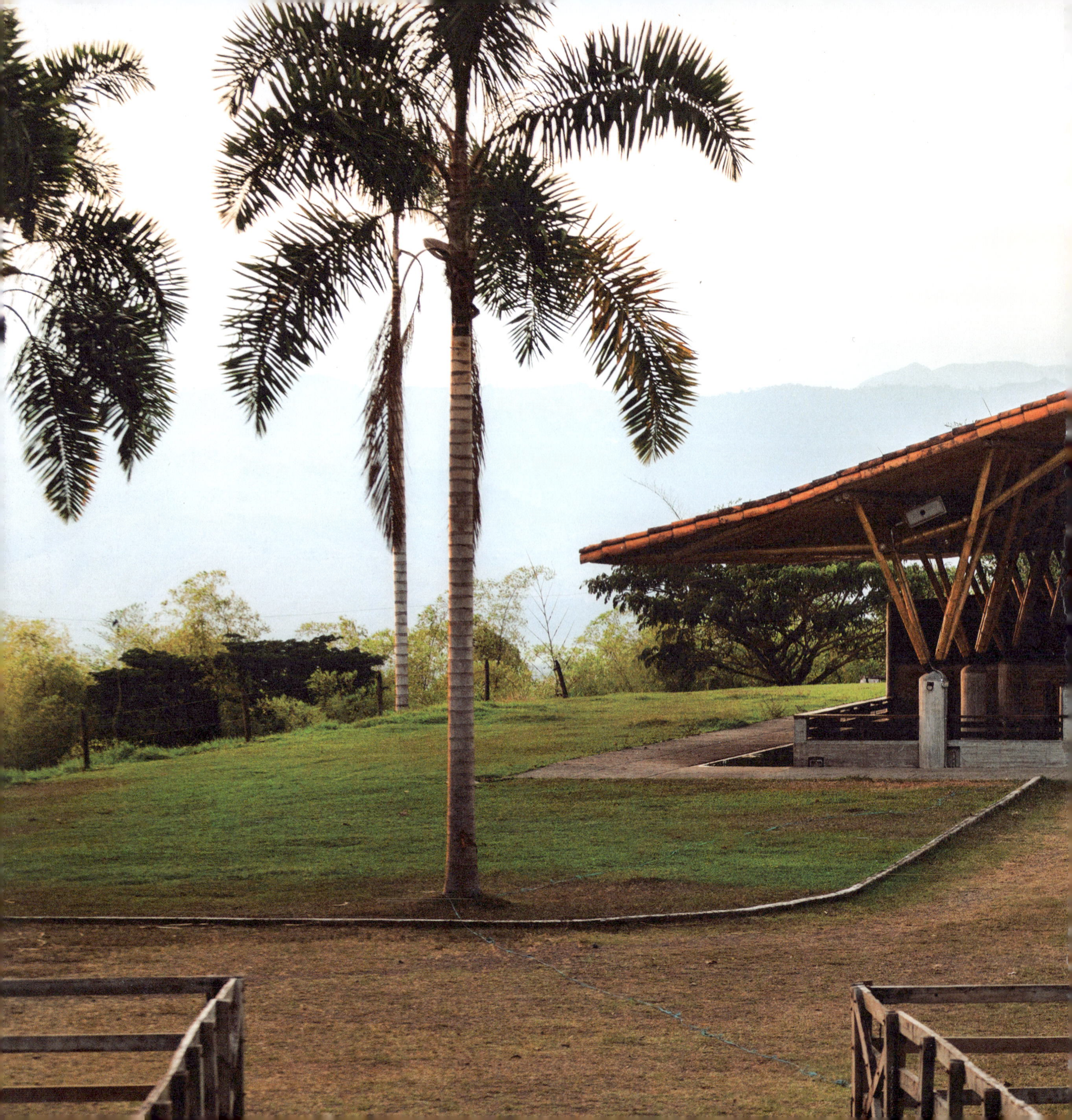